JOURNEY TO SOUTHERN THAILAND AND BURMA (1912)

Pierre Lefèvre-Pontalis

JOURNEY TO SOUTHERN THAILAND AND BURMA (1912)

Pierre Lefèvre-Pontalis

Edited by
Olivier Évrard
Aurore Candier

Translation by Olivier Évrard and Narisa Chakrabongse

First published and distributed in 2025 by
River Books Press Co., Ltd
396/1 Maharaj Road, Phraborommaharajawang,
Bangkok 10200 Thailand
Tel: (66) 2 225-0139, 2 225-9574
Email: order@riverbooksbk.com
www.riverbooksbk.com
@riverbooks   riverbooksbk   Riverbooksbk

Copyright collective work © River Books, 2025
Copyright introductory texts © Olivier Évrard & Aurore Candier
Copyright photographs © Lefèvre-Pontalis Archive
except where indicated otherwise.

All rights reserved. No part of this book may be reproduced or transmitted in any form or by any means, electronic or including photocopy, recording or any other information storage and retrieval system, without prior permission in writing from the publisher.

Editor: Narisa Chakrabongse
Production supervision: Suparat Sudcharoen
Design: Ruetairat Nanta

ISBN 978 616 451 099 9

Cover illustration: Boats on the Moulmein river. (Lefèvre-Pontalis Archive)

Printed and bound in Thailand by Parbpim Co., Ltd

Contents

Note on editorial choices	7
Foreword	9
Introduction	15
Transcription of Pierre Lefèvre-Pontalis' travel journal in South Siam and Burma	37
Acknowledgements	235
Glossary	236
Biographies of personalities	250
Index	255

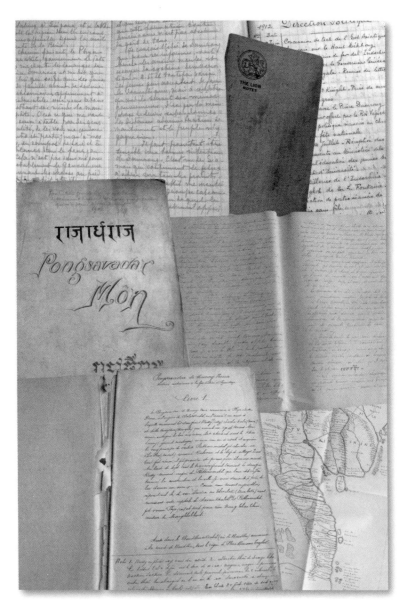

Research papers belonging to Pierre Lefèvre-Pontalis including the notebooks from the trip. (Lefèvre-Pontalis Archive)

Note on editorial choices

Pontalis took notes, sometimes quickly, by candlelight and also referring to texts of the time using different transcriptions of the vernacular terms used, in both Thai and Burmese. The notebooks in their original form reflect this disparity. We had to harmonise and make choices to achieve this transcription.

We have generally retained Pontalis' suggested spelling for ethnic terms, with the exception of Karen, which Pontalis erroneously transcribes as Kharen and Kachin, transcribed as Khachin. This is undoubtedly due to the influence of the Laotian context, well known to Pontalis, where the term *kha* referred to a myriad of mountain populations subject to the Thais.

As far as place and river names are concerned, we have followed a different rule for the Siamese and Burmese parts of the story. In the case of Siam, we have slightly modified the author's transcriptions of place names (which are often heterogeneous) to keep as close as possible to the current official spelling (Phatthalung rather than Pattalung, Chumphon instead of Choumphon etc.) except in the case of rivers (Mekong for Mae Kong, Mae Ping for Meping). As for the Burmese part, we have generally kept the transcriptions found in the notebooks, as Pontalis most often uses British colonial spelling. This is still used in Burma today, alongside the official transcriptions, which are much less well-known and pronounceable by European readers (Moulmein instead of Mawlamyine). The names used by Pontalis in the original text are given in the glossary at the end of the book.

Pontalis' transcription has been retained for personal names.

Readers can refer to the glossary of place names, institutional names and vernacular terms for contemporary spellings and definitions. A list of personal names with short biographies is also included at the end of the book.

Portrait of Pierre Lefèvre Pontalis, undated. (Lefèvre-Pontalis Archive)

Foreword

Pierre Lefèvre-Pontalis (1864-1938) was the son of Amédé Lefèvre-Pontalis (1833-1901), a lawyer, historian, businessman and politician, and a Legitimist MP for Eure-et-Loir. Pierre Lefèvre-Pontalis, perhaps inspired by his father's interest in Asia (his father was an influential member of the Comité de l'Asie Française, which published a monthly review, *Le Bulletin du Comité de l'Asie Française*, between 1901 and 1940), first studied law and then Vietnamese and Malay at the École Spéciale des Langues Orientales (now INALCO). He joined the Ministry of Foreign Affairs in 1889 and was appointed embassy attaché for the special mission to Indochina. He became deputy commissioner in Laos in 1894 and until 1895 took part in various border demarcation commissions in the Upper Mekong regions between the French and English colonial possessions. He is notably the author of the fifth volume of the Pavie Mission in Indochina, a work that is still invaluable to historians and ethnologists working on these regions, in which he demonstrates a remarkable understanding of inter-ethnic relations and local history.[1] In the years that followed, he published several works devoted to the culture and history of Laos, including *Recueil de talismans laotiens* (Paris, Ernest Leroux) in 1900 and *Chansons et Fêtes du Laos* with the same publisher in 1902.

Following this initial experience in Southeast Asia, Pierre Lefèvre-Pontalis was appointed secretary to embassies in various countries, including Cairo in 1896, St Petersburg in 1899, Athens in 1905 and Washington in 1909. He returned to Asia in 1912 as Minister Plenipotentiary

Henriette Pontalis. (Lefèvre-Pontalis Archive)

Part of Pierre Lefèvre-Pontalis' large collection of books in the Château d'Aulnaie. (Courtesy Lefèvre-Pontalis family. Photograph: Olivier Évrard)

to Siam, where he headed the French legation (which did not become an embassy in its own right until 1949) in Bangkok. He then held the same position in Vienna before retiring in 1921, still young at fifty-seven, to the Château d'Aulnaie in Eure-et-Loir, which his father had bought forty years earlier. He devoted the next seventeen years to publications on Siamese culture (in particular *Notes sur les amulettes siamoises*, Paris, Geuthner, 1926) and Khmer culture, the art of bookbinding as well as research into the history of the Châteaudun region in France, writing in the mornings and leaving every afternoon for long walks and discussions with the local people.

It was there, in the magnificent Château d'Aulnaie, that I had the pleasure of meeting his great-grandson, Patrick Lefèvre-Pontalis, in 2012. The meeting was no accident, quite the contrary. It was the culmination of a personal research that began in 1994 when I went to Laos as a volunteer for ORSTOM,[2] then as a doctoral student in anthropology. At the time, my dissertation fieldwork was in the Nam Tha valley, in the north-west of the country, a valley that Pierre Lefèvre-Pontalis had been the first Westerner to visit in 1894. His account had been extremely useful to me during my fieldwork, as it contained the names of several local notables and invaluable information on ethnonyms, toponyms and the history of social relations in the region. Several years later, when I had already defended my thesis and was attending the seminar given at the École Pratique des Hautes Études (EPHE) by Yves Goudineau, who had been my supervisor in Laos, one of the participants mentioned the existence of private archives belonging to Pierre Lefèvre-Pontalis and kept by his family. I made a mental note of the information, but it wasn't until 2009, taking advantage of a whole year spent in France between two long stays in Chiang Mai, where I was posted as a researcher for IRD, that I decided to investigate more seriously and try to make contact with his descendants. After I unsuccessfully looked up in the telephone directory, I contacted Jean-Bertrand Pontalis at Gallimard publishing house, who, amused by my request, explained that he did not belong to the same branch of the family as Aulnaie's heirs and gave me the right contacts. A few phone calls later, I finally managed to speak to Patrick Lefèvre-Pontalis, who explained the family

Part of Pierre Lefèvre-Pontalis' archive of unpublished papers.
(Courtesy Lefèvre-Pontalis family. Photograph: Olivier Évrard)

tree in detail. He confirmed that he had kept several of his grandfather's books and notebooks in the large family estate and very generously agreed to receive me there so that I could examine them. However, it wasn't until the summer of 2012 that, taking advantage of a holiday in France, I was finally able to visit the property and examine the archives.

In addition to a large library containing many old works on Asia, all superbly bound, Lefèvre Pontalis' personal archives contain four main categories of documents. Firstly, there are preparatory notes for the works he published, maps and handwritten copies of certain texts, such as the fifth volume of the Pavie Mission. A second group includes translations of Tai-yuan and Mon chronicle in relation with Chiang Mai, Chiang Saen and Lampang. A third group contains official correspondence with the Lao and Siamese royal authorities, the earliest concerning the delimitation of borders and the most recent ones concerning the period during which Lefèvre-Pontalis headed the French Legation in Bangkok. Finally, the fourth category of documents consists of the originals of his notebooks, some of which were written during his trip to northern Laos in 1894 and others during a trip to southern Siam and Burma in 1912 just before he took up his post in Bangkok. While, as I mentioned earlier, I was familiar with the account written during the Pavie Mission, the second set of notebooks immediately piqued my curiosity as they had not been made public. Patrick Pontalis confirmed that these notes had never been published, as his grandfather didn't think they were good enough, but that he was willing to let me digitise and transcribe them if I thought they might be of interest. Thus began a project which, in the midst of my various commitments, meetings and travels, took much longer than I had originally thought and has only now come to fruition with the publication of this book, which also owes a great deal to my collaboration with Aurore Candier on the Burmese part of the manuscript.

Olivier Évrard

---

1 *Mission Pavie, Indo-China, 1879-1895: Géographie et voyages*, tome 5, *Voyages dans le haut Laos et sur les frontières de Chine et de Birmanie*, Paris, Ernest Leroux, 1902.

2 Office de Recherche Scientifique et Technique pour l'Outre-Mer, renamed Institut de Recherche pour le Développement (IRD) in 1998.

Château d'Aulnaie. (Courtesy Lefèvre-Pontalis family. Photograph: Olivier Évrard)

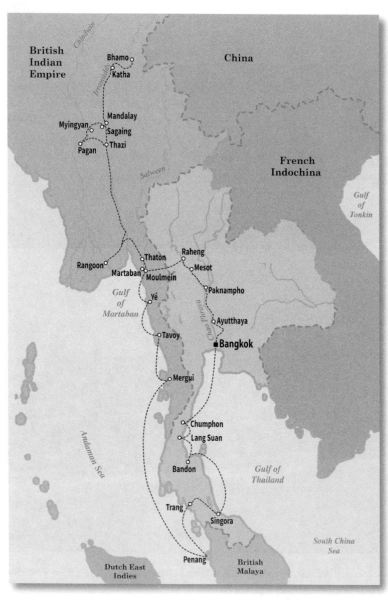

Itinerary followed by Pierre Lefèvre-Pontalis during his trip.

Introduction
Olivier Évrard and Aurore Candier

Written with pencil on more than five hundred pages of small bound notebooks, the diary presented here covers the period from 28 October to 18 December 1912, a journey of fifty-two days by boat, train, elephant, mule and sometimes on foot. Pierre Lefèvre-Pontalis left Bangkok on 28 October by boat and travelled down the Gulf of Siam to Songkhla, in southern Thailand. He then crossed the Isthmus of Kra to Trang, on the west coast, meeting many Siamese dignitaries, before sailing to Penang and from there to Mergui (now Myeik). He then took the train to Rangoon (now Yangon) where he met up with his wife, Henriette, and their friends, Philippe and Mélanie Vilmorin; Phillipe was a renowed botanist. Henriette Lefèvre-Pontalis brought an early Kodak camera with her and documented the second part of the trip, during which the four friends visited Mandalay and Pagan as tourists, then travelled by boat and train to Rangoon and on to Moulmein (now called Mawlamyine). From there, they made their way east to the Siamese border, reaching Myawadi (now Myawaddy) and then Mae Sot, by elephant and on horseback. Finally they arrived in Tak and the Chao Phraya basin, where they took a boat that brought them downriver to Ayutthaya, before finally taking the train to Bangkok for the last few kilometers of their trip.

Although the journey is occasionally a little adventurous, particularly when the group reaches Siam via Mae Sot by elephant, horse and sometimes on foot, it generally follows well-marked routes and is in no way an 'exploration' similar to that which the author had undertaken almost two decades earlier in northern Laos as part of the Pavie Mission. The Burmese part of the journey to Mandalay and Pagan was booked through the Cook agency in Rangoon, and for the other itineraries in Burma and Siam, the author had numerous contacts on the ground who facilitated his travel. In the first part of the story, when he travelled through the southern regions of Siam, his status as *envoyé extraordinaire* and *ministre plénipotentiaire* enabled him to meet a number of local dignitaries and to travel comfortably: a delegation of twenty-four people was waiting for him when he arrived in Phatthalung; a driver was sent specially from Bangkok by the influential Prince Damrong (1862-1943) to accompany him to Trang and he spent his nights in cottages built shortly beforehand for the Queen's visit. The many official meetings provided him with a wealth of information on the political situation and economic development of these outlying regions of the Kingdom of Siam. The second part of the trip, to Burma and then to the central part of Siam as the small group of friends returned to Bangkok, was less official and more touristy. However, the author's knowledge of the orientalist literature of the time, his sense of ethnographic observation and his constant reflection on the geopolitics of the region are all evident. The boat trip down the Mae Ping, which becomes the Chao Phraya downstream from Raheng (nowadays Tak), gave him plenty of opportunity to digress on the history and culture of the Tai populations of the north, whom he sometimes referred to as "Lao" and with whom he was particularly familiar.

Although this travel account does not have the same academic pretensions as the texts published by Pontalis on Siam and Laos, particularly the Burmese part, we feel that it is valuable for different reasons. There are many details to be discovered in the pages, which may be uneven in content but are always full of anecdotes and first-hand accounts of Southeast Asia just before the Great War. The notebooks provide an insight into the orientalist and colonialist prism through which academics and politicians of the time viewed the region, with certain variations between French and English speakers, which Pontalis' account aptly captures. Moreover, it takes place in a particularly interesting context for the history of Siam, at the very beginning of the reign of King Vajiravudh (Rama VI, r.1910-1925), at a time when the kingdom was transforming its administrative and territorial organisation to better resist colonial influences, particularly British. Pontalis highlights in particular the way in which the Siamese government, under the impetus of princes trained in the West during the reign of Chulalongkorn (Rama V, r. 1868-1910), used foreign experts to modernise its administration and transport networks, and how it also relied on a few Chinese families to develop the southern regions and counter British political and commercial influence.

The orientalist and the colonialist

Pierre Lefèvre-Pontalis' notebooks reveal him as a key player in the orientalist project of his time, which was in full swing in the first decades of the 20th century. This project, shared by the European colonial powers, was based on the notion of "external Hinduisation",[1] which was emerging in the discourse of German and French-speaking scholars, very often eminent members of the École Française d'Extrême-Orient, indologists and buddhologists. Their work describing the Hindu or Hindo-Buddhist temples of Borobudur and Angkor, or their translations of texts and lithic inscriptions in Pali and Sanskrit, identified Indian influences throughout the Indochinese peninsula and the Southeast Asian archipelago. These discoveries fed into the imperial imaginations of Europeans, particularly the French, for whom the cultural influence of ancient India was akin to their own conception of the civilising mission they felt they were entrusted with in their colonies. In this teleological interpretation, drawn from a philosophy of history inherited from the Enlightenment, the expansionist work of ancient India – seen as the cultural cradle of Europe where Indo-Aryan populations thrived – prefigured the European colonisation of Southeast Asia.

The reader can see Pontalis' interest in all the features of Indian influence he detected during his trip, as each one refers to a pressing orientalist agenda to which he had to respond as a *ministre plénipotentiaire* freshly arrived in Siam. Angkor, previously under Siamese rule, had been attached to French Indochina since 1907, following the retrocession of the provinces of Battambang and Siem Reap to Cambodia, just five years before Pontalis was appointed in Siam. Tracing the path of cultural colonisation that led from India to Indochina via Burma thus became one of the main intellectual and political challenges of his narrative. Right at the start of the journey, Pontalis wrote: "There is no longer any doubt today that Ligor (Nakhon Sri Thammarat) was the first stop for the Hindus in their conquest of lower Indochina. The organisers of Cambodia and the first civilised settlers came from there" (entry dated 1st November 1912). He then methodically noted the Indian presence in every detail of everyday life, clothing, architecture (pagodas, monasteries) and the cosmopolitan population of the towns.

Orientalism and colonialism were underpinned by scientific concepts of "race" that combined biological, natural and cultural attributes, and aimed to classify peoples. This theory, which forms the basis of modern racism, is coupled with an apprehension of the racial decadence that would ensue from miscegenation, a thought developed by Arthur de Gobineau (1816-1882) in his *Essay on the Inequality of Human Races* in the early 1850s. At the end of the 19th century, eugenicist ideas were added, notably by the British scientist Francis Galton (1822-1911), who drew on the theory of natural selection developed by his cousin Charles Darwin (1809-1882) to propose a programme to improve humanity by controlling marriages and births. His ideas, set out in 1904, were widely disseminated in Europe and the United States, and then spread throughout the world. This "scientific racism",[2] a rapidly expanding transnational phenomenon, permeated the thinking of Pierre Lefèvre-Pontalis, who punctuated his diary with racist stereotypes that may seem extreme to us today, but which were also evidence of the vigour of imperialism and the rise of nationalism in the pre-war period.[3]

In these evolutionary representations, races, like all organisms, struggle for survival and some disappear. This is what Pontalis intended to show in his racialised analysis of the regions he travelled through. He attempted to retrace the history of each "indigenous race" he encountered on his journey, from the "Negritos" (Mani) of Trang to the Mon of southern Burma and Siam, and also to understand the process of decline of each of them under the influence of their interbreeding with the "foreign races" – Chinese, Thai, Burmese and Indian. As a good ethnographer, he deplored the disappearance of the "primitive indigenous races", but as a convinced orientalist, he also observed the omnipresence of the "Indian race" in the region, the proof of a past expansion which, according to the paradigm mentioned above, announced the future colonisation from Europe. Pontalis thus insisted on the decline of the Burmese and their replacement by Indians (27 November), a "suicide of the race" for which he blamed the Burmese women uniting with foreigners (5 December).

But Pierre Lefèvre-Pontalis, far from being an expert on Burma, had to base his ethnographic and historical interpretation on the work of British historians and archaeologists, who had been present in the country since the early 19th century. British orientalism is characterised by a cultural approach that is more racialised and territorialised than that of the French,[4] a tendency perfectly embodied in the colonial historiography of Burma. The British imposed a periodisation that established dynastic moments, often associated with ethnic labels, in order to draw parallels between the history of Burma and neighbouring kingdoms, notably Siam, whose history they divided into the Dvāravatī period – corresponding to the Mon hegemony in Siam – followed by the Sukhothai period, then Ayutthaya and finally Thonburi-Bangkok.[5] This way of reifying and classifying "indigenous races", of attributing domination to certain races over a defined territory, but also of plastering these ethnic conceptions onto a distant past, has its roots in British colonialism and orientalism, for which Pontalis acted as spokesman in his journal.

Before setting off, Pontalis obviously did his homework. Between the lines we can read that he was particularly inspired by, but did not quote, the major work by Arthur Phayre (1812-1885), the first Commissioner of British Lower Burma and a fine burmanologist, published in 1883 on the basis of his reading of Burmese, Siamese and Chinese royal chronicles. Pontalis also borrowed from the work of Emmanuel Forchhammer (1851-1890), a Swiss indologist and paleolithicist who held the Paleolithic chair at Rangoon College in the late 1870s and was appointed head of the archaeological department of British Burma at the beginning of the following decade. Pontalis often used pages from Forchhammer's *Notes on the Early History and Geography of British Burma* (1883) to trace the ancient history of Burma from the perspective of a constant struggle between the Burmese and the Mon, the perpetual oppression of the former over the latter and the primacy of the Mon as the cradle of Burmese Buddhist civilisation. Thus, as vectors of Indian expansion towards the peninsula, the Mon would have inherited all the subtleties of Hindu-Buddhist civilisation that Forchhammer found in the excavations of ancient sites and the translations of inscriptions that he undertook at the end of the 19th century.

Pierre Lefèvre-Pontalis' account thus echoes an English-language historiography that has contributed to the conceptualisation of external Hinduisation. In his history of Burma, Pontalis combines Phayre's vision of the power of the royal city of Pegu (Bago) between the 15th and 16th centuries, with that of Forchhammer on the importance of the city of Thaton considered to be the heart of the ancient Mon kingdom of Suvaṇṇabhūmi, receptacle of Indo-Aryan civilisation and Theravādin orthodox Buddhism.[6] This historiographical bias is most distinctly expressed when Pontalis travels in southern Burma from Moulmein to Martaban. On his way to Thaton, he digressed on the ill-fated destiny of the Mon kingdom and its lost civilisation: "It was in 1010 that the Pagan king Anuratha, the hero of Burmese legends, proceeded with this conquest and seized all that had remained since the foundation of Hangsawadi, of the ancient Hindu kingdom of Thaton. Hangsawadi also succumbed and all the chronicles were destroyed or taken away by the Burmese to erase even the memory of the past. The Mon or Peguans, also known as Talaings and who made up the population of Hangsawadi, have never forgiven the Burmese for this attack on their history"[7] (November 14). Further on, he repeated that: "The destruction by the Burmese during their various expeditions of all the existing Pegouan chronicles has deprived us of an important part of the history of Hangsawadi" (4 December), once again following Forchhammer who denounced the decline of Mon culture at the hands of the barbaric Burmese who had "burnt the Talaing literature, looked down upon their inscriptions, forbidden the use of the Talaing language, and destroyed every town and village".[8]

Pontalis' diary should therefore be read not as a reliable history textbook, since it sets out to retrace the historical trajectory of Burma from the angle of ancient Indianisation through the cultural intermediaries of the Mon, masters for a time of the imaginary Hindu kingdom of Thaton, but as a fascinating source for readers interested in the history of colonisation, cultural history and the history of representations.

A privileged witness in a frontier region

The southern regions of Siam through which Pontalis travelled at the beginning of his diary have long been known to Chinese and Indian travellers and traders, and then to Europeans after the 17th century, for their natural riches: spices, precious woods, rattan, ivory, metals, swallows' nests, coconuts, palm oil and seafood in particular. Right at the start of his diary, the author mentions the wild elephants coveted for their ivory and the economic importance of swallows' nests, prized above all by Chinese merchants, subject to taxes from the central government and control by local chiefs. This importance has never diminished, and while swallows' nests generated up to 80,000 baht a year in revenue at the beginning of the 20th century (Ministry of Communication, 2016: 55), a recent study estimated that Thailand was producing more than two hundred tons a year in 2014, with total revenue estimated at three hundred million dollars (Jandam, 2021: 275). Tin, which was used mainly for religious ceremonies, bronze cannons and mirrors, saw its demand increase considerably at the time of the Napoleonic Wars in Europe (it was used to make tin cans for soldiers and also to protect iron or steel exposed to the elements). As Lefèvre-Pontalis pointed out on several occasions, tin production had a profound influence on local economies, particularly on the west coast in Phuket (from where England imported most of its tin requirements). In fact, he insisted that his companions observe for themselves the traditional methods used by the Chinese in the Trang region.

Despite their wealth and importance for trade, the southern Siamese regions, like those to the north, experienced periods of prolonged instability, notably due to repeated periods of war between Siam and Burma: Songkhla was destroyed twice in the 18th century alone while Nakhon Sri Thammarat (known previously as Ligor) was abandoned and refounded several times from the beginning of its history. The first Western visitor to Nakahon Sri Thammarat in 1826 noted that "the area had few inhabitants, no trade and negligible resources" (Baker and Pasuk, 2014: 23). Throughout the 19th century, the dispersal and mobility of the populations, and sometimes their revolts (particularly those of the Chinese workers in the tin mines, but also in the ports and towns such as Ranong and Phuket), made it difficult for Siamese central government to regain control of the southern regions. Even at the beginning of the 20th century, Lefèvre-Pontalis observes reminders of this precarious situation, for example when he recalls the conflicts between Phya Mahibal, governor of Bandon (now Chumphon) and his workers, who felled two hundred coconut trees on his plantations to protest against the drudgery he imposed on them. Further on, Pontalis also points out that attempts by local notables to impose cash crops such as coffee and rubber, or even to intensify tin mining, are subject to fluctuations in world prices and can sometimes lead to personal ruin and permanently hamper the authorities' development efforts.

Pontalis' journey took place at the beginning of the reign of Vajiravudh (Rama VI), when the administrative and territorial reforms undertaken by his father, King Chulalongkorn (Rama V), were profoundly transforming the political geography of the kingdom (Baffie, 2009). In addition to the gradual abolition of the various forms of slavery, the development of an agriculture more focused on cash crops and an education system more inclined to integrate foreign influences, Chulalongkorn's reign was above all marked by the overhaul of the bureaucracy (where salaried employment became the norm), the modernisation of the army and police and the introduction of a new system called *thesaphiban*, literally "territorial control". The old interlocking system of *muang*, with its porous peripheries and sometimes multiple jurisdictions (which Pontalis rightly remarked only constituted "momentary aggregations" in the history of Siam) was gradually replaced by a pyramidal bureaucracy in which governors were appointed by the central government and the revenue generated by local economic activity was better controlled. This reform was accompanied by a new territorial grid, in which the eighteen *monthon*, mentioned several times by Pontalis, grouped together several provinces, *changwat*, which were in turn subdivided into *amphoe,* districts. Although they were finally abandoned in 1933, the *monthon* played an important role at the beginning of the 20th century, as their leaders acted as relays for the centralising and modernising policies of the Siamese royal power.

The story shows the variable and very gradual success of the modernising ambitions of the Siamese rulers. It also highlights the importance of building infrastructure to really impose their reforms. When Pontalis set off on his travel, the journey from Bangkok to Songkhla took four days by boat but almost a month by road (Ministry of communication, 2016: 28). What's more, it was impossible to get from Nakhon Sri Thammarat to Phatthalung by road, even though they were only around a hundred kilometres apart. To the north, transport by boat was still the norm, and Pontalis points out during his visit to Raheng (Tak province) that it took eight days (at the time of low water) for a letter to arrive from Bangkok. This explains the enthusiasm with which he travelled along the road that had just been built between Phatthalung and Trang, observing the increasing number of clearings and plantations and anticipating the profound changes that would take place once the railway line linked Trang to the capital – which would indeed be the case in 1914. He also noted that the inhabitants of Trang and Phatthalung had only recently started using carts ("there were only three carts four years ago in Trang. There are now 200 in Trang and 80 in Phatthalung") instead of carrying goods on men's backs, and that this innovation owes much to the efforts of the High Commissioner of the Phuket *monthon,* Phya Ratsada (whose Chinese name is Khaw Sim Bee), who managed to convince the inhabitants to use them by bringing them in from Penang and hiring them out at low prices.

The construction of the railway to the south profoundly changed the political geography of the peninsula. In previous centuries, routes to the west and the Indian Ocean had been more important than those linking Siam to the Malay territories. These trans-peninsular routes, which appear to have been in use since the second century AD (Mills, 1997), were particularly important in their northern part for the kingdom of Ayutthaya in the 16th and 17th centuries, which was thus linked to the ports of the Mon region, notably Mergui (now Myeik), and from there to the Indian coast. For a long time, Mergui was the only major port on the route between Martaban and Malacca. Goods could be traded here, unloaded and transported by the most direct route via Phetburi, Pranburi or Kuiburi. The region produced tin, silver, lead, rubies, sapphires, benzoin and lacquer, teak, rice, salt, fish brine and precious woods (Lubeigt, 1999). As Pontalis notes, "this region has never been of greater interest than since the arrival of Europeans in the Bay of Bengal at the beginning of the 17th century. At the end of the same century, Dutch traders were already pointing out the route from Tenasserim to Ayutthaya as one of the most important trade routes in East Asia, with Mergui, the port of Tenasserim, in regular contact with the Indian coast". Portuguese, French, English and Dutch foreign governors were appointed with varying degrees of success by the Siamese kings to run the port of Mergui at different times (Smithies, 2012), as was the case further south at Phuket and Phang Nga Bay, from where other routes existed to Nakhon Sri Thammarat and Songkhla.

When Siam's control over this region came to an end in the 1760s, due to the wars between the Siamese, Mon and Burmese, Mergui lost its importance and Penang and Singapore became more attractive. Of course, crossings continued to take place, but most of them were between Phang Nga and Chaiya (which had also been under Siamese control since the end of the 13th century). Even after the development of Singapore, these routes remained important, not only because of the need for ports of refuge on the route to Malacca, but also because of the opportunities for trade with major cities such as Nakhon Sri Thammarat and Songkhla. However, the topography posed a problem on the eastern side for boats, with the presence of numerous sandbars, which Pontalis complained about (as they slowed down navigation and the unloading of boats) all the way down to Songkhla. Subsequent political and technical developments would never allow these small regional capitals to constitute serious alternatives to Singapore for international maritime trade.

In this sense, the development of roads and the railway network witnessed by Lefèvre-Pontalis marked the end of trans-peninsular networks whose fate might have been different had the idea of a canal linking the mouth of the Kraburi (which Pontalis calls Pak Chan) to Chumphon Bay been born in the mid-19th century. Originally formulated by King Narai (1656-1688) in 1677 when he commissioned a study from an engineer of King Louis XIV (1643-1715), from Lamar (but for a route further south, from Songkhla), it was mainly considered in the second half of the 19th century. During this period, several topographical studies were carried out, including one by the Franco-British commission, which included the diplomat Ferdinand de Lesseps (1805-1894), in 1883 (see document 17),[9] but their recommendations were negative. Apart from the technical difficulties, neither the British nor the Siamese wanted the project to be implemented, but for different reasons. The British did not want to harm the regional role of the port of Singapore and the Siamese, while not wanting to upset the British either, also feared that the canal would split the peninsula in two and call into question their control of the southernmost territories. Lefèvre-Pontalis also approved of the pragmatism of the Siamese, which enabled them to finance the railway line to the south ("By obtaining, through their complaisance for English ideas in 1909, the possibility of providing their own provinces on the Malay Peninsula with a railway, they have been in a hurry, that is to say, they immediately and definitively took possession of the corridor which, along the coast of the Gulf of Siam, so precariously linked Bangkok to the bulk of their Malay territories"), but he also regretted that France had not been able to better assert its interests in the region during the previous century.

Although it never materialised, contrary to Pontalis' expectations, the idea of a canal between the Gulf of Siam and the Andaman Sea has never ceased to be present in Thai politics (Doll, 2016). It continued to be the subject of numerous technical studies, during which six possible routes were proposed from Chumphon to Songkhla. The French thought of building it, the British blocked it and China is now showing its ambition to complete it. In 2005, the *Washington Times* revealed a plan for China to finance the entire canal, with Chinese port facilities and refineries, as part of its strategy to build infrastructure in the Indo-Pacific region, a strategy known as the "string of pearls" for its military and energy security. The Chinese project will take ten years to build and cost between 20 and 25 billion dollars. However, the Thai government officially abandoned this project in May 2020 and now favours the idea of a corridor (Thailand Bridge) between Chumphon and Ranong, two ports that could be developed in deep water and connected via a rail network for freight. Less costly (1.85 billion dollars), it is also a less politically dangerous option from the point of view of the Thai authorities, insofar as the country would not be symbolically "cut off" from the secessionist south. It would make it possible to shorten the sea routes by around 1,200 kilometres, or the two to three days normally needed for passage via Malacca. For China, it would also mean securing an alternative route in the event of the Strait of Malacca, through which 80% of its energy imports transit, being blocked. In Thailand, the Thai Canal Association, which supports the project and is close to Chinese circles, is trying to convince the government of the project's merits, but various diplomatic pressures and the major geostrategic stakes involved in such a decision have for the time being complicated any progress on this issue. An umpteenth feasibility study commissioned by the Thai government was approved by the House of Representatives in February 2024, and former Prime Minister Srettha Thavisin promised completion of the first part of the work by 2030, with the project scheduled for completion in 2039. The project could be buried again, however, as his government was overthrown a few months later, in August 2024, and the new Prime Minister Paetongtarn Shinawatra has yet to comment on the matter.

A reflection on Siamese identity and the appropriation of external influences

Pontalis' account also, and above all, sheds valuable light on a unique period which, at the turn of the 20th century, saw Siam transform itself into a modern nation-state by appropriating and reformulating two very different types of foreign influence: on the one hand, a Western technical, political and cultural 'model' – and the anti-colonial apprehensions and strategies it created; and on the other, the economic dynamism of the Chinese diaspora – with the political integration of its most influential members.

It could rightly be objected that this was in fact a continuation of an old paradigm which, from the time of Ayutthaya, saw the Siamese royalty using Persian, Chinese and Indian administrators to ensure its trade, Malaysian or Japanese soldiers to secure its palaces, Dutch craftsmen to improve its navy or French or Italian engineers to help build its fortifications and water infrastructures (Baker and Pasuk, 2014: 13). In a way, nothing had really changed at the beginning of the 20th century. Lefèvre-Pontalis met an Italian engineer by the name of Allegri who was working on a bridge project for the governor of Trang and then, on his return journey to Bangkok, a Danish captain by the name of Fabricius working with the governor of Tak to reorganise the Siamese gendarmerie. His notes on the ethnic diversity of the ports and towns in general, both in Siam and Burma, are a recurring theme in the historiography of these regions. The first European visitors to these regions had already considered that central Siam was mainly populated by Mon (whose presence predates the Thai) and Chinese. Between the beginning of the 18th century and the beginning of the 20th century, the populations considered to be ethnically Thai in Bangkok represented only a quarter to a third of the total (Van Roy, 2017: 24), the others being Chinese (mainly Taechiu) or belonging to other minorities, attracted by trade (Persians, Indians, Sikhs) or authoritatively displaced as a result of military campaigns (Khmer, Lao, Malay). Those campaigns in Southeast Asia had always aimed at repopulating centres rather than extending borders (Condominas 1980: 306). As mentioned earlier, some cities even had foreign governors, not only Mergui and Phuket but also Bangkok itself. Michael Smithies notes the presence of two Indian Muslims as governors of Phuket in 1676 and 1677, followed by a French missionary, René Charbonneau, in 1682. In Bangkok, three French governors succeeded each other between 1685 and 1688, and before them the post was held by a Turk (Smithies, 2012: 169).

Nevertheless, at the time of Pontalis' visit, the situation was substantially different from that which had prevailed two centuries earlier, for two reasons. Firstly, from the second half of the 19th century, Siamese nationalism was built, at least in part,[10] in reaction to French and English colonial ambitions that were much more concrete than they had been at the time of Ayutthaya. The Bowring Treaty in 1855 (and the many other bilateral treaties signed in its wake) had assured the Siamese royalty that the country would not be subject to outside interference and would remain independent, unlike its neighbours, in exchange for the liberalisation of trade and, in particular, the end of the royal monopoly on international trade. Nevertheless, fears of territorial interference remained, fuelled in particular by British commercial expansionism, both to the south and to the north, as well as by the military confrontation with French troops in 1893, as a result of which Siam lost the Lao regions it still controlled on the east bank of the Mekong, as well as the present-day provinces of Battambang and Siem Reap in Cambodia. Although Lefèvre-Pontalis does not refer to this episode, he does mention on several occasions the English attempts to control the tin and latex trade and the strategic interest, already mentioned above, for them in the construction of the railway linking

Bangkok to their Malay possessions. He also notes the presence of English consuls in Songkhla and Phuket and regrets that England benefited more from Siam's economic dynamism than France. His account also highlights the presence of a new player, the American Presbyterian missionaries, who had been absent two centuries earlier, and their growing influence in the fields of education (building schools and publishing books in Thai, the first one as early as 1836), health and public administration. He also wisely noted that their influence was in synergy with that of the British and annihilated any hope of seeing a French influence develop: "What is most certain is that by the spread of English education and Anglo-Saxon culture, the English neighbours in that part of Siam where the Americans work are called upon to facilitate their efforts. We have nothing similar in the French part of the Kingdom of Siam". The Anglo-Saxon influence was also facilitated by the fact that several of the princes who "modernised" Siam had received higher education in English, either in Bangkok or Singapore, and spoke the language perfectly, or at least used it more easily than French.[11]

More broadly, Siamese nationalism was built on a principle of "appropriation of external influences", as Lefèvre-Pontalis pointed out, which has subsequently been widely studied and described under various names (Harrison and Jackson, 2010): adaptation, duplication, reinvention, reinterpretation, imitation, internal colonialism, auto-colonialism or crypto-colonialism, all terms describing a capacity to absorb elements of Western culture in order to redeploy their meaning in a specifically Siamese matrix, or one considered as such, and thus legitimise a position of power or social distinction. The phenomenon is far from unique, and has been observed in many parts of the world and at different periods in history (Roman Gaul, Meiji era Japan), including in Southeast Asia among ethnic mountain groups in relation to the Tai populations of the valleys (Évrard, 2019). However, it was particularly noticeable in the Siam visited by Lefèvre-Pontalis, as shown, for example, by the energy and resources devoted by certain local notables in the south, at Trang and Phatthalung, to developing botanical gardens modelled on European "water city parks" and their ambition to turn them into sanatoriums for Westerners in Bangkok.

Chang's oasis, to which Lefèvre-Pontalis devotes several enthusiastic pages, still exists today and has become a royal botanical park. Although not a favourite destination for Bangkok expatriates, it is visited by many Thai tourists on their way from Phatthalung to Trang.

A second difference with the situation two centuries earlier was the scale of Chinese immigration and the crucial economic and political role played by some of its members. For a very long time, alongside the Indians and Persians, the Chinese had been the administrators of trade in the kingdoms of Southeast Asia and they mixed with the local populations in all the ports of the peninsula as well as on the coasts of the Indian Ocean. However, their presence increased significantly in Siam from the 19th century onwards,[12] during which time the various Chakri rulers (who themselves had Chinese ancestry) encouraged their arrival in order to develop infrastructure and extractive industries, increase their income and strengthen their political position. They excluded them from the corvée (Baker and Pasuk, 2014: 32) and entrusted the *jao sua*, or heads of merchant families, with the task of collecting taxes, particularly on swallows' nests, alcohol, opium and gambling. From the Bowring Treaty onwards, they also relied on the Chinese to limit European commercial penetration, particularly in the south (Leveau, 2003). King Mongkut (Rama IV, r. 1851-1868), for example, appointed five Chinese provincial governors out of fear of British covetousness over the tin trade and mistrust of the Muslim Malays.

As Bernard Formoso (2021: 103) points out, the Chinese acted as a buffer force for the Siamese sovereigns who, "by entrusting these disputed areas to subjects who showed great entrepreneurial dynamism, motivated by profit rather than status (...) succeeded in curbing Western expansionism and channelling towards foreigners the discontent of provincial squires whose prerogatives were threatened by the reform of the territorial administration". Several passages in Lefèvre-Pontalis' account echo this analysis, particularly when he writes that "the Siamese are very jealous of Europeans and that, while they are broad in their concessions of mines and land to the Chinese, they are extremely reserved towards Whites, which I understand". He also noted that in Siam there was no desire on the part of the central government to protect its citizens from Chinese economic competition, as the French colonialists were trying to do in Annam, and that on the contrary, the Chinese presence here was "a powerful stimulant".

Among the Chinese immigrants who played an important role in the economy and administration of the southern regions of Siam, the Khaw family is undoubtedly one of the best known in the 19th century (Cushman, 1986 and 1991). Khaw Soo Cheang (1792-1882), who made his fortune in the tin trade and became governor of Ranong during the reign of Mongkut (Rama IV), built up his initial capital by selling fruit in southern Siam. His son, Khaw Sim Bee, became governor of Trang and then of the *monthon* of Phuket under the name of Phya Ratsada (1857-1913). Lefèvre-Pontalis met him in Chang's botanical garden, which he had created, and devoted several laudatory pages to him. He emphasises the intelligence of his management ("to encourage the clearing of land for rice fields, he relieves people who have 10 rays of rice under cultivation of all drudgery, and to respond to their wishes or to the general interest, he facilitates land exchanges"), the apparent prosperity of the countryside around Trang and the people's confidence in their local leaders: "He is a benevolent and extremely open-minded expert in every respect. There are five or six governors or high commissioners in his family, all of whom have taken an interest in the fate of this region. They take an interest in the common work and make it their business in the most gentle and affable way. His relative, the Governor of Trang, has an excellent attitude towards everyone. I can still see this today in his dealings with the inhabitants".

The Khaw, like many other Chinese families settled in Siam, thus played the role of both cement and buffer for the Siamese government in the southern regions. They were able to establish matrimonial alliances with the great Siamese families while maintaining close links with the Penang elite (links mentioned several times by Pontalis). Alongside their economic and administrative successes in Siam, and their contribution to consolidating the power of the crown, they also developed mining and shipping businesses in Penang and were at the origin of one of the first Chinese conglomerates (Cushman, 1986). Their "dual identity" put them in a strong position to counter British influence in the tin trade, while also playing a role as public administrators and "globalisation brokers" for Siam.

Pontalis' trip, however, took place at a time when the attitude of the Siamese authorities towards Chinese immigrants was beginning to change. The drop in intermarriages (following an influx of Chinese migrant women) and the proliferation of associations aimed at preserving the culture of the country of origin gave the Thai leaders the impression that the assimilation process had broken down, generating xenophobic feelings towards them (Formoso, 2021: 103). This feeling was exacerbated in 1910 by rioting strikes in Bangkok during which the Chinese protested against the law imposing the same capitation tax on foreigners as on Thai subjects.[13] Lefèvre-Pontalis remains silent on these events – as he does on the other revolts by Chinese workers, particularly in Ranong and Phuket, towns under the control of the Khaw family, which punctuated the second half of the 19th century (Cushman 1991: 37-44), and on the anti-Chinese sentiment that developed during this period. At most, he notes that the Phya Ratsada "had the reputation of not even speaking Siamese" and that he favoured Chinese immigrants in the management of his *monthon*, charging them "a tax of only 3 ticals, instead of the 6 required in Bangkok". From this point of view, Pontalis' account can sometimes be considered too enthusiastic about Khaw Sim Bee's achievements and not sufficiently nuanced about the contribution of the Chinese to the development of the southern regions of Siam and their relations with the Siamese people, for whom the French diplomat often had harsh words full of colonial contempt. These few days spent with Khaw Sim Bee, less than three months before the latter's assassination,[14] nevertheless gave Pierre Lefèvre-Pontalis the opportunity to deliver a captivating account of the political and economic dynamics underway in this region and the links maintained by the Chinese notables with the nearby island of Penang.

Personnel of the French Legation, Bangkok 1913. (Lefèvre-Pontalis Archive)

Bibliography

Aung-Thwin, Michael (1998) *Myth and History in the Historiography of Early Burma: Paradigms, Primary Sources, and Prejudices*. Athens, Ohio: Ohio University Center for International Studies.

Aung-Thwin, Michael (2005) *Mists of Ramanna: The Legend That Was Lower Burma*. Honolulu: University of Hawai'i Press.

Baffie, Jean (2009) "Sous le règne de Rama V (1868-1910), l'adaptation du Siam à la modernité occidentale", in Gilles de Gantès and Nguyên Phuong Ngoc (eds.), *Vietnam. Le moment moderniste*, Aix-en-Provence: Presses universitaires de Provence, pp. 27-41, 308 p.

Baker, Chris and Pasuk Phongpaichit (2014) *A History of Thailand*, Singapore: Cambridge University Press (third edition), 323 pp.

Bayly, Susan (2004), "Imagining 'Greater India': French and Indian Visions of Colonialism in the Indic Mode," *Modern Asian Studies*, 38(3), pp. 703-744.

Condominas, Georges (1980) *L'espace social à propos de l'Asie du Sud-Est*, Paris: Flammarion, 539 p.

Cushman, Jennifer (1986) "The Khaw Group: Chinese Business in Early Twentieth-century Penang," *Journal of Southeast Asian Studies*, vol. XVII (1), pp. 58-79.

Cushman, Jennifer (1991) *Family and State. The formation of a Sino-Thai Tin-mining dynasty, 1797-1932*, Singapore: Oxford University Press, 172 pp.

Dobbs, Stephen (2015) 'Thailand's Kra Isthmus and Elusive Canal Plans since the 1850s', *TRaNS: Trans-Regional and -National Studies of Southeast Asia*, Volume 4 (1), pp. 165-186.

Évrard, Olivier (2019), "Re-reading 'Ethnic change in the northern highlands of Laos': notes on the Tai-ization of Khmu people," *The Australian Journal of Anthropology*, 30(2), pp. 228-242.

Forchhammer, Emmanuel (1883) *Notes on the Early History and Geography of British Burma*, Rangoon: Governement Press.

Formoso, Bernard (2021) *La production des cultures*, Paris: CNRS Éditions, 296 p.

Harrison, Rachel V. and Jackson, Peter A. (eds) (2010) *The Ambiguous Allure of the West. Traces of the Colonial in Thailand*, Hong Kong: Hong Kong University Press – Cornell University, 268 p.

Kulke, Hermann (1986) "Max Weber's Contribution to the Study of 'Hinduization' in India and 'Indianization' in South-East Asia," in D. Kantowsky (ed.) *Recent Researches on Max Weber's Studies on Hinduism*, Munich, Weltforum-Verlag, pp. 97-116.

Jandam, Kasem (2021) *Bird's nests*.

Business and Ethnicity in Southeast Asia. An anthropological study of business, Bangkok: Silkworm & TSRI, 395 p.

Leveau, Arnaud (2003) *Le Destin des fils du dragon : l'influence de la communauté chinoise au Viêt Nam et en Thaïlande*, Paris-Bangkok: L'Harmattan – Institut de recherche sur l'Asie du Sud-Est contemporaine, 288 p.

López Sanz, Hasan G. & Nicolás Sánchez Durá (2021) "Imaginaire colonial et représentation visuelle des populations noires africaines. Le cas de la Guinée espagnole (1880-1968)," in *Bérose - Encyclopédie internationale des histoires de l'anthropologie*, Paris. URL Bérose: article2346.html.

Lubeigt, Guy (1999) "Ancient transpeninsular trade roads and rivalries over the Tenasserim coasts", in Nguyên Thê Anh and Yoshiaki Ishizawa (eds.), *Trade and Navigation in Southeast centuries*, Tokyo: Sophia University – L'Harmattan, pp.47-76.

Mackay, Colin (2013) *A History of Phuket and the surrounding region*, Bangkok: White Lotus, 438p.

McCormick, Patrick (2014), "Writing a Singular Past: Mon History and 'Modern' Historiography in Burma," *Journal of Social Issues in Southeast Asia*, 29(2), pp. 300-31.

Mills, Janell (1997) "The swinging pendulum: from centrality to marginality- A study of southern Tenasserim in the history of Southeast Asia," *Journal of the Siam Society*, 85, pp. 35-58.

Ministry of Communication (2016) *Royal Siamese State Railway Southern Line 1917*, Bangkok: White Lotus, 210 pp.

Shaun, Cameron (2021) "By Land or Sea, Thailand perseveres with the Kra canal," *The Interpreter*, published on 22/09/2021.

Skinner, Georges William (1957) *Chinese Society in Thailand: an analytical history*, Ithaca: Cornell University Press, 459 p.

Smithies, Michael (2012) "French governors of Phuket, Bangkok and Mergui in the seventeenth century," in Michael Smities, *Seventeenth century Siamese explorations*, Bangkok: The Siam Society, pp. 163-180.

Van Roy, Edward (2017) *Siamese Melting Pot: Ethnic Minorities in the Making of Bangkok*, Singapore: ISEAS-Silkworm Books, 295 pp.

Wieviorka, Michel (1998), "Du racisme scientifique au nouveau racisme", in Wieviorka Michel, *Le racisme, une introduction*, Paris, La Découverte, pp. 13-36.

---

1 This concept, according to which the Brahmins were at the origin of a movement of "Indianisation" or expansion of Indian civilisation towards South-East Asia, was first developed by Max Weber (in *The Religion of India: Sociology of Hinduism and Buddhism*, 1920), then by specialists in South-East Asia from the 1930s and especially in the post-war period (Kulke 1986).

2 There is a vast literature on the subject in English. In French, we can refer to Michel Wieviorka's synthesis (1998) and Hasan López Sanz and Nicolás Sánchez Durá's work (2021) on the colonial imaginary and the visual representation of Black African populations.

3 The clichés about the "lazy Siamese", the indolence of the Burmese, the superiority of the Chinese or the sentences written on the boat taking him from Penang to Burma about "the people of Goa, blacker, fuzzier and dirtier, despite being Portuguese, than the most infamous negroes" are shocking today and may discourage some people from reading further.

4 Bayly 2004: 710-714.

5 McCormick 2014: 316; Aung Thwin 1998: 145-60 and 2005: 299-321.

6 The Indian king Aśoka (IIIe century BC), at the time of the third Buddhist council, is said to have sent the two monks Sona and Uttara to Burma to propagate Theravādin Buddhism, that of the Pāli canon. Forchhammer (1883: 4), taking up this Buddhist tradition, emphasises the Indian origin of local knowledge: "The sources from which the native authors drew the material for the ancient history of their country are the Buddhist scriptures written in India (...). The ancient history of British Burma (...) is really part of the history of the Hindu colonies in Suvannabhumi".

7 Pontalis here conflates Suvaṇṇabhūmi with Hangsawadi, the old name of the present-day city of Bago (Pegu), where the Kalyani inscriptions, deciphered by Forchhammer and constituting his main sources for the history of the Mon kingdom, are to be found.

8 Forchhammer 1883: 1-2.

9 Map from Loftus, A. J. (1883). *Notes of a Journey Across the Isthmus of Krà : Made with the French Government Survey Expedition, January-April, 1883. With Explanatory Map and Sections, and Appendix Containing Reprint of Report to the Indian Government.* Singapore: Singapore and Straits Printing Office.

10 In addition to external threats, the aim was also to regain control of a state apparatus that had been monopolised by a few families of senior civil servants or local lords.

11 In 1872, King Chulalongkorn enrolled fourteen of his cousins at the Raffles Institute in Singapore. In 1874, an English language school was opened in the royal palace under the direction of an Englishman, Francis George Patterson. This was the first truly modern Thai school, and a majority of the pupils were members of the royal family (Baffie, 2009).

12 In 1821, the British ambassador John Crawfurd estimated that there were 440,000 subjects of Chinese descent in the Kingdom of Siam, which he said numbered 2.79 million inhabitants, or 16.3% of the population (Formoso, 2021: 102). Subsequently, an estimated four million Chinese entered Siam between 1820 and 1950, but only 1.5 million chose to stay (Skinner 1957: 72-73). The Chinese minority, including mixed-race elements, now accounts for 13-15% of Thailand's population, but is over-represented in circles of economic and political power (Formoso, 2019: 112).

13 The Chinese were extremely privileged as they paid a capitation fee thirty-three times lower than the Thais, they were exempt from corvées, naturalisation was easy for them, they were free to move around and could buy land (Skinner 1954, cited in Tan and Grillot, 2014).

14 Khaw Sim Bee, along with his close relative, the new governor of Trang, Khaw Joo Keat, were murdered in Trang harbour in early 1913, allegedly by a man who was jealous of the advances that the High Commissioner of the *monthon* of Phuket had made to his wife. While Khaw Joo Keat was killed instantly, Khaw Sim Bee was taken to Penang where he succumbed to his injuries a month later (Mackay 2013: 343).

Agents.

The Siam Steam Navigation Co.
LIMITED.

WEST COAST SERVICE

For Koh Lak, Chumpon, Taku, Langsuen, Banden, Koh Samui, Lacon, Singora, Patani, Panarai, Telupin, Banguara, Kelantan, Bache, Semerak, Bisut, Trigganu, Berserah, Pahang and Singapore.

** s. s.	Boribat	29th	Oct.	1912
* s. s.	Yugala	2nd	Nov.	"
** s. s.	Asdang	5th	"	"
* s. s.	Mahidol	9th	"	"
*' s. s.	Redang	12th	"	"
s. s.	Prachatipok	16th	"	"
'* s. s.	Boribat	19th	"	"
s. s.	Yugala	23rd	"	"
" s. s.	Asdang	26th	"	"
s. s.	Mahidol	30th	"	"

(S. S. Mahidol and S. S. Boribat are calling at Kretay)
* Will not call at Koh Lak, Taku, Berserah and Pahang.
** Will not call at Koh Samui, Bacho, Semerak, Bisut and Tringganu.

EAST COAST SERVICE

For Siracha, Kohsichang, Koh Prah, Rayong, Koh Samet, Chantaboon and Kratt
s. s. **Chutatutch leaving here every Wednesday at noon.**
* s. s. **Krat** " " " **Saturday** " "
* Will not call at Kohsichang, Koh Prah and Rayong.

All the steamers are fitted throughout with Electric Light and have excellent accommodation for First Class Passengers.

For Freight and Passage apply to,
EAST ASIATIC COMPANY, LTD.
Managing Agents.

Extract from the Siam Steam Navigation Cie's shipping schedule between Bangkok and Singapore. October-November 1912.

Photo of the *Boribat*, on which the author sailed between Bangkok and Songkhla, 1908, Prince Damrong Bookshop.

Transcription of Pierre Lefèvre-Pontalis' Travel Journal

I left the Legation at 2 pm on the Banque de l'Indochine's *Luciole* longboat, which took me to the *Boribat* anchored in the middle of the river opposite the Danish East Asiatic Company.

Maugras, who will manage the Legation in my absence, Petithuguenin, Notton, Bonnafous and Tchioum accompanied me on board. It has been agreed that if Petithuguenin can escape at the beginning of December, he will meet me at Raheng so that we can visit Sukhothai together.

I took with me Patte, Petithuguenin's former travelling companion, who was very resourceful but didn't understand any language, and my Chinese valet Hahine, a young inexperienced man who didn't understand French very well but was just as willing as the other.

We set off at 3 o'clock. Hot and sunny day. At about 6.30 pm we passed Paknam. At 8 o'clock we reached the Bar, which we crossed easily. On our way down river, we passed the *Deli* bringing the post from Singapore and in the vicinity of Paknam we came across a crowd of pirogues full of people in very colourful festive clothes. The high river bank covered with nipa palms was also lined with a fringe of very colourful pirogues where the inhabitants of the area had come to watch the young men practise for the regattas of the water festival which will take place in the next few days. I'm sorry to miss it, but today's spectacle gives me an idea of what it will be like.

The sea was flat calm with a cool breeze despite the heat of the season. Great phosphorescence and fish shooting through the water like silver arrows.

30 October 1912

A good night. Cool weather. Calm sea. This morning the sky was overcast but it was not raining and the breeze is pleasant.

Around 9 o'clock we saw the fairly high, wooded coastline in the background and by 10 o'clock we were in the bay of Koh Lak, enclosed on the left by limestone islets with two sharp, wooded peaks dominating the sea. It's very picturesque. A few limestone boulders also line the bay as far as he other end. The plain between them extends a few kilometres deep as far as the next hills. The village is more towards the left with a few scattered houses on the water's edge further along to the right. This must be where the Europeans, for whom Koh Lak is a holiday resort, come.

I didn't go ashore. It was not worth it as it was only a short stop to drop off the post. Besides, the boat anchored close enough for us to see what the place was like. A few amusing boats with Chinese, Malays and Siamese live-aboard merchants swarmed around the *Boribat*. It's not much different from what you see on the Annam coast. The coast appears green, but there are no coconut or areca palms.

At 11am we left Koh Lak and followed the coast quite closely all day. At 6 o'clock at sunset, we rounded the rocky headland of Lem Chong Pra.

All night the weather continued to be very calm but I slept badly as we stopped several times and, although the stops were short and the crane wasn't used, the shouts of the sailors and the native arrivals kept me awake. The first stop was at 11 pm in Chumphon and the second at 3 am in Pak Nam Tako.

Phya Mahibal and his wife, n.d., National Archives of Thailand.

31 October 1912

At 6 o'clock in the morning, we anchored for nearly an hour off Lang Suan, where a few Chinese went ashore and where we loaded some sacks. This whole region does not seem particularly rich. You don't see any coconut palms, arecas or rubber. The seashore is generally occupied by low limestone uplifts, with the depressions in between them more wooded than cultivated.

Itinerary from Bangkok to 9th November. Adaptation of the Map of the Catholic Missions of Siam, Burma and Laos drawn and engraved by R. Hausermann. Missions étrangères de Paris/IRFA.

TRAVEL JOURNAL 39

The chain of not very high watershed hills is in the background and quite close up, with a plain stretching all the way to the sea.

At Chumphon, Phya Mahibal, who until recently was High Commissioner of Bandon, owns property where his wife he told me, wants to start serious rubber cultivation and especially coconut plantations. Every year she hunts elephants in the forest, the last time with great success.

She would also like to set up large-scale fisheries in Chumphon, as schools of *pla tu* are often abundant there. She has managed to make some good canned fish in oil and the smoked fish she gave me to taste were perfect. But it seems that Prince Damrong discouraged her. Perhaps he felt that this type of operation was not appropriate for civil servants. Or perhaps the Chinese, who are used to benefiting from fishing, were seeking to defend their interests. But if the rich and intelligent Siamese have to give up all initiative, who will take their place if not the foreigners? For my part, I feel rather indulgent towards Siamese civil servants of the Mahibal type, who are altogether too rare. Moreover, the Phya has just left the service; according to him, to regain

Right: Fishing boat in Chumphon, 1950, National Archives of Thailand, Prince Kavila collection.

Below: *Pla tu* and other fish caught in Chumphon Bay, 1950, National Archives of Thailand, Prince Kavila collection.

his independence; according to others, because some abuses were found in his administration and he was refused promotion.

At Lang Suan, we reached the region where the Siamese have retained both coasts of the peninsula and are no longer constrained by the divide created by the Tenasserim mountains. As a result, they are more active in these southern provinces.

We were very close to the Pak Chan fjord, which leads to the famous Kra Isthmus on the English border. This is a place I would have loved to visit, but due to a lack of time and means, it will remain off my itinerary in the Bay of Bengal.

At one o'clock we arrived in front of the confluence of the Bandon River, the capital of the province, and at 2 o'clock in the interior by boat up the river. Despite a stop which should be six hours, it was impossible to get off in these conditions, especially as this time we had anchored quite far from the coast and the local boats were slow coming to us.

The bay is very large, with the same characteristics as the rest of the coast and is more or less extended at its southern end by several islands, the two largest of which seem to be inhabited.

We dropped off our only European passenger in Bandon, a German who is on his way to a nearby rice mill, as there are apparently rice fields in the area.

A large Chinese junk with woven mat sails spent nearly two hours unloading its pigs, howling in their rattan baskets. They are put up at the front of the boat. It's lucky for me that I am not going all the way down to Singapore with them.

The boat coming to collect the post didn't arrive until 5 o'clock. We were so far from the river that it took a long time to reach us, even though the sea is unusually calm for the time of year. To reach the anchorage, she had to cross a high bar, which was only passable at high tide. The boat waited until 10 o'clock in the evening for the boat from Singapore, which always crosses with the one from Bangkok at Bandon.

The longboat brought an Englishman who, while waiting for the boat to Bangkok, came to spend the end of the day on the *Boribat*. He was very chatty and what he had to say was interesting.

On the subject of Phya Mahibal, he recounted that the East Asiatic Company, having heard in Bandon of land that was suitable for coconut cultivation, asked to buy it. They were kept waiting before finally being told that the land had been sold. It was Mahibal who had appropriated the land himself.

This Englishman, who is employed to survey the Siamese railway in the peninsula, finds that Siamese labour is ridiculously expensive for what it provides. Moreover, it is irregular, with the authorities diverting it for their own use, either for plantations or for carpentry work.

However, in his opinion, the line could be built under very satisfactory economic conditions. He has been in the region for six months and his current prospecting area is around 150 kilometres south of Bandon.

The forest provides excellent timber at a reasonable price, which the Siamese are very good at cutting. There are up to 10 species of valuable trees, of superior quality to teak. Logging is difficult at the moment because of the lack of regularity in the water regime of the Bandon river, but once the railway is built, logging will be incredibly easy, as the line goes through the forest.

According to him, no part of Siam is richer. Minerals abound, especially tin and antimony, but the Siamese are alert to this and don't let good concessions slip through their fingers. Neither do the Chinese, and when the Europeans used them as interpreters, they were soon deprived of the benefits of their discovery.

The Siamese are not as conscientious in monitoring the trade. As a Chinese junk approached the *Boribat* to drop off a load of hides, he pointed out that 6,000 buffaloes had recently died in the region from rinderpest. It was their hides, he added, that were being transported to Singapore.

It is said that the bar can sometimes play nasty tricks, and that some passengers disembarking from liners have had to spend up to three days on the islet in front of it, waiting for the tide to be high enough to cross.

As small bags of tin ore were being loaded on board the *Boribat*, the Englishman told us that he knew of five tin mines near his railway works, but that the Chinese who owned them were wasting them by drilling holes instead of exploiting them rationally.

As for the Siamese authorities, accustomed to cheating the customs to enrich themselves, they are very disappointed that the presence of

Europeans from the East Asia Company and on the railways has led to contols which have prevented them from cheating as much as in the past regarding the quantities of tin being exported and the duties collected on such occasions.

From top to bottom, the Siamese are the same. Of all the workers, he is the least industrious on the building sites, bending under his native bosses who exploit him, but taking revenge at the first opportunity. Thus just the other night, it seems the peasants felled 200 coconut trees on a plantation belonging to Phya Mahibal.

The Chinese, who spoil things when they are just passing through, work hard when they see a profit. They respond to promised rewards, get paid in advance on railway sites and then refuse to work as soon as it starts raining.

The Laotians of Chiang Mai constitute a particular class of railway worker, suited to certain special and not very hard jobs. They follow the work down the line and travel further and further afield, where their expertise is required, before those of them who have finished their employment return home with their earnings.

I asked the English engineer if there were easy communications between Bandon and Phuket along the Bay of Bengal coast. He replied that there were not. There is only an elephant trail, which is not very practicable. To get to Phuket, you have to go via Ligor or Singora, where there are roads. There are also roads in the whole of Phuket *monthon* because the High Commissioner, Phya Ratsada, is an intelligent Chinese who does as he pleases and can't even speak Siamese.

Bandon's Phya Mahibal, on the other hand, is a completely different story; he only thinks of plundering the inhabitants and doesn't care about the roads. In the past, however, there was a large tin trade between Phuket and the Gulf of Siam. Perhaps the roads were better. It is probable that most of the journey was made by junk on the river and that the journey by land was not made every day.

1 November 1912

We left Bandon yesterday at 10 o'clock in the evening. This morning, after a good crossing, our arrival at Ligor at 8 am was greeted by a squall which completely hid any view of the coast. A little later it cleared slightly so that we could only guess at the appearance of the place.

The mountain range with its many peaks that lies at the back of Bandon can be seen here closer to the shore and on its other side, but towards the south the coast is completely low for quite a long stretch.

The country is known in Siamese as Lakhon or, more accurately, Nakhon Sri Thammarat. The town is a few miles inland on the river and there are no dwellings to be seen on the coast. It's a completely open shore, barely lit and not at all practical. I find it hard to understand how, since ancient times, it has been the busiest point of passage and embarkation for travellers and emigrants coming to Siam from India or the Bay of Bengal.

This must be due to the political organisation of the country and the ease with which the masters of the country were able to create a solid settlement there from an early date. The fact is that under its ancient name, Ligor, Muang Lakhon enjoyed great power and prosperity in the past.

There is no longer any doubt that Ligor was the first stop for the Hindus in their conquest of lower Indochina. The organisers of Cambodia and the first civilised settlers came from there.

After having depended primarily on Burma, Ligor freed itself and the neighbouring principalities, which it eventually dominated. It was the domain of a powerful rajah, vassal of Siam for several centuries and hereditary prince.

It is only fairly recently that the Siamese have found it necessary to strengthen their ties with the head of the principality so as to make his domains one of the kingdom's provinces.

The main product is tin. It is brought to the Lakhon river via the Trang road. The railway is currently under construction and will soon link Lakhon to the central line of the peninsula. But for the time being, communication with Trang by car seems possible, as the roads have been improved following the Queen Mother's visit to the country a few weeks ago.

Lakhon is well worth seeing as it is an ancient city surrounded by walls and full of temples, some of which are very old and date back to the introduction of Buddhism in Indochina. Unfortunately, I doubt that the length of my stay in the peninsula will allow me to make this visit from Trang.

It's exasperating to remain at anchor for 10 to 5 hours without doing anything. The few barges that came quickly unloaded their bags of tin ore and we had no distractions other than to watch the comings and goings around the boat of a huge shark accompanied by its small satellite.

The Captain fired ten rounds from his Winchester without success. We also saw a small band of stingrays in our vicinity, but they were less frequent than the shark.

You can't imagine the care with which the two young Chinese who loaded their pigs onto the *Boribat* yesterday look after their charges. They take turns feeding them, sheltering them from the sun with latanier mats, and refreshing them individually with water. It seems that in these conditions very few succumb to the fatigue of the crossing. But what young European would know how to take such good care of his herd?

Departure at 5 am Flat calm. Radiant weather. At rest it had been hot all afternoon, but on the move the breeze was pleasant. For the first time since we started sailing along the coast of the Malay Peninsula, the coastline seems low.

2 November 1912

The *Boribat* dropped anchor off the islet of Singora at 5.15 am. The day was just beginning to dawn. When the whistle blew, no one rushed to respond. It wasn't until 7 o'clock that the first boats appeared, followed by the East Asiatic longboat, *Freya*, towing a large barge.

Seeing how the Danish East Asiatic has comfortable longboats here as well as in Bandon, I can't help making a comparison with the Messageries Maritimes who are so miserably provided for all along the coast of French Indochina. Everything is the same from top to bottom. During my last visit to Cochinchina, I learned that the port of Saigon had only one longboat for its own use, and it was still in a very poor state of repair. That says a lot about the maritime habits of those in power.

The *Freya* was soon replaced by a Siamese government longboat with an official on detachment in the front to receive me. The Prince of Lopburi, otherwise known as Prince Yugala, Prince of the King and High Commissioner, is currently away in Bangkok where his mother, one of the three Queen sisters married to Chulalongkorn, is suffering from uraemia and is being treated day and night by Dr Manaud. Orders have been given to receive me as if he were here.

From the anchorage where the *Boribat* is moored, it takes almost an hour to reach Singora, as the river that emerges between two hills forms a powerful bar in the sea that must be skirted. As you pass, you come across a few sandbanks. A few months ago, a junk loaded with oil, ran aground on one of them and was completely lost.

It is astonishing to suddenly find oneself facing the mouth of a vast river, hidden until then by trees and a hill. It was about 8.30 am when we entered it, with bamboo weirs for fishing on both sides. The right bank is low and sandy covered with a strange wood of pine trees somewhat reminiscent of the filaos of Ismailiah. In front of these pines are a few houses and flats. The longboat stopped at one of them, where the Singora government and its staff were waiting for me, as well as the governor of Phatthalung, in whose care I would be placed tomorrow. Also at the landing stage was the head of the engineering department, an Italian, Allegri, whom I know from Bangkok and who came to greet me with one of his compatriots, Canova.

While a motor van removed my luggage and boys, I left with the governor and his servant for the residence that was built two months ago for the use of the Queen and Prince Damrong.

It's a charming and wonderfully comfortable bamboo chalet, equipped with everything you could wish for, in the pine forest that stretches between the river and the sea. I find it to be very comfortable, with a large and stylish staff, and peace under this canopy reminiscent of the pines of Arcachon, the filaos of Ismailiah and the old gnarled olive trees of Greece.

By 10 o'clock, I had freshened up and was ready to go on an excursion in the surrounding area in my Renault Brothers car with the governor's secretary, who spoke English very well. The car bears the Yugala coat of arms and the driver, with all his bracelets, gold chains and marks of distinction, is obviously a gentleman in the service of the Governor.

We walked along the now almost completely destroyed city walls, on the left of which the railway station has been built and the railway line constructed. The recently built roads and streets are less reminiscent of the outskirts of Saigon.

First a few marshes, then a little further on, after some gardens, the crossroads of the roads leading to Patani and Kedah. The road to Patani is not yet finished, and if we were to take it, we would quickly come to a halt due to the lack of bridges to cross the rivers. However, we would soon reach Prince Charoon's rubber plantations, the new Siamese minister in Paris. He has just left to go to Penang with his family to pick up the boat that will take him to Europe.

We set off on the Patani road, which leaves something to be desired. But as it is, it represents a great advance for Siam, as it can be travelled by car. Several times we crossed the railway line and its branches. One leads to the wharf on the river, the other to a stone quarry where the Chinese railway workers are preparing excellent ballast. Another new development for me in this old country of Siam.

The road is lined with numerous *sala* where pedestrians can rest. Most of them are Siamese or Siamese Malays who have forgotten their language, but who wear turbans and whose women have not given up their buns.

We arrived safely at the seven kilometre point, the destination of our excursion, but then the car broke down, therefore putting our return into question, as the driver with his bracelets did not seem to know much about the mechanics of his Renault. My guide took the precaution of sending someone to town to ask for a spare car, but we didn't need one because during the hour we spent on the edge of a coconut plantation, the driver finally managed to repair the car. He came to join us at the owner's house where we were chatting over fresh coconuts with the Siamese workers from the plantation who were resting in between making fishing nets.

There are 10,000 coconut trees in full production on this plantation and 4,000 younger plants. It is owned by the widow of the former governor of Singora, who died two years ago and managed to run his business using prison labour. Whether this a was scandal or not, the work was done and the plantation is a living example for the lazy and indifferent populations of the region. It must be said that the governor who took this initiative was of Chinese origin. A Siamese would never have been able to do as much.

In good years, the plantation produced 1,200 coconuts per day during the harvest season, which lasts from August to November. Last year it produced only 800 and this year 600. Is this because the master has disappeared or because the rains have been less regular?

Fifteen consecutive days of rain are enough to compromise everything. It needs to be regular, but not too frequent and not too heavy. The nuts collected are spaced out for a short time, then opened and women can shell up to 300 a day, extracting the pulp which is then sent in baskets to Singapore where it is processed into copra and then vegetable butter. The profits are so high that they may have attracted more than one Siamese prince or governor who is trying to do the same. Fifteen Siamese coolies are enough to run this plantation which, in European hands, would undoubtedly look much better, but which nonetheless represents a serious effort. The owner lives in a Chinese house in town and comes from time to time to look after her property.

Coconut transport on an EAC Liner Ship, 1950, National Archives of Thailand, Prince Kavila collection.

The car that had come to meet us took us back to the chalet without a hitch at half past noon for lunch. It was served with an excellent Bordeaux by Prince Yugala's stylish servants. My guide praises the prince highly and says that he rivals Chakrabongse, Rapi and Chira in ensuring progress in the new Siam. Unfortunately, he comes up

Princes Chakrabongse, Chira and Rapi, n.d., National Archives of Thailand.

against people happy with their lot, with few needs and for whom nature satisfies their most urgent necessities so easily and so cheaply.

He himself was brought up in Penang and has travelled in Burma and Java, so he knows where he stands regarding the examples of progress set by his neighbours. Prince Yugala married the daughter of Prince Bhanurangsi so that he is as close as possible to the throne. One of his sisters is the famous princess who was said to be destined to become the first wife of the present King but at the time of his coronation, he seems to have definitively discarded her. Was it impotence or the need to abandon the traditions of royal consanguineous marriages? So much has been said on this point!

Prince Yugala is a Cambridge alumnus and very proud of it. Although he is younger, he may bring shared memories to Dunn, the English Consul who has just arrived in Singora and whom I went to see in the afternoon. However, Dunn feels much better acquainted with Prince Charoon, who has just been in the country and who was his classmate at Cambridge and a member of his sailing team. Dunn complains of having little to do and to lack resources in Singora, while in Phuket, the former Junk Ceylon, where his colleague Fitzmaurice also now in Singora, goes to run the English consulate, there is a large group of European settlers busy tin mining. What's more, according to Fitzmaurice, Phya Ratsada is far superior to the Siamese leaders of the neighbouring *monthon*.

With the governor and his colleague from Phatthalung, we set off

TRAVEL JOURNAL 49

for another car ride through the town, and for a climb on foot with the governor of Phatthalung to the top of the wooded hill overlooking Singora. We climbed the hill by stairs, stopping first on a terrace where a roof had been erected over a small golden *phra bot*. Higher up, by a tougher staircase, you reach the summit with its Buddhist pyramid and lighthouse. The view is magnificent and well worth the climb, with an expansive horizon of sea, wooded shores and Singora stretching out below its hill like Luang Prabang around its Tiom Si.

Inland, the river and lake stand out like silver slices against the wooded hills. At sunset, it's a truly Japanese landscape, something like Nagasaki or the Inland Sea. And one begins to dream of a great natural harbour, which may have sufficed in ancient times for the limited needs of sea-going boats and junks. This is no longer the case today since the lack of depth in the lake and the difficulty of access to its entrance mean that the Singora river is unapproachable at any time of year for ships of any tonnage. During the northern monsoon season, the situation is even worse. Ships can only get close by anchoring briefly near the island in the open sea, where they can drop off travellers like they do in Bandon.

However, it is on the hill I climbed this evening that one of the two wireless telegraphy stations that Siam has ordered from the German company Telefunken will soon be installed. It is Western Siam that will benefit from this innovation, as well as from the progress currently being made by the development of its railway network.

Despite the improvement in its relations with Indochina, it is still always British trade that stands to benefit from Siamese improvements. When the Siamese do something on our side, it is a torpedo boat station

Singora lighthouse on the Kao Tang Kuan hill, private collection of Chao Kawilavongse na Chiang Mai.

that they are planning at Chantabun, or a penal establishment that they are trying to create at Koh Kut on our Cambodian border. If I can manage to change this trend, I'll be very happy, but I'll need a bit more help than I have had for Indochina.

My guide Luang Peo interests me because his conversation is typical of Siamese bureaucrats who have been trained in English and European ways. He is fluent in all the issues. Those concerning Japan and China are particularly close to his heart. He has a great idea of China and what it could do with a little union, unity and discipline. Japan seems to strike him less, and perhaps he's right. As for scientific inventions and the results that can be expected from them, Europe retains its prestige. This is still how we hold the world together, and that's a good thing, because without it, where would we be?

3 November 1912

By 7 o'clock I was on my feet and it was really nice to be on the veranda of this pretty royal bamboo pavilion, after a good night's sleep enjoying the morning light, filtered by the branches of the old pines that separate the chalet from the sea.

After lunch, the governor of Singora arrived, flanked by his colleague from Phatthalung. They came to pick me up and took me by car to the longboat, while my boys took my luggage away in a cart.

It's impossible to leave the slightest tip. I am in the King's house, or at least his brother's, and when I wanted to give money to my servants adorned with bracelets and medallions, I was politely but forcefully refused. Where in this country do you draw the line between secretary, servant and slave? It's not always easy to tell.

At 8.30 am the boat left after a great exchange of compliments with the Governor of Singora. The Governor of Phatthalung was on board. He speaks good English. He is 60 years old. His brother, he told me, died at 97. He is a kind and thoughtful man who once commanded at Phixaie. If he came all the way to Singora to meet me, it was on the express orders of Pince Yugala, who seems to have arranged every detail of my stay in his *monthon* from afar.

On the lake the light was soft and the air was fresh for most of the journey, which lasted from 8.30 in the morning to 4 in the evening.

In reality, this lake is a double lagoon fed by several streams flowing down from the mountains and ending in a very large arroyo lined with fishing villages. The first lagoon, that of Singora, is partly bordered by hills and bisected by a large island filled with fruit trees which have the best reputation. It was 10.20 am when we left this first lagoon to enter the arroyo and precisely midday when we left the arroyo to enter the Phatthalung lagoon, which is twice as large as the first.

In the meantime we had lunch on board and were able to stretch our legs in the delightful little Siamese-Malay fishing village of Pak Payun, which lies at the narrows where the large arroyo emerges. We spent half an hour there, then entered the Phatthalung lagoon, which gradually widens and spreads to the point where you can barely make out some of its banks.

The most distinct bank is the Western one: it backs onto the watershed line or is at least separated from it by a lightly wooded plain. On the Singora side and towards the sea, the line is less clear and on the Ligor side, it disappears completely and merges with the horizon, which this afternoon lent itself to mirage.

It was towards the watershed line that my attention was mainly focused. Here I could see the outline of the ridge I must cross to reach Trang. But in the plain between this range and the lake, a few small isolated limestone massifs stand out, with jagged shapes, one of which, Kao Chay Son, is quite curious and would seem to deserve a serious visit. It contains some remarkable caves that Prince Damrong admired and that I too would love to visit, but it would take me a long time and a very tiring day would not even be enough as there is no dirt road to get there. Another more important massif is the one near which, at the end of the lake, is the Phatthalung river, at the mouth of which is the village of the same name. We saw this group of limestone heights growing and becoming more defined as we advanced nearer to Phatthalung. But before that, towards the middle of the lake, we passed a fairly large group of islands whose core is also made of limestone and which is not lacking in picturesqueness. This group is known as the five Ko Si Ko Ha Islands and is said to be famous in China for the swallows' nests that are found there and harvested at such great expense. In reality, the market is in Bangkok, where the harvest is leased to a Sino-Siamese group who has been doing very good business for a long time. But China is definitely leaving! Swallows' nests are no longer in fashion, and last year the Bangkok syndicate couldn't make ends meet. It seems that the swallows' nests in Chumphon, north of Bandon at Phya Mahibals' property are also very famous.

It is in this same Chumphon that such great fortunes could be made by better organising *pla tu* fishing. The governor of Phatthalung knows the hopes and disappointments of his neighbour Mahibal, or rather of his wife, and as he knows all about them, he laughs rather mischievously under his breath.

Aerial picture of Singora-Phatthalung lake over Pak Payun and Koh Si Koh Ha, private collection of Chao Kawilavongse na Chiang Mai.

The governor of Phatthalung is less ambitious. If only he could persuade his constituents to cultivate their rice fields and prevent weeds to grow there; if he could get more of them to plant fruit trees and especially coconut palms, he would consider that he had done enough. But most prefer to indulge in the pleasures of fishing, abandoning the fields for the fisheries in the middle of the lake and the nets they have all set out in front of their houses on stilts. This will not change the appearance of the country, which in many respects has a bush-like appearance while it would lend itself so well to cultivation. The population may not be abundant either. It has been decimated or abducted en masse many times in the past and even after more than a century the inhabitants still remember with terror the old wars with the Burmese.

In any case, it's not easy to restore farming habits to a population that has lost them and is content to live on so little. It's true that without well-being and rice fields, the population has less chance of multiplying. It's a vicious circle. Tigers are not uncommon, nor are wild elephants in the marine marshes of the Phatthalung lagoon. It is at the place called Thale Noi, beyond Phatthalung, that you can encounter, especially at this time of year, bands of wild elephants that have come to graze. The Governor would like to take me there one of the next days, but I have no time to waste chasing after uncertain elephants.

About half an hour before reaching Phatthalung, the Governor pointed out to me a clearing on a peninsula where a *phya* from Bangkok had just started a coconut plantation. It's a good example. Judging by the numerous plumes of coconut palms and sugar palms rising above the villages of the first lagoon, the region is favourable for this crop.

As for profits, that's another matter altogether. Won't there one day be a coconut crash, like the one expected for rubber? What is certain is that, given the country's needs and habits, consumption is assured, and nothing can do more to populate and develop the region than to develop a crop that is also used for food.

The Governor has certainly done things very well. Even though Saturday was his day off, he insisted that all his staff be present to greet me on arrival. So there were more than 24 of them, greeting "My Excellency" as best they could as soon as I disembarked, and once again I had great difficulty distinguishing the heads of government departments from the servants who bowed to the master in the old-fashioned way. Admittedly, the spit holders, fire holders and parasol holders of the old days have disappeared, but many gestures have survived.

In any case, I was delighted to find a car here, albeit of German make, and a driver with sufficient experience.

As for the residence, it is sumptuous, for Phatthalung, which is not a holiday resort like Singora. In any case, it's brand new, having been built for the late king or even for the Queen's recent visit. My mosquito net doesn't close with pink satin ribbons like in Singora, but nothing is missing. The Queen spent three nights here less than two months ago, and we could house a regiment in the bamboo cottages attached to the main house.

The Governor didn't let me waste any time and as soon as the official introductions had been made, we set off by car to inspect the town and its surroundings.

A great road builder, he laid out the network for the future town, but it has yet to be built, because apart from the main street, where a few shops are scattered around, the population seems to prefer living in the countryside. At least it's a good thing that they don't seem to dread the immediate vicinity of the Trang main road, along which there are now quite a few gardens and houses.

Apparently, this was not always the case. The Governor says that at first the inhabitants were most resistant to the work of building the road, which imposed many chores on them, and then to the residence next to the road. But little by little they got used to it and understood the value of this type of work, which in the future will make up most of their chores. The number of carts increases and transport by hand decreases accordingly.

Actually, a year like this one is not going to reduce their drudgery. The Queen's month-long journey gave rise to endless requisitions and forced labour for the construction of new tracks, the refurbishment of old ones and the building of rest cottages and houses wherever the satisfaction of her every whim could be anticipated.

So there was nothing tender or trusting in the gestures and eyes of the natives when they saw the government car arrive. Many still maintain the traditional crouch as a sign of respect and obedience, but others have abandoned it and almost all have a sullen look.

The Governor, although complaining about his eyesight, does not close his eyes. In passing, he gave his secretary a few helpful comments and was delighted to see that the rice fields are still promising. He told me how many have sprung up from the jungle since he took charge of the district. And in truth the country as a whole is a pleasure to see, with its lush green fields alternating with fruit tree gardens and beautiful *mai yak* groves with shiny trunks. It's like being in a park.

What makes this landscape even more interesting is the presence of the vegetation-covered limestone boulders that had caught my eye from the lake and drawn my attention throughout the last part of the trip.

The Governor had me get out of the car and go to one of them, the Tham Ha, which is preceded by a more or less abandoned pagoda in a thicket of superb vegetation. At the foot of the pagoda is a beautiful rounded grotto with stalactites, filled with seated Buddhas of various types and colours, with a larger statue on the left and a large reclining Buddha. It's all very picturesque and impressive.

What is no less impressive is the band of black, vigorous, long-tailed monkeys frolicking in the trees and creepers around the bend in the cave, jumping up and down with terrible cries when they hear the sound of a blast in their immediate vicinity. It is in fact the construction of the railway that is attacking their beautiful limestone rocks, provoking the discontent of these quadrumanes, and my goodness, I understand them. These rocks are so beautiful and until now they have been the only ones to share ownership of them with Buddha, in whose honour the faithful have managed to erect, God knows how, a small pyramid at the top of the highest and steepest conical block overlooking the plain.

If only the railway could be of some use to me. But I won't have to use it at any point on the line, and the ballast train that brought Fitzmaurice, the new British Vice-Consul from Phuket, here today, whom I saw yesterday in Singora, has left again. So I've been unable to organise tomorrow's excursion to Kao Chay Son by this means and have had to give it up.

Fitzmaurice too has had to give up a lot of things. As his trip coincides with mine, he is bound to be sacrificed. Phya Ratsada in Phuket told him from Trang that he could not send his car, so he was obliged to walk from the railway line to the bungalow where we happened to meet him, a route that his more fortunate luggage followed on one of those rather precarious trolleys that seem to be a novelty here.

Phya Ratsada's car is reserved for me, of course, with a planned excursion to Ligor, which is becoming decidedly improbable. A telegram from Trang told the Governor about the insurmountable obstacles to this project: bridges cut, broken roads, continuous rain, etc. In short, there is nothing I can do. I'm only half angry about it, because since my breakdown yesterday I have been somewhat reluctant to embark on a two-day journey by car for 7 hours a day, at the end of which I was likely to miss my arrival in Penang for the boat on the 9th of November.

The Governor, whose goodwill is unalterable, gave up trying to do the impossible. Too bad for Fitzmaurice who is not asking for anything at all. As the only person in Phatthalung who speaks a European language, he would at least have liked the government to provide him with a few interpreters to cope with all the new needs created by the arrival of Europeans attracted by the work on the railway or the recently discovered attractions of the region. But not one of his staff spoke a word of English. And yet he has some well-educated young people among those who this evening served us at table with as much care as distinction and elegance. This evening, at least, I learned for sure, because he told me himself who these young people were, how interested he was in watching them make their administrative debut and how keen he was that they should take advantage of My Excellency's presence to learn about European customs, which they know absolutely nothing about.

I'm ashamed of it, but I didn't have the chance to change my clothes to come to the table and I made stains on the tablecloth when I cut a mango. What a fine example for the young son of the Ubon High Commissioner and brother of one of the King's secretaries, in residence in Dusit! Serving curry to the Minister of France in the village of Phatthalung, where last night crocodiles from the lake came to raid the Governor's henhouse in his absence, is a strange way to start a career.

What a misfortune not to find myself in the presence of one of these terrible animals! After all, I can't complain. I saw monkeys roaming free in a way I had never seen before in Indochina: once in the Angkor forest and once on the Hà Tiên canal, I found myself in the path of these interesting jumping masters.

4 November 1912

If I don't die of indigestion tonight, it won't be the fault of my Siamese hosts. From 7 o'clock onwards, I had to eat eggs, coffee and jam. At 9 am I had to eat a full breakfast with European and Siamese meat courses. Then, on the road, twice, on arrival once more and

Portrait of Khaw Sim Bee, who became Phya Rastada, 1908, National Archives of Thailand.

in the evening at Phya Ratsada's in Tehong a sumptuous meal. I have begged them not to feed me so much tomorrow.

We left Phatthalung at about 10 o'clock in the morning, the governor and two others with me, in yesterday's car driven by a chauffeur specially sent from the Bangkok palace for my visit by Prince Damrong. The two boys are with the luggage in one of the three car vans that have been serving Phatthalung, Singora and Lakhon throughout the region on official business since the Queen's visit.

Along the way, Phya Wittanakit, governor of Phatthalung, sings the praises of Prince Damrong and tells me that it is he who demands that young family men, before becoming civil servants, learn to make themselves useful in the eyes of everyone by dirtying their hands with work themselves. This is why I was served at table by people of quality, and saw them drive me in their cars and carry my boxes to the van wearing silk *sampot* and white stockings.

This bothers me and probably the Governor too. He strictly obeys the Prince's orders, but nevertheless shows his friendship for some of his subordinates and, at my request, he told me that this all-American training was not to everyone's taste.

I can understand Damrong's idea that his reforms should break away from the old worlds and try out the democratic system. But is he right? These young people agree to act as servants, but only on condition that when they themselves become governors, they demand the same of their subordinates. The administrative distances are maintained and the people gain nothing.

But you have to appreciate Damrong's good intentions. He is one of the Siamese who continue to improve things in every respect.

Phya Wittanakit shows me in passing a limestone chasm whose destruction the Prince is absolutely opposed to for artistic and sentimental reasons, as opposed to the utilitarian sense of the road builders.

He's a kind-hearted man who knows how to take an interest in these young people whom he pretends haven't reached the required level. To one of Phatthalung's best, who is from an upstanding family and who, honest and discreet, keeps to the shadows with dignity, he said that with such reserve he would hardly make his way in life and that he behaved like a woman. The Governor told me that "he was trying to encourage this perfect and fundamentally honest boy whom I love like my own son".

The Governor, whose attentions to me are endless, told me how pleased he was with my visit and naively added: "at least it won't be said that we don't have roads, because we even have railways and cars". And it was with real joy that from his car, in which he travelled in all directions along the road from Phatthalung to Trang, he observed the state of maintenance, the repair of the bridges with hard wood, and the hard work, at least for the moment, of the people gathered in the rice fields. But having been away from home for several days, he was dismayed to learn that not a drop of water had fallen on the rice fields for five days.

For my part, I could see that right up to the edge of the non-irrigatable land, people were working hard everywhere, and a lot of forest had recently been cleared.

On the other hand, there were many huts and gardens along the road, buffaloes and oxen and carts, and on the road itself there were pedestrians in both directions, many of whom take their produce to Trang.

We came across traders selling pigs and poultry, and Malabar cattle buyers who knew the outlets in Penang and Singapore. Before long, with well-established communications, the Phatthalung region will be a beautiful agricultural country.

However, in an hour and a half by car, or even a little less, we had crossed an entire cultivated area. At a quarter to twelve, having already crossed several strips of advanced forest bordering the dry plain, we reached Na Wang at the bend in a ravine where a clear-water torrent flows around the partly deforested hillocks.

TRAVEL JOURNAL

It was here that Phya Wittanakit chose, at the foot of the wooded mountains of the watershed range, a place of rest and seclusion for visiting princes, and where the Queen recently spent several days, with great pleasure. Two years ago, everything had been prepared down to the last detail for the announced visit of the late King. But just as people were expecting him to arrive, they suddenly learned that he had just died.

So much effort had been wasted, but the Queen's visit this year put everything back on track. The authorities did better because they knew the terrain better and since the works on the road, the bridges and the railway had brought them more into contact with the country, they had a clearer understanding of its resources. It was barely a year ago that Prince Damrong drove the first car in this region, and since then there has been a great deal of progress in improving the road, in maintaining it and in its daily use! The governor of Phatthalung is well aware of this, having been at work all the time, but he is not unhappy that, in addition to his chiefs, a few foreigners have noticed it.

His masterpiece, or at least the one he is most proud of, is the Na Wang oasis, which he has carved out of the forest and which he continues to embellish every day. A number of small chalets overlooking the wooded mountain and the torrent have been built on the slopes, some of which have been cleared of trees and planted with grass. The entrance to the estate is marked by majestic trees, gigantic jars with straight shapes like immense columns. At the top of the paths, the Phya has accumulated all the ferns and curious plants of the forest with multicoloured foliage, pink periwinkles etc. and under the Queen's windows he even managed to grow European roses.

You'd think you were in a water city park. That's exactly what it feels like. It's a completely new experience for travellers to Indochina.

Phya Wittanakit would have liked me to stop there for the night, so that I could get a good feel for the charms of this estate, where he himself often comes for a short holiday. But as it was only 12:30, we needed to go on. And Fitzmaurice, whom we met on the way walking in front of his ox carts, told us that this was where he intended to spend the night. The Phya tends to dislike him more and more and grimaced as he said, with a tone that was hardly Siamese, that while he could not prevent the English consul from sleeping in the Queen's cottage this evening, he found it regrettable that it would be in the company of his native mistress.

So we continued on our way. At Na Wang, before arriving, I was surprised to see a huge lizard measuring at least 1.5 metres across the road. I thought it was an alligator emerging from the stream, but it could well have been an iguana. On a tree in the park, I also saw a lizard much smaller than this one but much bigger than our average beasts.

We then entered the most beautiful and thickest virgin forest to be seen in these parts. The deep and infinitely winding road follows all the folds of the torrent and passes over numerous bridges. It is very beautiful, not in terms of mountain views, as there are none at all, but in terms of vegetation and the local landscape. Beneath the most majestic giants of the forest, superb sago palms display their magnificent leaves.

In barely half an hour we reached the end of the Phatthalung territory under the woods, which is also the boundary of the watershed. I wouldn't call it a pass, because the climb was so gentle that it hardly felt like a mountain.

Barely 200 m from this point, we managed to puncture a tyre. The presence of our driver, who had come from Bangkok and was the only one able to repair the accident, was a great stroke of luck, especially as we had stopped nearby in front of the rustic triumphal arch erected for the Queen's visit, on the boundary between the two territories.

In the shade of a *sala*, we waited patiently while the Governor and I ate. By 2 pm, everything was fixed and we were back on the road, this time descending towards Trang, still in the middle of the forest, with slightly more sensitive switchbacks.

However, a clearing appeared after about ten metres in the forest. This is the area where Phya Ratsada, High Commissioner of Phuket, has set up his oasis named Chang.

Chang is older than Na Wang. It served as a model and is more complete and better finished. Initially, we had planned to go as far as Tap Thieng, but I had insisted on stopping at Tehang. So that's where we stopped, and it was a good thing we did, because as soon as we arrived at the chalet, which the governor of Trang pointed out to me, a torrential downpour began that continued almost unabated until nightfall.

Waterfall in Chang's garden, 1950, National Archives of Thailand, Prince Kavila collection.

We had been chatting for some time on the veranda with the Governor of Trang, the same man who last month drove Maugras in his car to Phatthalung, when I saw a large round ball, a belly escorted by two Siamese officials and a European, advancing under a Chinese parasol.

It was Phya Ratsada himself, who had just finished his nap and was arriving with a young Italian engineer whom he had been keeping attached to his service for some months. I had been told that Phya Ratsada was the most intelligent of the Siamese High Commissioners because he was not Siamese but Chinese, and that he doesn't even know the language of his constituents.

This is a bit of an exaggeration. He speaks Siamese with his native entourage, but enough English with Europeans to make himself easily understood. As for his Chinese character, it shines through in his general appearance and in the smallest details of his attitude. He seems to be singularly independent of the central authorities. Perhaps this is true. In any case, he must know how to conceal himself very well when he needs to, because above this majestic belly and in this puffy face appears, in spite of his damaged left eye, the finest and most intelligent look imaginable.

I have heard that his *monthon* is marvellous and very well developed. From what I am able to see of his behaviour, this is surely true. He has lucid and happy ideas which he easily executes. Having completed

Phya Ratsada artificial lake in Chang's garden, 1915, National Archives of Thailand.

his masterpiece of Chang, he is now dreaming of a sanatorium for the Europeans of Bangkok on one of the neighbouring peaks. And that's why he's holding on to his young Italian.

I complimented Phya Ratsada on everything I had seen since my departure and on the impetus he has given to all this work. Like the Governor of Phatthalung, he admitted to me that the most difficult thing had been to motivate the local people, who were not at all interested in getting paid for the roadworks and who did not understand the ultimate usefulness of the project. He gradually succeeded, just as he succeeded in getting the inhabitants interested in improving their buildings. He brought the first carts from Penang, which he requisitioned for official use. Then, in order to encourage the inhabitants to have their own carts, he lent or rather rented them out at low prices. Four years ago, there were only three carts in Trang. There are now 200 and 80 in Phatthalung. So the momentum is there. The inhabitants have realised the benefits they can get from the road and the oxcart, and from the oxen themselves, which they can use or sell.

In my opinion, this is the best and most convincing result of all the work undertaken by the Siamese in this region. Alongside the railway, which has a more general aim and whose economic future is as yet unknown, the road not only lives for itself but is a prodigious source of local progress.

It's an example that the builders of the Tourane-Savannakhet road in Laos should learn from. And Phya Ratsada to whom I spoke about it, emphasised the way in which he succeeded in introducing the local people to the advantages of the oxcart.

Perhaps it wouldn't be so difficult in Annam and Laos when you consider how the existing section of the Kratieh road is already being used.

The Governor of Phatthalung left us at 3 pm to return home before dark. I parted from him with many thanks. And they are well deserved. Didn't the good man promise to send me some monkeys, angus and prehistoric stone instruments to Bangkok? And this morning, before leaving Phatthalung, he presented me with the most beautiful angus feather one could ever dream of.

According to some, this forest, which has been transformed into a kursaal and an English park, abounds in strange wonders. An hour before I arrived, several of the Negritos of the peninsula, the old inhabitants of the country, could be seen in Chang itself. They are now taking refuge in the thickest part of the forest where they don't even have any houses and where they flee society. They kill birds and monkeys with blowpipes, don't understand the value of money, and don't appreciate anything handmade except red-dyed cotton. It seems that those who came today had a request to make to Phya Ratsada. When the Queen came, she was shown some, but it was only the old who came, while young people and women did not. Their numbers are dwindling by the day. I'm not surprised if they have no houses, no fields and no means of escaping the effects of the terrible humidity in the forest. Their language, I'm told, is all bristling with "r" of the hoarsest sound. I'm not surprised. In terms of language, they are very much of the same species as all the primitives in the rest of Indochina.

In the forest, I'm told, deer, antelope, wild boar, monkeys and tigers abound, as do peacocks and pheasants. Phya Ratsada has built up a whole menagerie of tigers in Phuket. It was he who sent Prince Chakrabongse a hideous tapir found in the forest and he says that there are also many rhinoceroses in the hills.

Phya Ratsada comes from Penang. His house there was next door to that of the Hardouin family and he was and still is a close friend of our former Consul in Bangkok, whom he asked me about. He also told me about Deloncle, whom he met in 1883 when French engineers came to the region to study the construction of a canal in the Kra isthmus.

He wears European-style white trousers and a little black jacket over a big belly, like many other Chinese now. He seems to be a great pleasure-seeker, eating a lot, and likes to get people to work around him to embellish and improve everything. In Chang, for example, he dreams of storing mountain water in vast basins to create clear bodies of water. He collects curious plants from the forest and he has brought rose bushes from Penang. He is interested in wildlife and in the design of his buildings. But in this he is much more European than Chinese.

Prisoners serving six-month sentences are employed as labour. He uses them to work on the road and its construction. Some are even sent to him from Bangkok. He built them a prison in Tehong and had them sow a vast vegetable garden where they now grow vegetables that the monkeys from the mountain come to steal from them.

Behind the royal chalet and close to this vegetable garden are two streams that meet at the foot of extremely dark, wooded hills. One of the streams forms a small waterfall in the undergrowth, which we went to see after the rain at the end of the day. The Queen is said to have loved this place. The King, who came here after the death of his father, but before his coronation, spent several hours bathing in the clear waters of the torrent and said that if we could transport Chang to Dusit he would never leave.

Phya Ratsada himself lives in a tiny cottage below the King's and has the Governor of Trang as his immediate neighbour. He loves this place and stays here as often as possible, preferably in Phuket or Trang. He loves the solitude and charm of Chang, and I can understand that. He has only just returned from Bangkok, where he had been for the meeting of the High Commissioners, and it was there that Damrong himself was able to tell him about my visit.

5 November 1912

It is hard to imagine the degree of care with which Chang is looked after. As soon as we woke up this morning, a large number of people and prisoners were busy picking up leaves and twigs that had fallen during the night onto the green lawn.

After a hearty first lunch, the Governor of Trang took me on a walking tour to the large waterfall. Through a shaded entrance, it takes ten minutes to reach a wide torrent where the water flows in tiers over rocks, forming pools deep enough for easy bathing. The King apparently took great pleasure in it and the German chargé d'affaires De Reuth, who passed through here a few weeks ago, repeated his bath several times a day. After such a hearty lunch, I regret not being able to do the same.

On the way back to the chalets, we saw Phya Ratsada coming towards us, rolling his little hump and on his feet since 5 am. He showed us the water feature he created at the confluence of the torrents from the two cascades and told us of his intention to create a similar one on the other side of the park at the point where a third torrent arrives.

When he first came here seven years ago, it was complete bushland. He was seduced by the picturesque site at the foot of the mountain and near the waterfalls he built a bamboo chalet which was the starting point for the foundation of Chang. Four years ago he began to implement his plan, which has continued to develop ever since. Today, he is multiplying the number of bungalows to make them available to holidaymakers, cutting down sections of bush to turn them into English meadows and decorating all the areas around his buildings with rare, artistically planted plants. To this end, he has a sort of bamboo and foliage greenhouse near the pond, where he gathers and cultivates all the curious plants of the forest. He collects ferns, begonias and orchids.

His dream will only be fulfilled when, on the wooded mountain overlooking Chang, he will have built new chalets constituting a sanatorium that can be reached by car, where people can enjoy a European climate and from where they can see beyond the jungle and the forest to the two gulfs of Siam and Bengal. It is this project that he wants to develop at the foot of the aforementioned mountain, in the presence of a young Italian engineer whom he is going to leave on this bushy summit as soon as the end of the rainy season will allow. But the seasons are deceptive. I expected to find the rain settled on the Singora side and completely at an end on the Trang side. I could see yesterday, barely over the hill, that the monsoon had not changed. It looks like we'll have to endure some rain again today.

Phya Ratsada's cottage in Chang's garden, 1915, National Archives of Thailand.

The plan for the day having been decided at the last moment, I was unwise enough to let my boys leave with all the luggage directly for Trang, where I wouldn't meet them again until tomorrow evening. At a quarter to 9, taking leave on the main road of Phya Ratsada, whom I would meet again in Trang, where he was due to come down with Allegri, who had come to study a bridge project, I left with two towels and my pyjamas in the company of the Governor of Trang.

He was driving himself in his latest model Zedel torpedo, which arrived a few weeks ago. He is very proud of it and drives very carefully. In fact, from Chang onwards, the road is so flat, so straight and so well maintained, that you would think you were driving through a park under a canopy of greenery skilfully reserved in the medium-sized forest that borders the road. There are a few clearings, and the recent rubber plantations seem to be doing well.

A little further on, the first wonderfully green rice paddies begin, looking very good in the perfectly cleared bush from which they have recently been plucked. These rice fields are as impeccable as can be and the further we went, the more beautiful they became. The marvellously maintained road is full of pedestrians laden with food, poultry or fruit, or driving oxen, buffaloes or pigs by hand to sell at the Tap Thieng market. All this showed a remarkable state of prosperity, which has only recently begun to develop. The friendliness of the people and their politeness also indicated that the population is no longer as fearful as that of Phatthalung or Singora and that they understood the reason for all that has been done for them and by them. There is hardly a place in Indochina where I have had the same impression. It is singularly encouraging.

By 9.30 am we were at Tap Thieng at one of the resting places prepared for the King two years ago and where the Queen stayed this year. It is no longer the grandiose solitude of Chang and Na Wang, but has a view of the rice fields and the road where the peasants parade against a landscape background of wooded watershed mountains. It seems that the Queen enjoyed this view of the fields and the proximity of the people for two or three days. As for me, I stopped only long enough to visit the group of bamboo chalets painted white and green and to receive greetings from the notables of the *ampheu*.

The car set off again and passed through the bustling Tap Thieng market, where a few women wearing sarongs and Malay hairstyles caught my eye. There were a lot of Chinese, like everywhere else. All the roads were busy. There are three intersecting roads in Thap Thieng: Chang, Trang and Khao Kao. As the market takes place alternately every day in each of these three towns, the same bustle must be present every day.

We set off along the Khao Kao road. It merged with the road to Tang San and Lakhon (Ligor), and all the time more or less closely followed the new railway line from Trang. The railway had been temporarily opened to half-traffic but it has recently been closed to await the definitive opening of the line to Tang San, which should take place within the next three months.

Leaving Tap Thieng, the road passed through a number of Chinese-owned pepper plantations. Unfortunately, the Chinese are not considerate enough. When the price of pepper falls, they stop cultivating and when it rises again, their plantations are in decline. Near the station, I meet one of Hardouin's cousins, Mr Mathieu, originally from Penang, who was manager of a rubber plantation for some time.

I chatted with him for a moment and he told me that Hardouin is only waiting for his retirement to come and finish his days in his family's properties in Penang, which doesn't surprise me.

A little further on, the rain surprised us, but the car hood is down and we arrive safely at the Khao Kao pavilions at 11.15 am. They are designed in the same spirit as the previous ones but along the road and without any view. The upkeep is also rather primitive. These pavilions, where the Queen nevertheless spent three days, seem to have been built to make it easier to visit the Khao Kao caves, which are, however, still seven miles away. But this is the most important inhabited centre in the vicinity of the caves, and the brand new road leading to them is a fork from the main road to Lakhon, which you leave just outside Khao Kao. Prince Damrong, who is very fond of these caves and has visited them several times, took the new King there more than a year ago. He would also have liked to show the caves to the Queen, but it rained all the time during her stay in Khao Kao, and although she tried to take advantage of several sunny spells, she was never able to complete her project and finally had to give up visiting the caves.

We weren't as tactful and although I had nothing to change into, we decided to leave for the caves immediately after the tasty lunch that the young and kind secretary of the Governor of Trang, who had come especially for this purpose, had prepared in my honour in the accommodation designated for me.

At half past noon, we were back in the car. The rain stopped for a moment but started up again very soon after we left. It's a pity, because the new road is not very solid and one still gets stuck easily. It seems however that it stimulates economic development since on four separate occasions we saw new clearings and rice fields along the new route, indicating the proximity of villages ready to take advantage of the example set by those on the road to Chang.

At 1.30 pm we came up against a fairly strong river. People saw us from the huts on the other bank and hurried to find us in the rain by pirogue. Bravely, Chinese parasols in hand, we set off on foot accompanied by the village elders and two sedan chairs, which we wouldn't be using for the caves, which were a good half-hour's walk away. The scorching sun, which soon followed the rain, didn't make the excursion any less arduous. But I'm not averse to a bit of exercise, and the visit to the caves was an interesting enough reward for my trouble.

There's nothing archaeological or artistic about them, but from a natural point of view, there's something very curious, albeit not particularly new. A limestone massif without particularly picturesque forms rises above the forest clearing and rice fields that are coming back to life. But as in a Greek or Oriental convent, the route is signalled by staircases and balconies, which here are made of bamboo instead of wood and are preceded by a few coconut and areca trees replacing the palms or anchorite cypresses.

These stairs take the visitor up to the first cave, where there are still a few uninteresting Buddhas, but where the monks have disappeared. Just as in Europe, they have been told to move away from the cave, on the pretext that they were damaging it with the smoke from their torches and gravel. A strange mistake, but the same everywhere: "Propter vitam vivendi perdere causas". Our dear Damrong was rather misguided on this one.

From the first cave, you go up inside the rock to another, much larger and higher cave with bays open to the outside. It is decorated with hanging plants and begonias. Stalactites abound. The effects are grandiose.

Permanent seepage forms columns in several places where petrification continues.

View from inside one of the Khao Kao caves, 1909, National Archives of Thailand.

Our notables followed us. They presented us with delicious fresh coconuts, which are not to be missed. They were pleasant and good-humoured, like all the inhabitants since we arrived in the territory of the *monthon* Phuket, and I admire how confident and simple they are in the way they converse with the Governor of Trang. We are not used to this in the rest of Siam. And yet throughout the region, there is no shortage of respect. Nowhere have I seen so many formal greetings as those we have received since this morning all along the road.

All this seems to be the result of the wise and beneficent policy of Phya Ratsada and his entourage. He has done a lot of good for the whole population, who, after apparently resisting, has finally understood. Nowadays, the authorities get everything they want. They have implemented a compulsory but paid corvée to maintain the roads. The inhabitants obey, without being fined, when officials demand that each person plant every year a certain number of coconut trees on their own land and raise at least five chickens. This is the adorable system of the debonair and benevolent tyrant, the best one for all countries inhabited by lazy or indifferent people.

At 3.30 pm we finished visiting the caves and were back in the car on the same road, regretfully leaving on our left a path that apparently leads to a lake of clear water on another limestone knoll. The rain has definitely come to an end, but has done nothing to improve the roads. Nevertheless we were at the Khao Kao chalets before 4 am, me dirty and wet. Fortunately, God spared me a bout of fever. Since I've been on the road, I've started taking quinine again as a preventive measure.

After a short rest and before the 5 o'clock tea, I asked the secretary of the Governor of Trang to accompany me to the village and the market. He did so willingly, but we saw nothing curious there. A few Chinese shops like everywhere else, and that was it.

It is impossible to go as far as the tin mine, which is said to be located half an hour from the village, because of the mud and the state of the paths. However, we did go to meet the Chinese, whose job is to smelt the tin ore brought to them into ingots.

The process is extremely primitive, but that makes it all the more interesting. Under a bamboo loft, a man uses his arm to lift a forge bellows that feeds a charcoal-based fire into a cement furnace at the bottom of which the ore has been deposited. The ore is made up of grains similar to small dark pebbles, which at first sight appear to be of good quality, and which the smelters buy from the villagers, who bring them to the smelter in varying quantities. Six men, each working for two hours at a time, keep the bellows going day and night.

Below the furnace, the incandescent metal flows out through a hole in the side and falls onto a pile of ash mixed with slag, which is removed in fairly large blocks from time to time.

When there is a large enough quantity of liquid metal on the sand, a wooden mould is used to make a hole in a nearby pile of sand and the metal is spooned into the hole. When the metal cools, it forms a powerful, heavy, clear and sonorous ingot, inlaid with Chinese characters indicating its origin, which bears little resemblance to the ore we saw earlier and is astonishingly perfect when you consider the primitive methods used. It's a small-business system and the Chinese proceeding in this way have very few expenses. However, serious mining operations seem to proceed quite differently. They do not smelt their ore on site and find it advantageous to dispose of the ore en masse and in its natural state. It was in this form and in small bags that I saw tin ore being loaded at Bandon and Lakhon.

The system used by the Chinese of Khao Kao does not allow anything to be lost and therefore the resources of the mine are barely scratched: the slag is fired three or four times to exhaust every last trace of tin.

I was very pleased to have been able to see this way of doing things, because I didn't know whether I would have another opportunity to see so much during this trip. The Governor's secretary told me that tin prices are very high at the moment.

After this walk and tea, the rest of the day was spent talking, writing and drying off. The excellent thing about these good Siamese is that as soon as dinner is over, they consider their task accomplished. They did not let me out of their sight for a moment all day and are very considerate of me.

They seem to be passionate about all issues relating to the region's economic future, and are happy to listen to what is being said.

These two seem to me, especially the young one, to be well educated, and there is no doubt about their intelligence. They talk endlessly about China and its current political affairs. They are prodigiously interested in the future of the Chinese republic in a federal form, the only one possible. You get the feeling that it is no longer Japan that is at the forefront of their minds. However, they know too much about the divisions among the Chinese themselves to believe that they will easily come to an agreement for the common good.

6 November 1912

The rain yesterday and last night did not improve the roads. However, the governor of Trang, Phra Sathorn Sathan Phithak, was very proud to be able to reach Trang in two and a quarter hours after stopping for about half an hour at several points on Tap Thieng.

Several coconut and rubber plantation trials on the Lakhon road, which is still fairly new and needs to be improved, show the country's openness to new efforts, which can also be seen in the clearing of some villages at the junctions of certain centuries-old roads. Once the railway line is open, the rest will be easy.

Tap Thieng is a particularly favoured location at the crossroads of several roads, where fruit gardens are abundant and highly productive. Not only pepper but nutmeg is grown here with great success. Unfortunately, the price of this commodity has fallen sharply, and what was once worth 80 ticals per picul is now worth only 10. Many growers, especially in Penang, have become discouraged. This is a pity, because the tree is very beautiful and the nut, with its yellow bark and pulp, its coral-red thread and its brown kernel, is a sight to behold.

Tap Thieng is one of the central stations for the American missions, which maintain a hospital there. Yesterday, on the road to Tehang, I saw one of these Americans on horseback with his wife. Today, after a short stop at the cottages where we thought we would find Phya Ratsada, we were surprised to meet him in the car, near the Tap Thieng market, in the company of Fitzmaurice and Dr Dunlop, one of the main members of the American mission, whom I had met in Bangkok.

The mission seems to have been much more successful in civilising the country than in converting it to Christianity. In any case, it seems to have good relations with the authorities and with Phya Ratsada, because to replace the American hospital at Tap Thieng, which seems rather modest, the government is going to build another one and it will be entrusted to the mission's doctors. This solution interests me enormously because it is the one suggested in Ubon for the employment of our French doctor by the Siamese government.

The Americans also seem to have some involvement in the organisation of the schools, of which there are more than 60 in the Trang district alone. Dr Dunlop is on the committee and the free school system is used for the study of Siamese and the teaching of manual skills which should make the present youth an intelligent agricultural population. The Governor says that the children love going to school. Passing by the school buildings, I have more than once noticed that they are indeed very busy. What's surprising is to see these schools so different from the pagodas. In fact, there are very few pagodas here because a large part of the population is of Malay and Muslim origin. So the pagoda is not there to keep the child away from the first elements of reading and Buddhism.

The Queen has donated 3,000 ticals to set up a school in Tap Thieng. Once it's built and running, the Queen has promised another 3,000 ticals.

On leaving Tap Thieng on the road to Trang, the gardens continued for some time. We reached a beautiful avenue of tall trees at the end of which a pagoda was erected not long ago. This is where the seat of the local government used to be before it was moved to Trang.

Indeed, Phya Ratsada told me that about twenty years ago, Tap Thieng's remoteness from the part of the river accessible to steamboats coming from the sea had struck him, and he therefore decided to move the district centre further down the river. In doing so, he seems to have remembered Muang Ranong's origins near the Pak Chan confluence, which was created by his family and where he himself was born, as was the current governor of Trang, his relative. In these maritime provinces, easy access to the sea is essential. In fact, Phya Ratsada and his entourage are constantly thinking of Penang. On the other hand, he thinks that there is not a single place on the Siamese coast suitable for the creation of a port, Singora less than any other, since there are no more Chinese boats travelling there during the favourable season. Chumphon, which others had consdered as a natural end point for routes from the west to the east, does not seem to him to be an obvious choice either. The only one that seems logical to him, which does not surprise me, because it is in line with what I know about the past and the geographical layout of the country, is Bandon. Before the existence of Singapore and Penang, he told me, Siamese boats or European ships came from Macao to Bandon; from there to Phuket and from Phuket via Malacca, merchants sent products from the Far East to the north of Sumatra. It is therefore very likely that Singora will not benefit from the transit movement created by the railway.

We spent an hour from 9.30 am to 10.30 am at Tap Thieng and, then leaving the railway station on the right, the road headed towards Trang through rice fields intersected from time to time by a small patch of bush or coming up against quite a few wooded knolls. Rubber plantations are currently being tested on some of these knolls. As for the rice fields, they have continued to develop and improve since the road was built. In 40 minutes we reached Trang, which still seems to be a sparsely populated and scattered centre. It's very hard to make sense of it, as the public buildings set in parks hardly give the impression of a village at first glance. It was only when I took a drive in the afternoon with the Governor of Trang that I was able to realise that, in fact as in logic, the river, which is hardly visible on arrival, is and will increasingly be in the future the point around which the town will cluster.

The new railway station is already close by and is linked to the Chinese street along the river, where the shops and wharves are located.

Roads, which may one day become streets, lead from this side to the second row of gardens, where the administrative buildings, the court, the *ampheu* and, a little further on, the police station are located on the slightly open, grass-covered heights. The latter will be built of brick, as will the prison a little further down, next to which a young tiger caught in the forest is now caged.

The King's cottage, reached by a monumental staircase, is the only one with a view of the official buildings, the river and its mouth, some ten miles away. Like all the cottages in the park, its main façade faces the road and the grassy slopes that border it.

I was happy to find my boys and my things in one of these chalets, because having brought nothing to Khao Kao, I really needed to clean up and change.

At noon I lunched with the Governor and in the afternoon I received a visit from the High Commissioner who had come with Fitzmaurice. The English captain of the Siamese government yacht placed at my disposal by Prince Damrong also came to announce that to take advantage of the tide our departure for Penang should take place tomorrow morning between 8 and 9 am. This yacht is delightful. She was built in Hong Kong. I saw her a little later on the river and she is bigger and more comfortable than the mail boat that will be leaving loaded at about the same time. It is used by Phya Ratsada to travel back and forth between Trang and Phuket and has just taken Prince Charoon to Penang on his way to Europe.

Phya Ratsada was keen to talk, so I got him to tell me how he managed to get the resources he needed to carry out the considerable work he was doing on all fronts in his *monthon*. He told me very simply and without making a fuss that the Ministry of the Interior provided him with more money than others, but that he was trying to make the inhabitants understand the usefulness of what he required of them and that little by little they would come round to his views and support him.

The prisoners he employs are taught a useful occupation and when they are released, they make a living from it. Naturally, there is no question of perverts or criminals.

On a trip to Java, he found that the inhabitants all had to work 24 days a year absolutely free of charge. He did not want this system to be introduced in his *monthon*. With 15 days of drudgery per inhabitant, during which the latter is fed at the *monthon*'s expense, he is able to cope with everything.

From the Chinese, he only asks for a tax of three ticals, instead of the 6 demanded in Bangkok and the 15 dollars collected from them in Saigon. It is true that he has no reason to use a prohibitive tax to keep them away, as we have to do in Indochina in the interests of the indigenous Annamese, because here the neighbouring Chinese are a powerful stimulant for the Siamese.

To encourage the clearing of land for rice fields, he relieved people who had 10 *rai* or more of rice under cultivation of any drudgery, and to meet their wishes or the general interest, he facilitated land exchanges.

In every respect, he is a benevolent and extremely open-minded expert. There are five or six governors or high commissioners in his family, all of whom have taken an interest in the fate of this region. They oversee the common work and make it their business in the most gentle and affable way. His relative, the Governor of Trang, has an excellent attitude towards everyone. I could still see this today in his dealings with the inhabitants.

He took me to see the boys' school. He also took me to the roads recently built to serve the new rubber plantations on the cleared slopes of the neighbouring hills. This is where Prince Naret and his son Prince Charoon have recently set up theirs. However, passers-by and the children in particular showed us genuine respect without any over-exaggerated demonstrations. I had the explanation of this fact at dinner in the evening. The High Commissioner had gathered in my cottage the Governor, his secretary, Fitzmaurice and Dr Dunlop who is all about the schools and to whom it is appropriate to attribute the good habits given to the boys who, according to the Governor, after having at first shunned him, have now taken him into great confidence and friendship. From the conversation, I realised that the Siamese authorities had more or less tied the knot with the American Missions, who very skilfully step aside when the Siamese have a personal project, as in the case of the Tap Thieng school, which they insisted on making a royal foundation.

At this dinner, at which the High Commissioner did his utmost and gave me a toast, we ate oysters (with pearls) from the Bay of Bengal, which were very bad by the way, and swallows' nests from Phuket, with orange blossom, which were more bland than pleasant, but very expensive. Naturally, we talked about a lot of things, and Dr Dunlop, who has lived in the region for seven years and travelled all over it, pointed out some very interesting things.

I learnt that the Trang River can be rowed upstream for seven days and is divided into three rivers; that in the Tehong region the number of Negritos decreases from year to year, but that as far north as Muong Chaiya there is still a group of around 500.

According to him and Phya Ratsada, the journey from Pak Chan to Chumphon would be easy even though the country is sparsely populated. Within two years, the High Commissioner is determined to establish a motorway between Chumphon and the Pak Chan valley.

There are herds of wild elephants on this side. Dr Dunlop told us of a massacre of seven of these pachyderms.

Limestone massifs abound both on land and in the sea. On this side of the sea, there are cirques enclosed at high tide by immense walls, as in Halong Bay.

Not far from the Khao Kao rock is another outcrop where his colleague Kennedy from Bactau found some beautiful ancient Buddhas with Hindu inscriptions in a cave.

There are also hot springs here in Trang as in Ranong. The garden where the Trang cottages are built is a sort of botanical garden, with palm trees, orchids and all kinds of plants from the region. There would be some very interesting studies to pursue here. But it seems that nothing in the region beats the botanical garden in Penang. In order to take me to the Chinese temple or to his son's home in Penang, the High Commissioner demanded that the Governor's young secretary accompany me there tomorrow. I let him do so, because the ever-indulgent Phya Ratsada does not want to abandon me to my fate so soon.

I don't know how to thank all these people, and as Fitzmaurice left me this evening, he promised me the same support from his compatriots in Burma.

Here in Trang, I have received all the news since I left Bangkok of the Turkish war from the Penang newspapers. The Turks' disasters are multiplying at an astonishing rate. The Serbs seem to have behaved very brilliantly and are masters of the Sandjak, in other words the whole of old Serbia. The Bulgarians have also won brilliant victories and the Greeks are also gaining ground.

So far, Russia has only moved to congratulate Serbia and Montenegro. As for Austria, which must be astonished, it is showing goodwill towards Serbia and claims that it is only looking for economic interests beyond its natural border. If this point of view is sincere, it may well facilitate a solution.

My Siamese are following this inevitable conflict with interest, and perhaps they will be wise and flexible enough to avoid it when the next event comes.

7 November 1912

I telegraphed Henriette yesterday, who must have arrived in Colombo, to tell her that I was here and would be leaving Penang on the 9th. She is due to leave Colombo on the 11th, I think, after travelling around Ceylon with the Vilmorins, who arrived on another boat two days after her.

Phya Ratsada, the Governor and their entourage accompanied me aboard this morning. Before we parted, I presented the High Commissioner with 100 ticals for the school in Trang. It was the least I could do after all that had been done for me.

On arriving at the embarkation point, the High Commissioner explained his latest plans to me, namely to build a hotel on the hill near the station and opposite the avenue leading to the river dock; then to transform the rice fields that stretch between the river and the hotel into an inhabited district, the liveliest centre of which would remain the quay, which is currently lined with Chinese wooden houses and huts, but where he would build the post office, customs office, etc. He would also have the course of the river regulated and deepened. But in his mind, Trang should remain a place of pleasure and administration like Saigon, with Tap Thieng playing a sort of Cholon role.

There is already a sizeable trade in poultry and livestock between Tap Thieng, Trang and Penang. It is monopolised by the Chinese Eastern Navigation Company, which serves Trang and Penang two or three times a week. The company gives advances to the natives, who pay in poultry, so much so that the price of chickens in the country has apparently risen considerably.

The company's boat left Trang today at 10 am. I preceded it by at least an hour on the very pretty and much more comfortable Siamese government yacht. She is called *Thalang* after the former Junk Ceylon, now Phuket. She weighs 350 tonnes and was built three years ago in Hong Kong at a cost of 80,000 Mexican dollars by the Chinese

Shipbuilding Company. It's unfortunate that in Indochina we don't have any similar vessels.

The captain, the only European on board, is a very proper Englishman. The engineer officer is a native. The Governor's secretary accompanied me to Penang, where I was preceded by telegrams of recommendation from the High Commissioner.

We weighed anchor at 9.30 am. The river is wide but shallow, lined with bushy trees, some of them quite tall. Water palms of various species stand in the midst of other trees.

On the left, on the hills of Trang, we could see the various clearings for rubber plantations – those of Prince Naret, Prince Charoon, his son, and also those of the Governor, who had not shown them to me but who only stopped planting rubber trees when he had reached the figure of 50,000 trees. The Commander says that the Siamese are very jealous of Europeans and that, while they are broad in their concessions of mines and land to the Chinese, they are extremely reserved with regard to white people, which I can understand.

Many sandbanks obstruct the course of the river and we passed the remains of a Chinese steamer that got lost on the sands. The yacht moved forward slowly and cautiously, sometimes through a fairly narrow channel that brought us very close to the flooded forest where large trunks stand on mighty bald roots.

Drawing of the *Thalang*, n.d., Naval Education Department Archives.

Just before reaching the confluence, we passed a number of huts inhabited by Chinese who trade in wood here. They cut logs and planks and also sell water palm leaves for roofing the huts.

Apart from that, there is no life. The Siamese are too lazy and too inexperienced to go fishing in the sea, which is full of fish, and besides, the coast seems extremely sparsely populated.

Around 10.30 we were at the mouth of the river. The weather was superb. Two large limestone rocks in the middle of the sea point the way. Their strange shapes evoke mythological memories or primitive paintings. They are also rocks with sea swallow nests, where the harvests are good.

A fairly large wooded island on the right, called Pulo Telibong, is said to be inhabited by wild oxen and deer, which are sometimes hunted. As for fishing, which could be admirable, the Siamese have not developed it under favourable conditions.

Little by little we got closer to these sheer rocks that tower so high above the sea. You would expect to see Polyphemus or some Oriental sea god, some Leviathan on the summit. Yet everything is green where the rock is not visible, and at the bottom there are little beaches that beckon you to bathe. It is said that there are Malays in the region who only leave their boats to go and grill the fish they catch on the small beaches of these islets. The English call them Sea Gypsies, but they have nothing to do with the Chinese traders whose junks pass us by, recognisable by their brown sails made of woven bamboo.

At 3 o'clock we arrived near Pulo Teratau, the last Siamese island after the 1909 treaty extended British territory northwards to include the Malay state of Perlis. Teratau is separated by a narrow strait from Pulo Langkawi, an island or rather a group of islands that in all fairness should have remained Siamese. The king had visited it and Prince Damrong went down there more than once. But the British insisted on having it because they knew that the Germans had made attempts to secure it for themselves in order to take advantage of a natural bridge formed by the neighbouring islets, where they would have set up a coal depot.

Pulo Langkawi is bigger than Penang. Volcanic in formation, its outer edges are of the purest limestone, orange from the waves, and of a picturesque finish. The northern and eastern parts are not very usable, but the southern part is suitable for tropical cultivation. Before the cession, it was almost uninhabited, but since the British occupation, it has become increasingly populated and Chinese and Hindu coolies are multiplying rapidly. Plantations have apparently been started there. Hot springs and a lake of fresh, pure water in the mountains add to the charm of this admirable island. A little further inland, a group of flat islets mark the Siamese border. Here begins the state of Perlis and a little further on that of Kedah, both of which have become British. They are rich in tin ore, especially towards the northern tip of Perlis, which runs into Siamese territory. From Kedah a road leads towards Singora where I noticed that the Siamese are also building a road on that side.

After Langkawi, night began to fall and the weather turned bad. It rained and stormed until 11 am, when the *Thalang* anchored in Penang harbour in front of the municipal buildings, separated from the old fort by a beautiful meadow used as a cricket pitch and where there is a Sports Club.

I spent the rest of the day reading my little volume dedicated by the American missionaries to Hamilton King, the former American minister in Bangkok who died a few weeks ago. He was himself a former member of the Missions, still affiliated with the very special work being carried on in Siam by his countrymen and co-religionists.

Some of his writings have been grouped together in the book. One of them is an appeal to the members of the American mission to show them the path they must follow if they are to succeed. Making good use of the work of religious propaganda and conversion, in spite of the protests of the sponsors in the mother country, Hamilton King recommends that the missionaries pursue a work of high civilisation which will prepare the Siamese, more than any preaching, to adopt the most immediate benefits of Christian culture by breaking down prejudices.

In Hamilton King's view, this should be done through schools, by caring for the sick, and by setting an example for the natives to improve their intellectual and material lives. He was delighted with the way in which his companions had already confirmed their role and the enormous influence they had acquired with the authorities in the organisation of public administration and hospitals. Nothing is done in this area without consulting them and asking for their cooperation.

I now understand the significance of the sixty or so schools in the region, which they helped to found. According to Hamilton King, Prince Damrong greatly appreciates this competition and is keen to extend it. Why are we not in the same situation with our own missions! It's true that, from a religious point of view, we can wonder what the final result will be. The Jesuits also started down this road in the 17th century. The vague deism that can bewitch will obviously bring the Buddhist Siamese closer to the Christian foreigners, but to what extent? What is most certain is that by the spread of English education and Anglo-Saxon culture, the English neighbours of this part of Siam where the Americans work will facilitate their efforts. We have nothing similar in the French part of the Kingdom of Siam. It's unfortunate for our influence. Our efforts have even been negative since we have prevented American missionaries who would have worked for the consular influence from settling in Luang Prabang. We were unable to prevent them from setting up establishments in Chiang Hai but on our side, we have not established anything French in the Siamese Mekong basin. Our missionaries have fallen well short of the civilising work of the Americans and their relations with the French authorities there are poorer than anywhere else in Indochina. From the point of view of French influence, the results are even more inadequate in the Nam Mun region, where there is so much to be done. Here, on the other hand, as seems to be the case in Chiang Mai, there is complete intimacy between Americans and English. In Phuket, Singora, Lakhon and Trang, the American missionaries have made the task of the English consuls much easier and, whether they realised it or not, have been working hard for English assimilation and annexation.

In another memoir, Hamilton King also studied the role that the United States should play in Siam in the distribution of administrative functions entrusted by the Siamese to foreigners.

On the face of it, this system was repugnant to him, but he believed that the question should be considered from the point of view of facts. American trade can do little in a country where the political influence of certain countries is so pressing. It is therefore necessary, according to him and with a view to trade, to secure for the Americans an equal share of influence with that of other countries, and not to disregard the

TRAVEL JOURNAL 83

system of influence in the councils of government as is practised in its present form. America must be able to defend the principle of the open door against disguised monopolies. America must also be able to react against a financial system that results from treaties and only allows the Siamese to collect 3% on foreign goods. Forced to find resources to live on, Siam has to rely on alcohol, gambling and opium. This is a situation which is primarily attributable to foreigners and which does more than anything else to undermine the esteem in which they should be held. Hamilton King wanted to see this situation changed and he encouraged his missionaries to create a current of opinion to this end. He encouraged them to publish. They now have printing works; they were the first to write and print books for the Siamese: they aim at giving them the means to exist by themselves and to do without foreigners. In this way, the missionaries will be doing useful work and they will gain sympathy that will benefit not only Christianity but also American trade. Their presence in the country is already doing a great deal. Bicycles, sewing machines and American machinery have followed in their wake. We couldn't be more completely Chicagoan. What a joy to be rid of this plague!

8 November 1912

By 7 o'clock I was on my feet and leaving the *Thalang*, accompanied by my young Siamese secretary, who will not be leaving for Trang until this evening, and Mr Newbrunner, who, from father to son, performs consular duties in Penang on behalf of Siam, and whom Phya Ratsada had informed by telegraph of my arrival.

This kind old man took me in his car to the Eastern and Oriental Hotel where he put me up and then took his leave of me to go and spend the end of the day at one of his plantations in the mountains. It's a holiday here today, tomorrow and Sunday. All the European offices and shops will be closed in the afternoon, which is rather inconvenient for me. I was therefore obliged to take advantage of the morning to do some shopping in town and to reserve my place on the British India *Zaïda*, which leaves tomorrow morning at 8 am. So I ran around town in a rickshaw and met lots of Germans.

You'd be hard-pressed to find Malays in the city. As in Singapore, they can only be found outside. Everywhere there is a swarm of Chinese and Hindus, especially Malabars, with a higher proportion of Hindu women than in Singapore. The Malabars wear coloured loincloths and light silk scarves that are unknown further south.

I had fun browsing in a few native shops similar to those in Bangkok. Malay jewellery, although also made by the Chinese, is very different from that of the Siamese. I bought a rather nice specimen of gold brooches.

My boys say that their compatriots from Hainan are rare here and that the Cantonese and Fu Kien people are in the majority among the Chinese of Pulo Penang.

In the town, I was shown some sumptuous European colonial-style houses belonging to Chinese owners. The streets are more built-up than in many parts of Singapore, and the business district is extensive. It ends in a series of very wide lanes shaded by centuries-old trees on the edge of the countryside, where there are plenty of comfortable bungalows.

The quays on the housing side are very crowded and lined with large buildings starting from the citadel, which the current authorities unfortunately want to knock down to give more air to the military buildings. The official English town has its usual beautiful colonial appearance, bordered by a small stone esplanade beyond which magnificent trees have grown. The Eastern and Oriental Hotel is located in one of these areas, in a former property belonging to the family of Mr Newbrunner.

The garden and windows of this tropical hotel look out directly onto the sea, with beautiful trees that provide protection from the sun but don't block the breeze. My yacht, anchored almost opposite, is superb, and close by you can see the dry land that protects the harbour and can be reached by a ferryboat that puts Penang in direct communication with the peninsular railways in just a few minutes.

I can't help dreaming of a Phu-Quoc that would be thus linked to the Cambodian or Cochinchina coast and which a little more initiative on our part could ensure such a bright future. But Phu-Quoc is not just a few minutes from the coast like Penang.

At 4.30 pm the young Siamese secretary Nai Chit Preecha came to see me in the car of Phya Ratsada's son, who lives in Penang but regrets not having been able to come himself as he too is on his plantation today. Nai Chit is in charge of taking me to the botanical gardens and showing me the most beautiful avenues in Penang. He was unable to come and have lunch with me, as he was held up in town by his friends.

He was educated at the superb French college Saint François Xavier run by the Catholic priests. And he left there without knowing a word of French, only English! The French foreign missions seem to be on a much firmer footing here than in Bangkok. Their buildings, their church and their two schools are in the most upmarket part of town and are well kept. The priests even have a club for their former pupils with extensive grounds for games. You feel they are on the same footing as their English and foreign rivals. Why should Bangkok and French Indochina be any different?

I was delighted by this walk through the botanical garden. It is wonderfully situated in a high valley formed by several wooded slopes with a torrent cascading down to a reservoir where water is filtered for use by the town.

The vegetation is more beautiful than that of Singapore and the place is better laid out. This is really the place to come to judge the value of such a garden. The one in Trinidad that I saw two years ago is too small, although very pretty, to produce the same effect. Besides, it's not everywhere that you can see monkeys roaming free as they do here.

The avenues leading to the botanical gardens are sumptuous, shaded by immense trees. The villas are large and beautiful, surrounded by vast gardens with flowers and plants of choice. The most beautiful are by the sea. Others are close to the vast, well-kept racecourse, through which golf links have been laid.

Many are owned by Chinese people. They are richer, more modern and more enterprising here than in Singapore, no doubt because they feel further from home. It is here that the group of Phya Ratsada and his family, who are currently having such a powerful influence on the destiny of Siamese Malaya, are exiled.

These Chinese love luxury, but more in the European style than anywhere else. Maybe it was because today was a holiday, but I saw a lot of them driving around in cars, and even young people dressed very much in European style, with their very elegant Malay-style wives sitting beside them.

The governor of Trang, who is himself of Chinese origin but the son of a Siamese woman, and whose son is being brought up in Penang, told me that he knew Chinese people here who were married, one to an Irish woman and the other to an Australian.

Today's festival is a Hindu one. So the people were particularly dressed up with new, brightly coloured loincloths and scarves, the likes of which I had never seen before. The little girls in their coloured ruffled dresses and dark Second Empire-style jackets were particularly amusing.

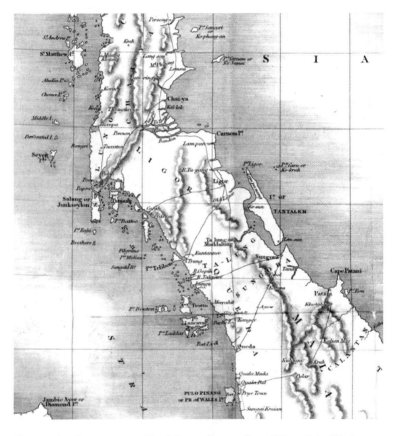

Transpeninsular routes over Kra Isthmus. Extract from "Map of the Kindoms of Siam and Cochin China", compiled by John Walker, published in Crawfurd, John (1828), *Journal of an Embassy from the Governor-General of India to the courts of Siam and Cochin China exhibiting a view of the actual state of these kingdoms*, London: Henry Colburn, page VIIIB.

Itinerary from 9th to 19th November. Adaptation of the Map of the Catholic Missions of Siam, Burma and Laos drawn and engraved by R. Hausermann. Missions étrangères de Paris/IRFA.

In more than one corner there were also Hindus gathered around the musicians and strolling actors in masks. Bernard would have found there some of those colourful effects that he collected so successfully in India last year.

At the end of my walk, when I got back to the hotel, the sea beneath my windows beyond the tall trees was delightfully inviting. Had I had more time, I would have gone by ferryboat or canoe to explore the approaches on the other side, towards the mainland. As it was, I had to make do with a trip to the docks and the pier.

9 November 1912

It didn't stop raining in torrents all night, so with the idea of an early start, I couldn't sleep a wink. In fact, although departure was set for 8 am and I was on board British India's *Zelaya* from 7.30 am, where only an insignificant load of peanuts and dried fish was carried on board, the anchor was not lifted until around 10 am.

The weather has been damp, grey and cloudy all day. I am the only passenger on this cargo ship, which is quite large but not used to carrying passengers, and where everything is dirty and unkempt. The food is as unappetising as possible and the service is provided by people from Goa, who, despite being Portuguese, are blacker, fuzzier and dirtier than the most infamous negroes. Four Englishmen and a doctor made up the European staff on board. The crew is black and disgusting. It's a bit of a cheap shot that I've taken by embarking on this coastal navigation. But it's the only way to see Mergui and its archipelago and to go ashore at least once, as I'm assured that I'll be able to do so in Mergui.

In Tavoy and Ye I won't have the same luck because these towns are inland and the boat is loaded at the mouth of the river. In truth, when you don't have your own yacht, travelling is very difficult.

It's quite something to follow the coast closely enough to be able to make out the contours and the most striking points. In the afternoon, we followed the west coast of Pulo Langkawi from a little further away than with the *Thalang*, but I became perfectly aware of the shape of this island and the other one near it.

The Siamese complain that by taking Langkawi and leaving them only Teratan, the English have secured the best part for themselves. But what will they themselves do with Teratan? They lack the manpower, whereas in the English possessions there is never a shortage of Hindus or Chinese. As for their initiative, we know what it is worth. Wherever there is a hint of activity, it is a foreigner who has come up with the idea or provided the capital. The former Governor of Singora is Chinese, the Governor of Trang is Chinese, the High Commissioner of Phuket is Chinese. And the Chinese are always kept on their toes by the proximity of the Malay Peninsula and by the example of Pulo Penang, which sums up all the experiences in the eyes of even the most backward and least far-sighted people.

Who will ever say what has been done for the development of civilization by the practical example and by the spread of ideas, points of limited and concentrated action such as Hong Kong, Singapore and Pulo Penang where the English have set up sorts of "nurseries" where all their initiatives have been fertilised and germinated. Nothing theoretical, but a practical example that is gradually spreading and leading to prodigious developments, while remaining within everyone's reach. People like Phya Ratsada saw their families' fortunes born and grow in Penang under the shelter of excellent institutions. They understood the teachings and found themselves in a position to try similar experiments on neighbouring land. Transport them elsewhere, far from the plantations, roads, sumptuous houses, gardens and flowers of Penang, and they will no longer be in the same position to succeed. Penang is always on their minds and on their lips. If, instead of Phya Ratsada or one of his descendants, the Siamese government appoints a Siamese prince like Mahibal to Phuket, we will see what he is capable of despite his European education and long stays in foreign courts. On the contrary, let the work begun continue with the people who started it, and there is no reason why progress should not gradually be developed along the entire Siamese coast of the Bay of Bengal, from Pak Chan to Perlis. Of course, there are drawbacks. The autocratic King of Bangkok, the formalism of the Siamese mandarins, the absence of capital and also of natives capable of applying the experiments of European science themselves, the laziness of the Siamese peasant, the inadequacy of the coolies. Easy. The Siamese Malays have already proved that they can grow rice and fruit gardens like their neighbours. A good public works company, well managed by Phya Ratsada and initiated by his neighbours, could make the country accessible. As for industries, they could be born from the association of European capital and the work of foreign engineers with the help of Siamese civil servants and Siamese holders of concessions. This seems to be the really practical future. Prince Damrong seems to see it more or less that way, and I know Frenchmen like de la Jonquière would be willing to go along with these views rather than put all their eggs in the same basket of English Malaya.

The English way of doing things too big, especially in Malaya, where people like to take risk and gamble, is not suited to all temperaments. You are subject to market fluctuations that have their origin outside you and that bring about your ruin, without you being able to do anything about it. From coffee, which had been pushed to excess, rubber was suddenly thrown in with the same exaggeration. As for tin, the government is not moderating the movement. Perhaps there is already too much competition on the spot. Who knows whether a system of enlightened protection that would moderate sales or production, and which the Siamese would be able to impose through its governmental procedures, would not benefit the beneficiaries. They are already stingy with their concessions, so won't they remain cautious once they have glimpsed regular sources of profit for themselves and their associates? *"By and by"* is the motto of enlightened Siamese like Prince Damrong and Phya Ratsada, while in British Malaya, *"go ahead"* is the order of the day.

It is this difference in viewpoints that makes it easy for the English on this side to believe that the Siamese hate them. No. Not so much. But not wanting to be eaten, they don't want to be dragged too far or too fast.

10 November 1912

My solitude aboard the *Zelaya*, the lack of conversation from the ship's officers and the monotony of the journey left me free for my reading. This morning we passed a certain distance from Phuket and all day we continued to follow, but from too far away to be able to enjoy it, the Siamese coast in the direction of Pak Chan.

To our left, we began to skirt the first islets that heralded the approach of the Mergui archipelago, where so many pirates have found places of refuge in the past. From now on, these islands and islets would multiply. Pak Chan, whose mouth we will pass tonight, almost played a role in our history 30 years ago. Didn't the French imagine, a few years after 1880, that they wanted to open a canal between Kra and Chumphon, which would have been the most direct link between the Indian Ocean and Bangkok? We would have escaped the control of the English in Singapore and Penang. But would we have escaped the control of the English of Tenasserim, masters of the sources of the Pak Chan and riparians of this watercourse along its entire northern bank?

From a transit point of view, the affair would have been unquestionably detestable. From a political point of view, the British were quite wrong to be frightened. But at a time when we were getting our hands on Tonkin, they were able to believe in a serious project to form a partnership with Siam, to create interests for us there, to provide us with an access route independent of them as far as Bangkok, and finally to limit their economic and political advance southwards by creating French interests on their borders. I like to think that before embarking on this project, our compatriots, Deloncle, Mahé de la Bourdonnais etc., would at least have considered the practical aspects of the affair. Phya Ratsada, who still remembers Deloncle, must have pointed them out, because when he told me about Ranong, from where his family had spread, he said that these regions are still little exploited, but that tin abounds there. I wouldn't be surprised if, as far as he was concerned, Phya Ratsada regretted the failure of the French venture. He insisted on taking me there one day to show me these places and the fact is that if he carries out his project for a road from Ranong to Chumphon, suitable for automobile use, as it is understood nowadays, this would be the most direct route in Siamese territory from the Bay of Bengal to the Gulf of Siam. A branch line of the Siamese railways would soon follow the opening of the road. This would provide a much more direct route from Bangkok to Europe than the one that seems likely to prevail in the near future.

As long as the Trang River, which is clogged with sandbanks and closed off by a bar, is not accessible to liners larger than the Eastern

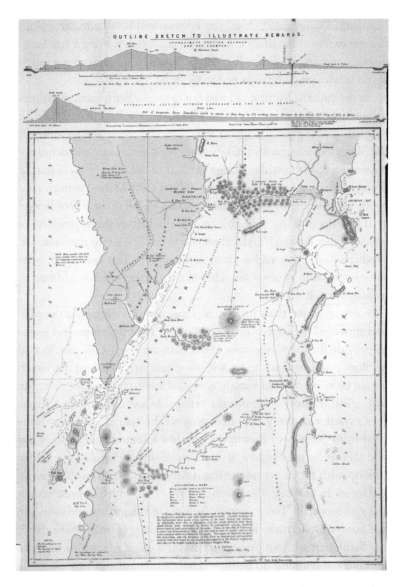

Kra Isthmus. Map from Loftus, A. J. (1883). *Notes of a Journey Across the Isthmus of Krà: Made with the French Government Survey Expedition, January-April, 1883. With Explanatory Map and Sections, and Appendix Containing Reprint of Report to the Indian Government*, Singapore: Singapore and Straits Printing Office.

Navigation Company's clogs, the railway will be able to serve Pulo Penang two or three times a week and, if necessary, bring a few long-distance passengers. From Pak Chan, however, it seems that a much better service could be obtained to Ceylon.

In the end, the Siamese did well not to arouse British susceptibilities by not insisting on creating a railway line along the Pak Chan. When, in 1909, they were given the opportunity to provide their own provinces in the Malay Peninsula with a railway, they took immediate and definitive possession of the corridor along the coast of the Gulf of Siam that so precariously linked Bangkok to the bulk of their Malay territories.

By establishing their first point of access by rail to the Bay of Bengal at Trang, the Siamese were able to give the British the satisfaction of believing that Penang is and will remain the end point for the economic products of the new region that is opening up. This will not prevent the construction of other branches in the future, which could lead to new access points.

Conceived for their use by the English, who suggested the plan and provided the money for its execution, the English project seems to provide for the connection of the Siamese line to the province of Wellesley and to Penang, by a section coming from Singora which would cross the state of Kedah. A road already exists in this direction in English territory. Without the bridges, it seems, from what I have seen myself, to be very close to ending on the Siamese side. As for the road from Singora to Patani, the first few kilometres of which I saw and followed from Singora, it seems more or less destined one day to link up with the as yet non-existent network of roads in the State of Kelantan. In any case, the English railway line, which at present does not go beyond the Trang river, in the State of Pahang, should soon join the border of Kelantan in the North, and there is little doubt that if the Siamese road from Singora to Patani is one day transformed into a railway, it will end up being welded to this Eastern branch of the English railways of Malaya.

But this line is only of purely local interest. The other is singularly more interesting for the future of Siamese Malaya, because the future of the port of Trang or any other port that the Siamese government would like to create on its behalf on the coast of the Bay of Bengal will depend on the link between Singora and Penang.

It is difficult to appreciate the degree of pressure that Siam has been or is still being subjected to by England since 1909. But what is certain is that whatever hopes the Siamese may have of the complete and most immediate development of their Malay provinces for the connection with Penang, they have everything to fear for the independence of this region from an English economic hold, and once it has produced all its effects against them, it will be very difficult to create in their turn on the Bay of Bengal a Siamese exit door which for many centuries has been one of the main objectives of their commercial policy.

When the powerful but short-lived kingdom formed by the Burmese conqueror Bureng Naung began to crumble at the end of the 16th century, the Siamese regained possession from Martaban to Malacca of the entire Tenasserim coast, which had been one of their first and most important conquests after the 13th century, when the kingdom of Sukhothai was built. This region had never been of greater interest than since the arrival of Europeans in the Bay of Bengal at the beginning of the 17th. At the end of the same century, Dutch traders were already reporting the route from Tenasserim to Ayutthaya as one of the most important trade routes in East Asia, with Mergui, the port of Tenasserim, in regular contact with the Indian coast.

At the beginning of the 18th century, a Portuguese Jesuit arrived in Ayutthaya via this route, followed by a Siamese embassy on its way to Goa. Then it was the first emissaries of the English East India Company who got to know this route. Tavernier, in the middle of the 18th century, mentions it as being in common use. And from then on, ambassadors, missionaries and trading company employees followed this same route until the Burmese conquered Tenasserim in 1767, which put an end to Siam's direct relations with India and was closely followed by the destruction of Ayutthaya, thereby interrupting European trade with Siam for a long time. When trade resumed, the Siamese no longer had Tenasserim or Mergui at their disposal, and the Burmese were extremely reluctant to facilitate their enemies' commercial communications through a devastated territory from which they could not, however, derive any profit for themselves.

The tradition had been broken and was not re-established when, in the first part of the 19th century, the English replaced the Burmese in their possession of the coastal region. Trading patterns had changed. The English already had points of support for their trade with Siam to the south. The possession of Penang, then Singapore, led them to use the straits route to trade with Siam. From all points of view, their navigation was now so safe that there was no need to reopen communications between Mergui and Bangkok, which after all had never been extremely easy.

And yet they had made every effort in the past to ensure free access to this route! In the second half of the 18th century, when France and England were vying to secure a monopoly of the India trade, it is fair to say that, especially after the cession of Bantam to the Dutch in 1682, it was on the Siamese coast around Mergui that some of the most serious games were played. Although the King of Siam, Phra Narai, who was himself a trader and was ably assisted by Constantin Phaulkon, his minister, who was well acquainted with Indian affairs, played a considerable personal role in the Bay of Bengal at this time, he unconsciously served as an instrument of rivalry between the two European powers.

At Mergui, Phra Narai not only maintained commercial ships that traded with Coromandel and Sumatra, but also a war fleet that successfully fought more than one battle against the English East India Company and took the war as far as the states of the King of Golconde. It was the policy of Phaulkon and his king to fight to the bitter end against the monopoly of the English East India Company. But neither of them intended to deprive themselves of the services of the Company's English competitors. As a result, Burnaby and White were appointed governor and head of the port at Mergui by the Siamese. Frenchmen had also held similar positions: Charbonneau and then Rouillé, from 1677 onwards in Junk Ceylon, and this was one of the things that most infuriated the agents of the English Company and made them see in the arrival of the French in Siam a Machiavellian plan of conquest and monopolisation devised in Versailles.

And yet, it is unlikely that Phaulkon would have sent to Mergui one of the detachments of French troops brought to Siam at his request by Desfarges and La Loubère, if the English Company had not declared war on Siam and opened hostilities and if an order from James II himself had not imposed on the English in the service of Siam the obligation to withdraw. They were not given time to do so and a large number were massacred at Mergui.

It was only then that the French took a leading position in Mergui with the soldiers of de Bruan and Beauregard, who even built their fort there. But their stay in Mergui, which should, at least in the minds of the English, have turned into a conquest, did not last. It came to an end, as far as we can be sure of the true intentions of Louis XIV's government, when Phra Narai died and Phaulkon was overthrown by a palace revolution. The Siamese party, which had recently come to power, put an end once and for all to these somewhat dangerous foreign occupations, both in Bangkok and in Mergui.

Since then, Anglo-French rivalry has had its permanent battleground in India, where the great battles of the 18th century took place and Mergui lost its international importance. However, Siam was able to make the most of its position until the Burmese conquest, and its policy underwent a major change when it could no longer be directed towards the East Indies and supported by a maritime trade which, at certain times, had attained real importance.

As soon as the Burmese occupation meant that the road from Mergui via Tenasserim to Bangkok was no longer free, the English looked elsewhere for an alternative, and this is how they came to set their sights on Junk Ceylon, today's Phuket, which, because of its island nature and its immediate proximity to the mainland, was much better suited to their needs for a permanent settlement than Mergui or Tenasserim, which were much more difficult to defend.

During the first war against the Burmese, which led in 1825 to the cession of the Tenasserim coast, the English officers who visited these regions, Low for example, did not have enough regrets for Junk Ceylon, but despite the unfriendly nature of the relations they then had with the Siamese, jealous of their occupation of Moulmein and Tenasserim, the English were not at war with them at the time and had to give up possession of Junk Ceylon, which would have offered them advantages similar to those of Penang, Singapore and Hong Kong.

Today, however, Junk Ceylon, known as Phuket, is one of the places in Siam where you can meet the most Europeans, especially the English, who even have a vice-consul there.

At the end of the day, we sailed fairly close to the shores of Chance Island, which appears to be uninhabited and most of which is made up of wooded, peaked hills. Although the mainland coast is Siamese, this island is English. It is the first island of any importance in the Mergui archipelago and, if the Kra Channel had been dug, it would have dominated the shores of Pak Chan from afar.

These islands in the archipelago have long been a haven for pirates. In the middle of the 17th century, Mendes Pinto heard of a band that ravaged all the surrounding coasts and which appears to have been formed by the crews of three rebellious Portuguese ships. Since then, many others have taken advantage of these islands, as well as the Andaman and Nicobar islands further south, which navigators were reluctant to approach due to the reputation of their ferocious inhabitants.

English peace has changed all that. As far as pirates are concerned, there are now only the Selang, a population speaking a Malay dialect, who no longer attack anyone and are content to live by fishing, leaving their boats only when the monsoon forces them to build miserable huts on the small golden sandy beaches of the archipelago's islets. They sometimes hunt wild boar in the woods that cover these steep, rocky islands.

11 November 1912

By nightfall yesterday we had passed Chance Island. This morning at 8 o'clock I was surprised to find myself at the entrance to the most crowded part of the archipelago. By 9 o'clock we were even north of Bentik Island and skirting the south of Court Island. In the Company's prospectus, arrival at Mergui was only announced for the 12th, but as we arrived there today at 3 pm, I expressed my surprise and satisfaction to the Captain. "The Company," he told me, "arranges its programmes as it sees fit and so do I." That's fine but when, in a case like mine, the authorities are informed of the expected date of arrival of a boat, it can present more than one inconvenience. As far as I'm concerned, I'm delighted because I'll have two days more than I'd hoped in Moulmein, where I'll be on the 13th instead of the 15th, and as long as we can't get off at either Tavoy or Ye, all the time we can save en route is advantageous.

This archipelago is magnificent. It doesn't look particularly exotic from the sea, but as the islands are all wooded, infinitely variable in size and very well indented, the eye is continually treated to a very pleasant spectacle. For yachting enthusiasts, there would be an opportunity for lovely excursions with bathing, fishing and hunting. Some islands are said to be inhabited. The Captain showed me one where there is a village of pearl fishermen who somewhat falsify their products by making artificial pearls, although it is nature that takes care of covering the balls they put into the pearl oyster with mother-of-pearl. What can be done now to shame people with the things they choose to wear or eat, if the natives themselves lose the habit of exploiting and seeking out the direct products of nature?

In the large islands such as King, a little further north, there are apparently rubber plantations.

The Commandant told me that Mergui has become a very unimportant port that is only linked by a regular service with Burma and Penang and has no direct communications with India. What a difference from the Mergui of the late 18th century which had so many links with Masulipatam where the English East India Company imported so many elephants from Tenasserim. Aceh, Bengal, Golconde, the Persian Gulf and the Red Sea all had regular trade links with Mergui. The Shah of Persia sent his embassies to the King of Siam via Mergui and Tenasserim.

Whatever the French missionaries may have said, the overland route from Mergui to Bangkok cannot have been a practical one, especially for travellers like Mgr de la Motte Lambert for instance, who took 18 months to reach Mergui by following the normal route from Marseille (27 November 1660), Malta, Cyprus, Alexandria, Aleppo, Baghdad, Basra, Ormuz, Surate and Masulipatam, where he arrived on 6 March 1662, reaching Mergui on the following 28 April.

Once at Mergui, the travelers went to Jelinga on the Tenasserim river in canoes, and from there in 10 days by ox cart to the Siamese village of Menam. Six days later they reached Couir (Koney), 10 days later Pram (Prang) and then another five days to Phipri. Two days later they accessed the mouths of the Menam by river and then by sea, and after a final journey of five or six days they finally arrived in Ayutthaya.

It wasn't fast going, but it had been so long since they left Marseille: what did it matter if they arrived a little earlier or later when there was so much to learn along the way?

Since then, the route from Mergui to Ayutthaya has been followed by many other missionaries and travellers and described by many others. Sometimes it was at Koney (Couli / Kin / Couir) that they left the overland route, without going as far as Phipri to reach the mouths of the Menam by boat.

In 1826, the Englishman Leal, bringing with him, after the conquest of Tenasserim, some populations abducted and then returned by the Siamese, described his itinerary in the opposite direction: eight days by sea from the mouth of the Menam to Bangnarom on the west coast of the Gulf of Siam, north of Ban Tapan. From there, five days by land to the foot of Mount Kasun, whose ascent was the sixth day. The next morning he crossed the border at Sing Khon Tha Pe. On the 8th day, following a good route, he reached the banks of the Tenasserim river, which he descended in rafts to Mergui, reached in five days. In all, it took 16 days from the Menam mouth to Mergui, but Leal pointed out that the journey could have been considerably quicker had it not been delayed by the presence of a large number of people, many of them women and children. Didn't the French, when they occupied Mergui, once complete the journey in 10 days under conditions that were hardly any easier?

As for the substitution of Bangnarom for Phipri as the starting point for the overland route, this dates back to the last years of the 18th century, when the King of Siam had created a military route reaching the border that could be used by elephants in order to be able to invade Burmese territory.

Prior to the 11th century, it seems that there was no place on the Tenasserim coast for masters other than the Hindus of Dravidian origin who had come from Kalinga and the southernmost districts of India. It was these Hindus who had not only colonised the Malay peninsula, where they had created the principality of Ligor, but who had also founded a kingdom in the north-east of the Bay of Bengal, which was the origin of the kingdom of Pegu, and on which the entire Tenasserim coast depended.

Between 1050 and 1057, this kingdom was destroyed by the Burmese of Pagan, and it was from this period that the first conquerors from the north took hold of the region. The Burmese of Pagan were the first and preceded the Siamese, but although they possessed Tavoy and Tenasserim at the time, there is no evidence to suggest that they extended their domination further south. It was at this time that Ligor, which nominally depended on Cambodia, which then still controlled the entire Gulf of Siam as far as Palembang, extended its authority over the Malay Peninsula to the detriment of its neighbours, including Junk Ceylon, which was no longer conquered by the Burmese.

This state of affairs lasted until 1282, when Wareru's conquest of Martaban brought the mouths of the Salween and the Tenasserim coast under the rule of a Thai king who was himself a vassal of another Thai king, that of Sukhothai. This is how Tenasserim became a tributary of Sukhothai for several centuries, and then of the kingdom of Siam, which grew out of it, although several times at the beginning of the 19th century the princes of Martaban, before the kings of Pegou and Burma, tried to detach it from Sukhothai.

When, in 1257, Siam finally shook off the yoke of Cambodia, it replaced its authority, not only in the Menam basin, but along the entire west coast of the Gulf of Siam and as far as the Malay Peninsula, where Ligor and all its dependencies, including Junk Ceylon, came under the suzerainty of the King of Siam. Thus, through Martaban as well as through Junk Ceylon, the Siamese held both ends of Tenasserim and, through the Menam basin, they surrounded it.

However, even as a vassal, Ligor continued to exist as a flourishing Hindu principality. It was from here that the Thais derived their civilisation and their Buddhist religion and they prided themselves on this in their capital of Sri Satchanalai, as can be seen from the famous inscription of Ramkhamhaeng. Some of these Hindus from Ligor had found a way of slipping into the central Menam. Tenasserim, which had once been enslaved by the Burmese and had been devoid of Hindu princes for several centuries, was not in a position to play the civilising role vis-à-vis Siam that Ligor did. However, its geographical location gave it great importance. It is not surprising that the Thai, who were so anxious to secure a gateway to the sea from Martaban, did not understand the importance of using Mergui commercially until so late in the 18th century. First they had to spread out into the Menam valley. On that side, they had an open exit to the sea and on that side too, many more rice fields to cultivate and prospects for future conquests towards the East.

In short, Mergui never attained the degree of importance that its geographical location implied. However, the French and the English both saw it as an opportunity. Their rivalry neutralised their efforts and the Siamese, who had the hinterland at their disposal, were unable to turn Mergui into the major centre it should have been. Perhaps it would have been different if the streams that form the Tenasserim River, instead of running parallel to the coast, had provided a real route to the centre of Indochina.

Instead, the watershed so close to the coast, which eventually became the Siamese border, is a high chain of mountains, bisected by very rare passes and covered with thick forests. This was not a favourable terrain for Thai expansion. And the fact is that even today the lower valleys of this region are occupied by Karen, not Peguan or Burmese. For a long time, the Siamese, like the Burmese themselves, limited themselves to raiding the inhabitants from time to time and transporting them to the Menam. It was a concept like any other.

The ancient town of Mergui was once located 35 miles upstream compared to the present town on the Tenasserim river. The Peguans called it Brit, the Burmese Mrit or Brit Myu. Europeans gave it all the names they could think of: Meguim, Merguim, Merguy, Myrghy, Mergy, Mergi, Mergen and Margen. Along with Tenasserim, it is currently the only town in the province. Tin is still found here. The archipelago that precedes it is made up of a wide variety of features. In addition to the submerged and wooded mountain peaks, but without any special limestone features, which make up most of them, there are higher and more extensive islands such as King Island and undoubtedly also Kisserang, which are perfectly habitable and partly inhabited. Others are nothing more than alluvial deposits formed by the Tenasserim River. They are covered with low, green vegetation.

Just before noon, we left the area of emerged peaks and began to find shallow waters. Skirting the large King Island, whose heights are wooded but partly cleared for plantations and whose lower parts are extending like the neighbouring islets of alluvium from the Tenasserim, we entered an interesting, fairly narrow passage that already had all the appearance of a river. The alluvial deposits of the Tenasserim will eventually all come to rest on King Island. The area around this island, with its half-cultivated, half-wild landscape and almost no visible dwellings, is very attractive. The green varies on the summits, in the clearings and on the shore, and its foothills are beautifully designed.

After passing King Island at about 1.30 pm, we found ourselves in the open sea with the alluvial deposits of the Tenasserim on our right and Mergui at the far end, backed by a fairly distant chain. The blue and green sea is superb. To the north, towards Tavoy, the mountain range is more pronounced. At around 2 o'clock, the whole area was lit with a lovely brightness.

At 3 pm, we dropped anchor in the river off Mergui and I went ashore. There was only one wharf and one serious street along the river. A pagoda with official buildings stood on the highest knoll overlooking the market. There were a few streets behind with houses in the folds of the hillock. That's all there is to Mergui, which has little more than wooden houses and straw huts. As for the port's activity, it says it all that there is only one steamer on the river apart from ours and that the *Zelaya*, which arrived almost empty, is only waiting to take on a few loads in the direction of Moulmein, and barely a little more on the way back in the direction of Penang.

As it is, Mergui is extremely interesting and instructive. If it were a French port, one might think that its state of stagnation was due to our way of doing things. But it's an English port and a port with a great past, so its decline is due to the causes I mentioned earlier. Mergui is no longer a gateway or an outlet. The region produces neither rice nor tin in sufficient quantity to ensure regular freight. As for the port's location, it is excellent in itself, especially since it is at the mouth of the river and sheltered from the front by a hillock and further away by King's Island.

It seems that rubber plantations have multiplied so much here for some time, that for half a century Mergui has not had such important commercial movements as in the last two years. Little tin is produced, but the recent discovery of wolfram mines in the vicinity of Tavoy, a new metal used to harden steel, promises new fortunes for Mergui, especially when the planned coastal railway, to be extended to Victoria at the mouth of the Pak Chan, will enable all the region's products to be centralised at the port of Mergui, which is easily accessible and well protected.

It is true that Victoria Point will perhaps benefit as much as Mergui from all this traffic, especially as its installation at the exit of Pak Chan will prevent any Siamese port in this region from prospering and will monopolise transit from Bangkok. This is something I had not foreseen, unaware at the time of the English coastal railway project when I examined the future of Pak Chan above.

I stayed ashore from 3.30 pm to 6 pm and visited as much of Mergui as I could, which was not difficult. I was surprised at the multiplicity of types and races as well as at their tendency to blend together. Chinese, Burmese, Malays, Klings, Hindus of other origins live side by side and their children now have cropped hair, parted hair and Malay-style sarongs. This is the result of the Chinese reform and also of the education provided by English schools, which in mixed areas such as this tends to make young Burmese abandon the use of the chignon. There is really as little difference as possible between a Burmese of this type and a young Chinese 'nouveau style' and both have a striking analogy with the Siamese. What sometimes distinguishes the Siamese is the raised tail of the *panung* while with the Malay is his velvet cap.

In addition, Mergui has a permanent population of Klings, blacks from the Malabar who, having come at their own expense as coolies, some with their wives, stay and create a very cheap workforce in the country, quite different from that of the temporary coolies imported by the companies in Singapore and the Straits.

The rubber companies are benefiting from this for their plantations, some of which were quite expensive to begin with, having been bought from the government, which had carried out trials in the Mergui region long before the Straits rubber rush, and which put its plantations up for sale at a relatively high price once the rush had begun.

It seems that there are about ten Europeans living around Mergui on their plantations. A dozen or so others live in town, including the Deputy Commissionner and the British India agent. The Club has around twenty members.

A few years ago, the pearl trade attracted a number of Australian fishermen to Mergui, who were very expert divers, but the Japanese came and proved to be even more skilful. They eventually ousted them, although the people who employ them are not very happy about it, as they are not honest and are very good at hiding their finds.

As for the scientific exploitation of artificial pearls, this was undertaken by an Anglo-American company in Rangoon and the results are said to be surprising.

Some very competent commercial travellers often pass through Mergui, and not long ago a Frenchman came and made some major purchases, it seems.

Although there are no shopkeepers selling pearls in Mergui, I had been told that I could find some by talking to certain Chinese in the market street. A young Burmese man who spoke English and was a pupil at the local school, knowing of my desire, took me to three or four houses. Burmese women married to Chinese men showed me a number of isolated pearls that were quite large and beautiful but rather expensive for what they were. One was quite round and cost 500 rupees. Others, from an old Chinese who kept them in a dirty piece of newspaper, were offered at 500 and 600 rupees respectively, which was extremely over priced. Generally speaking, opportunities are rare, it seems, because at the market this type of individual is on the lookout and doesn't let anything pass him by.

Although I didn't have the chance to take advantage of an opportunity, I took great pleasure in witnessing the pearl dealers' market procedures on the Place de Mergui. Of course you can't find many pearls at these prices and in these circles. They all told me that in ten days or so, a return from fishing would provide more favourable opportunities. But where will I be in ten days?

Since Mergui was moved by the British, it goes without saying that this is not the place to look for the former French port built by de Bruan for his soldiers in the service of King Phra Narai.

Here, or rather on Kings Island, it seems that the easternmost bay has retained the name of French bay. This was probably where our ships from Pondicherry were concentrated or stopped. We may also have had a settlement there in de Bruan's time. An oral tradition says that the French taught some of the natives how to build boats. It has also been said that Kings Island was ceded to us by Phra Narai. This seems to be completely inaccurate. If any point in Siam was ever offered to us, it was Singora on the Gulf of Siam in 1680 by a letter from Phra Narai to Louis XIV on gold leaf. We have never taken advantage of it. Yet Singora would look good on the other side of the Gulf of Siam, opposite Cambodia. It is true that Kings Island on the other side of the Bay of Bengal, opposite Pondicherry, would have been a good opportunity also in the 17th century, but judging by the way Desfarges understood his role vis-à-vis first Phaulkon and then the usurper, I find it hard to believe that the intentions of the King of France were very clear at the time. It is true that from 1688 onwards the continental war took on such importance for France that colonial issues inevitably took a back seat. When Desfarges and then Father Tachard returned to Mergui after the events, they had some fine assets and neither of them dared to do anything. By then, the Dutch had regained all the influence in Bangkok that they had had at the beginning of the 17th century before the arrival of the English and then the French. What a fine revenge we could have taken here on William of Orange!

I got back on board at 6 pm but we didn't leave Mergui until 10 pm. The load was insignificant. We only took a few deck passengers. The other steamer that was in port also belonged to British India. It was going to Victoria Point. If it is so lightly loaded, this does not indicate that British India's business on this coast is flourishing. It's easy to see why they're trying to kill off all competition and get their hands on the 50 Eastern Navigation boats, which are more or less owned by Chinese capitalists from Penang.

12 November 1912

As the *Zaïda* did not go as far as Tavoy, the commander planned his time to coincide his arrival at the mouth of the river with the most favourable time for the tide, as a longboat was due to meet us from Tavoy to bring the goods and passengers. At about 6 o'clock in the morning we dropped anchor at the entrance to the large arm of the sea which forms the mouth of the river and at 6.30 am. I went down in a dinghy with the officers of the ship to take a swim in the sea and play a game of ball on a small beach below the lighthouse perched on the right bank at the top of a wooded hill. It was unfortunate that there were no monkeys in the area at that time of day, as it seems they like to hang out in these parts. The bathe was excellent, although the water was a little warm and the bottom muddy. On the way back, the sea was rough and it took us half an hour to row the short distance back to the boat. The jokes were non-stop throughout this amusing game.

The coastline is extremely rugged, but there are a few low-lying coves at the mouth of the river, giving access to streams that flow down from the very high mountain where the tributaries of the Amta, the main river from the north that flows into the Tenasserim, originate. It is through this massif that one of the roads leading from Tavoy to Kanburi, and from there to Bangkok, passes. What a beautiful sanatorium could be set up on these heights for the use of the Europeans of Bangkok!

For about an hour and a half from 9.15-10.45 am, we traveled up the river to the small village of Sim Jan Bine on the left bank. The valley remains just as straight and wide but alluvium has gradually been deposited at the foot of the hills on both banks, and on the left bank a few emerald green rice fields appear. On both sides of the dark but well-lit hills, you can make out the light patches of numerous clearings and the tips of a few pagodas. In the background on the left bank, but very close up, are the blue slopes of the high wooded mountains in the direction of Siam. It's a very cheerful and unusual landscape.

The bottom of the bay towards Tavoy, around 15 miles away, appears in the distance to be less rugged.

The river boat joined us at Sim Jan Bine. It was full of Burmese boarding the boat. Far fewer got off. As for the cargo, there was not the slightest trace. It seems that's not the way they travel.

Tavoy is said to lie to the east of the river. When the British took possession of it in 1825, it was a town of around 25,000 inhabitants surrounded by an inner brick wall and a less solid wall sheltering the suburbs.

The population was made up of Burmese, Peguans, Chinese and indigenous Christians. The dilapidated church with an open presbytery and no priests that I saw yesterday in Mergui obviously belonged to this group of former Catholics. The site was a good one, about half a metre high and in the liveliest part of town, indicating an ancient settlement.

The country is agricultural, but is said to be less fertile than Martaban. As in Mergui, the majority of the farming population is of Burmese race. Among those who came on board, the older men wore coloured turbans on their buns, but several young men had their hair cut. Beyond the fairly limited rice-growing region, the country is very wooded and rugged.

The region is said to have been first settled by people from Martaban and others from the east, and then by immigrants from Arakan who came in search of iron. Today, as in the past, iron is one of Tavoy's specialities.

Tavoy remained under Siamese and Burmese rule until the 18th century. When the English seized it in the first part of the 19th century, they had to contend not only with the Burmese, who were masters of the country, but also with the Siamese, who regretted that they no longer owned it and frequently raided its inhabitants.

One of the roads leading from Tavoy to Siam crosses the Nayé Daung pass, which is particularly rugged. At the time of the British occupation, the border was marked by a pillar at the Myi-Kya-Kyauptein point. Captain Low went to check this boundary, but the road was as impassable for elephants as it was for horses. He was told that there were tin mines on this side, 3 miles down the road.

I do not know if this was the route indicated by the English interpreter Leal in 1826, following his journey from Martaban to Rangoon via the Nam Kuei Noi, one of the branches of the Meklong. On the way and not far from the Siamese fort of Menam Noi, he was told that Chayok (probably the Tchu Yok on the Pavie map) was the starting point for the Tavoy road, a mountain route through thick forests that was very difficult, although fairly short as the crow flies. Leal relates that two sepoys carrying official English dispatches from Bangkok made the journey from Chayok to Tavoy and back in eight days.

What is certain is that although the road from Bangkok to Tavoy is no longer used regularly for trade, it is considered to be the most direct and shortest route from Bangkok to the coast of the Bay of Bengal, as the telegraph line passes through there. It is true that it is often interrupted in rainy weather by falling trees or damage caused by elephants. In such cases, we can use the Singora or Moulmein line, or the Saigon line.

At 2 pm we were at sea again and this time I could see clearly, which I had not been able to do last night, the long straight coastline closely hugged by several rows of mountains, which stretch between the mouths of the Tavoy and Tenasserim rivers. This is indeed the compact barrier that the maps seem to indicate. On this side, the sea is much clearer of islands and islets than to the south of Mergui.

In 1568, the Venetian traveller Cesar dei Federici, on his way from Malacca to Pegou, got lost in the Mergui archipelago. He was accompanied by several Portuguese who had previously been to Tenasserim. Several of the passengers wanted to reconnoitre Mergui by canoe, but they were unable to find the port and for eight days they wandered around, feeding on a little rice and turtle eggs, until they found themselves in the Gulf of Tavoy where they met some fishermen. Pushing on to Tavoy, they hoped to find the boat they had left, but it had not arrived. When they went to look for it, they found that it had had to fight against the winds, and that the passengers had run out of water and food because there was no boat to take them ashore, since Federici and his companions had taken the only canoe on board.

Leaving the Gulf of Tavoy, we followed the coast very closely, with its pretty little bays, jagged, green and formed by hills overlooking small golden beaches. Nature is pretty, especially in fine, cloudless weather like today's, but isn't it surprising that all along this coastline since leaving Penang, there has been no trace of villages or seaside dwellings on the islands and even, except at Mergui, at the river mouths?

Before 5 o'clock we started to sail along the outer edge of the Moscos archipelago. These are still hilltops covered in vegetation, but nothing particularly picturesque.

As night fell, as on previous days, the wind freshened but it did not bring bad weather. Since the Mergui archipelago, we have entered the zone where the monsoon change is complete, which promises us some security for our overland journey.

13 November 1912

From 3 am to 6 am last night, the *Zaïda* remained at anchor in front of the mouth of the river Ye. There's nothing particularly striking about the place. It is reminiscent of certain confluences in the Gulf of Siam. Wooded hills line the seashore, with some forming islets in front of the bar. Behind, along the river, is a plain of little extent, because although it is not as high as at Tavoy, the dividing range is not far away.

Ye is an ancient dependency of Tavoy of relatively little importance, although in the last century the country still produced a lot of timber used for trade.

I regret not having seen the town, which is said to be 15 or 20 miles inland, in a picturesque situation on a hill above the river. At the mouth of the river, I didn't see the slightest trace of cultivation or construction, and as the boat from the river came to visit us in the middle of the night, I don't even know what it loaded and unloaded. It must have been very little, judging by the lack of noise caused by this visit.

According to tradition, Ye was founded by the daughter of a prince of Tavoy, who settled there in 731 CE. In 1438, the town was embellished and fortified by the Prince of Tavoy, Naratha Jedi Men.

That's all I know of its history, except that Ye followed the fate of both Tavoy and Martaban. There was more than one battle on its territory between the Siamese, the Pegans and the Burmese, and for a very long time until the treaty of 24 February 1826 in which Burma ceded Ye, along with Tavoy, Mergui and Tenasserim, to England. The Siamese, who had lost this territory as early as the 18th century, kept up their habit of raiding some of its inhabitants.

The mountains directly behind Ye in the east, which appear lower from the sea than those of Tavoy, are the source not only of the Tavoy river but also of the two streams that form the Moulmein river and, especially on the Siamese side, of the main tributary of the Nam Kuei, whose waters irrigate Kanburi, Ratburi and Meklong.

Here is where one of the historic routes between Martaban, Moulmein and Bangkok passes through. This is the route of the Three Pagodas, known to the Burmese as Phra Song Chu and to the Siamese as Phra Chedi Sam Ong, in reference to the monuments that mark the most important point along the way.

The pass is apparently not as steep as Nayé Daung on the road from Tavoy to Siam. According to Captain Low, it takes about 23 regular stages to reach Bangkok, starting from Martaban or Moulmein, but the natives take much less time to cover this distance.

The first two or three stages are on the Attharam River. Then to reach Menam Noi, on the Siamese river of that name, takes six to eight days. The travellers then reach Kanburi, which at the time of the British conquest of Tenasserim was an important border post at the junction of two branches of the Meklong. Two days later, travelling down the Meklong, they reach Ratburi and the beginning of the canal by which the Meklong is linked to the Menam branch which flows into the sea at Tha Chin. It then takes another two or three days to reach Bangkok from Ratburi.

Today, Ratburi is linked to Bangkok by a railway, but the road to Moulmein via the Meklong does not appear to be very busy.

The English interpreter Leal followed the route in question in April 1826, having embarked in canoes on the Uttaran river near Moulmein. He passed through the following places: M. Uttaran, Klong Bangwilai, Klong Peli, Phra Mongue, Klong Mykut where he crossed a large teak forest, Klong Mysikleet, Mykesath where navigation on the Uttaran ends and where he encountered a Siamese post. It had taken him

Three Pagodas Pass from *Royal Siamese Maps*. (Courtesy River Books)

seven days to get there.

The next day he reached the border by land at the place known as the Three Pagodas. The exact point of the border was difficult to determine. The same day, Mr Leal reached Songola, a Siamese village of about 150 souls on the eastern bank of one of the main branches of the Meklong. There was a Siamese guard post there, made up of around a hundred Peguans.

The next stage ended at the fort of Lumchang, also guarded by Peguans and Siamese soldiers. It was a place that began at the confluence of three tributaries of the Meklong, and Leal was able to find boats there to take him down the river.

Despite difficult navigation, they reached Menam Noi, where there were two Siamese ports, in a region where cotton was successfully cultivated. Menam Noi was a short distance from the post of Chayok, from where a mountain road leads to Tavoy.

Via Thakuto, Sam Sing, Danclai and Ban Chiom, navigation continued on the Meklong. Ban Chiom was a fairly important centre, inhabited mainly by Pegouans at the confluence of the Sissovat.

Pak Prek, also known as Kanburi since the Burmese destroyed the old Kanburi on the Sissovat in 1766, had a population of 8,000 at the time of Mr Leal's visit.

Via Ratburi and Ban Chang, he eventually reached Meklong at the mouth of the river of that name. It was a major trading centre with a population of 13,000.

Further along the Tha Chin river, inhabited mainly by Peguan and Chinese, he joined the Menam, following the Klong Menang Luong, and thus arrived in Bangkok by a route he was probably the first European to have explored.

Leaving at 6 am from the mouth of the River Ye, we were by 1.30 pm in front of the immense Salween estuary and stopped in front of the green island of the Amherst lighthouse and signal mast to take the pilot on board. The native village of Amherst disappears completely under the coconut trees. All that can be seen are a few small naval establishments backed by small green hills, to the north of which lie a few alluvial terraces, the whole still dominated fairly closely by the heights which form the background to the picture and whose precise line we follow, extending on the other side of the estuary by the Martaban massif.

When you look from afar across the yellow bay of the estuary, which extends several hours out to sea, and see the mountain of Martaban with a line of low-lying coastline below it to the north-west, you immediately understand the geographical reasons for the first events in the history of this country.

For an invader coming from the south and by sea, the Tenasserim coast with its mountains so close to the sea could not be a centre of colonisation. The same is true of the Salween valley, with the river muddy at its mouth, narrow in its course and with no cultivated land. The only slightly larger area available was at the foot of the Martaban massif, not towards the Salween, but towards the point in the gulf where alluvial deposits from rivers flowing in from the north had undoubtedly already formed land suitable for cultivation. The idea of emigrants from the north or east, guided by the course of the rivers, following the valleys, settling on their banks and being satisfied once they had made contact with the sea, must have been quite different. Hence the construction of Martaban itself on the river, at the junction of several river mouths, but next to the river where the previous inhabitants had their rice fields and settlements.

In settling in Amherst and Moulmein, the English were not subject to the same requirements. They settled where the necessities of navigation and their personal convenience drew them. They did not have to be guided by the size of the fields. This explains better than any book the history of this country.

Moulmein, an English creation on the site of a former native village, is now a town of about fifty thousand inhabitants on the left bank of the Salween. It stretches for about seven miles along the river, but is very narrow and only has stone quays for a mile. It is far from being a busy port. Apart from the *Zelaya*, there is only one small steamer, the *Amapura*, which was loading at that moment and appeared to be on the regular Rangoon service. There were also a few Chinese junks, six rather elegant but small sailing ships and a fairly large number of steamers plying the river and its tributaries. There is no major inland waterway service on the Salween, where, because of the rapids, steam navigation can go no further than 60 or 80 miles.

Moulmein's fortunes were made for a time by teak, but here, as in Siam, things have been done too quickly. The forests have been devastated and, as it takes around 50 years for a tree to be ready for felling, it will take at least a generation to achieve results from the efforts currently being made by the forestry department to restore this important source of income.

The area around Moulmein produces a certain amount of rice, but not enough to compete with Rangoon, which owes much of its superiority to the excellent navigability of the Irrawaddy.

It is therefore a town in decline, exporting a little rice and metal and a small quantity of rubber, and importing a number of everyday items for use by the Shan and Karen of the upper region. Judging by the number of rice mills established along the river, however, there is a big difference between Moulmein and Bangkok, although rice production in this region has been more abundant than anywhere else in Indochina in recent years.

What was most striking on arrival was the number of teak sawmills, which is still considerable, although there are very few logs on the river. In some of these sawmills, however, elephants work and pull up a few logs along the bank.

At 5 o'clock when the *Zelaya* docked, Moulmein appeared at its best, with the pagodas that dominate the surrounding hills, one of which is brightly gilded, well lit by the setting sun.

Warned of my arrival by my English colleague in Bangkok, Arthur Peel, who had written and telegraphed to Rangoon, the Commissioner of Moulmein, Mr Dawson, was waiting for me at the landing stage and very kindly offered me hospitality in his house.

Before that, he took advantage of the little time we had left before nightfall to give me a ride in an English dog cart along the quayside and through the commercial districts of the town, and to make immediate arrangements for the excursion I'm planning tomorrow to Thaton.

He then took me to the Club to meet the people who could give me the most useful information about the journey I was going to make between Moulmein and Raheng in a fortnight's time.

We met Mr Russel, a tall, solid Englishman, a very pleasant man who is one of the Bombay Burmah agents here and who has made this journey more than once. Another member of the Club who had also made the journey gave furthur directions, but as is usually the case, the information was not all in agreement, either on the mode of transport to be used or on the stages where it was important to stop. Russel, for his part, prefers mountain walking to elephants or even horses. But neither I nor my companions are cut out like him for walking. As for horses, we would have to buy them either in Moulmein or Rangoon, with the idea of selling them in Raheng, which would be impractical for travellers passing through as quickly as us, and very expensive.

Russel obligingly offered to enquire at Kokarit about the possibility of hiring horses or mules there. It is impossible to make use of the mules of a caravan from Yunnan on the return journey, as they do not descend to Moulmein until December.

In any case, the journey to Raheng, which can be expected to take ten days, although Russel completed it very quickly in four nights, seems perfectly feasible, even for ladies, especially in this cool season when the rains are over, with excellent roads to the Siamese border and a varied choice of well-equipped bungalows. Luggage will have to be transported by ox cart to Myawadi, the last station on British territory.

Once we had this information, we made a vain effort to meet Father de Chirac, a French missionary living in Moulmein, whom Mr Dawson would have liked to invite to dinner. He was not at home. So, we went home to freshen up, then had dinner with Mr Dawson's brother, who had been a civil servant in Moulmein in 1897 and was now a judge there.

There was a most courteous welcome from the two brothers, in the absence of Mrs Dawson who is with her two children in England. My host is of the phlegmatic sort. He has an inert, dreamy air, with a rubbery figure, despite being very thin. He has nonetheless a precise mind, which lodges every detail in his brain for the right moment and is not lacking in judgement. It didn't take long for me to realise this from the painstaking care he took in organising my day tomorrow, and from his final conclusions about the Raheng journey. They are perfectly practical, even though he has never travelled in the mountains himself, and are in line with my own views and with those in the letter of information he has received from Rangoon about me, which he was willing to share with me. These instructions state that if I cannot find horses to buy in Moulmein, elephants should be made available as far as the Siamese border. This is by far the solution that seems most practical to both of us and which we have decided on. If, in the meantime, Russel comes up with something better, there will still be time to adopt his scheme.

All Dawson asked was to be informed in good time of our final decision, as well as of the number of carts we will need to transport our baggage. No arrangements need to be made on the other side of the border with the English, as the Siamese will have their own system all organised.

I'm really pleased that I was able to stop in Moulmein before arriving in Rangoon to sort out all these details.

With the greatest kindness in the world, Mr Dawson is keen to offer us hospitality when we return, however many of us there may be at the time. This is not to be ignored, as Moulmein has only a mediocre boarding house and it is much more convenient to be under the same roof as the authorities who make all the decisions.

14 November 1912

By 6 o'clock I was on my feet after a good night's sleep, and at 7 o'clock, having had my bath and coffee, I found Dawson and his brother ready to accompany me on the elevated pagoda road to give me a general view of the town and its surroundings.

The Commissioner spent part of his night and morning providing me with letters for the Thaton authorities and securing for me the official boat to Martaban, then a 1st class wagon to Thaton and this evening a berth in Thaton for the Rangoon train. He also provided me with the number of rupees I needed to get to Rangoon, as I only have Siamese ticals and the bank here seems reluctant to accept them. This is a striking symptom, which had already been pointed out to me, regarding the lack of importance of trade relations between Siam and Burma in these parts.

Our morning walk was delightful. On the fairly low wooded heights that dominate the long ribbon of Moulmein, the Burmese have built several pagodas and monasteries that are very picturesque in their glitz and glamour, despite the deplorable zinc roofs that are increasingly replacing the old gilded carved wood. It's a jumble of staircases, terraces, chapels and monastic dwellings, surrounding round pyramids ending in royal crowns. One of these pyramids has been very recently gilded. Another, near the Commissioner's house, was covered in bamboo and will soon be gilded again. One of the neighbouring chapels is entirely covered in mirrors cut in a diamond pattern, with a reclining Buddha on a bed in the same style, covered with a golden lobster which appears to be encrusted with stones. It's a lovely piece of imitation that's not lacking in style.

Although the type and style of the Burmese pagodas, which are less classical than the Siamese ones, were fairly new to me, since I saw the first ones at Mergui, I was above all interested, but passionately interested, in the marvellous panorama that unfolded around us, all along this marvellous walk. It is one of the most beautiful views you can see of the various rivers that meet near Moulmein before flowing into the Bay of Bengal; of the plain cultivated with rice fields or covered with beautiful trees; of the mountains in the direction of Siam, on the Thaton and Martaban ranges and finally on this limestone range which looks like a curtain in the direction of the Salween, with this fissured rock whose shape is reminiscent of the head of a reclining, shaven man, so much so that it is called the Bonze's Head.

It's a truly remarkable sight. As for the town that stretches along the river at the foot of the hills, part of it disappears into the trees, but you can make out more than one monument that I passed in front of last night. They are not beautiful, but they were of some interest to me because there are two Catholic churches, one of which is French and is waiting for some money to be rebuilt, as well as a large French friars' school, which my companions speak very highly of. I'll try to visit all that on the way back.

An English church, a new prison, a rather meagre clock tower in honour of Edward VI, a very mediocre statue of Victoria, these are the features that distinguish this shady and rather primitive town, which has nothing to compare with Pulo Penang. It does not appear rich. The few hundred Europeans who live here are not accustomed to luxury. There are few cars, or even any cars at all. There are sports, of course, but simple and unpretentious. The gymkhana club is large but quite primitive and the Commissioner's accommodation is old and unpretentious. It is even rented from a Chinese merchant.

Moulmein's only sparkling feature is its remarkable site. Despite my host's insistence on keeping us here for a long enough time when we return, there isn't a good reason for a second stay.

At about 10.15 am after a substantial breakfast, Mr Dawson took me to the quay and installed me on his longboat. It took me about twenty minutes to get to the other side of the river and a little higher up, Martaban, whose name recalls more than one memory: not only that of the kingdom of Farua or Wareru at the beginning of the 14th century, but also the visits and early accounts of Portuguese travellers in the 16th century.

Of Martaban, the temporary capital of a kingdom that had more significance in the history of the Thai race than in the general history of the world, very little remains, but more than seen by de la Jonquière, whose hasty visit to the village on the banks of the river did not allow him to spot all the ruined pyramids, some covered in earth and trees, which are spread out over all the hills behind the river above the new railway line.

This railway has only existed since 1905 and no one in Bangkok was even able to tell me for sure that it had been built. Today, Rangoon is linked by rail, if not to Moulmein directly, at least to Martaban, but it takes 13 hours to go from one point to the other, whereas it only takes 9 hours, but only three times a week, by sea. As for extending the railway via Moulmein and the Tenasserim coast to Point Victoria at the confluence of the Pak Chan, that's another matter. Mr Dawson admits that it has been talked about more than once, but he does not believe that the project will be carried out any time soon. It's true that once the railway is built, people in Bangkok may still remain unaware of its existence, or pretend to be.

As it stands, the railway from Martaban to Rangoon serves the capitals of several kingdoms that were once very flourishing and which I think are well worth a visit. I was delighted to have this opportunity to stop at Thaton.

From Martaban, the railway line runs extremely close to the foot of the hills that border the Salween basin and end in the final spur opposite Moulmein. The rice paddies grow right to the foot of the hills and extend continuously across the flat land as far as the sea. There are many white pyramids on the heights, from which a few cascading streams emerge amidst the trees. At its base, villages surrounded by fruit trees lie along the way near their rice fields, where the grain that is forming promises to be excellent.

It was at the foot of these hills that the subjects of the King of Martaban cultivated their fields, but long before the Siamese conquerors of the 13th century, other princes had had their capitals in the vicinity of these rice fields.

Remains of monuments dating from the 3rd to 4th century CE can be found at Thaton and are said to have a distinctly South Hindu character. The people who built these monuments came from the east coast of southern India when the Kalinga kings of the Cālukya dynasty ruled this part of the peninsula.

These foreigners, who brought southern civilisation to the Bay of Bengal, created colonies and trading ports in this region. With the fall of the Tharekkettara kingdom, whose capital was near Prome, around the 1st century, it was possible for these Hindus to form a kingdom between the Salween and the Irrawaddy, which included the entire delta of the Irrawaddy, although the capital was Thaton, quite a distance from this great river.

The kingdom of Thaton, or Saton, Xatan, Satan, depending on the pronunciation, was called Suvannabhumi and the capital itself, in Sanskrit, Saddhammanagara, a distortion of Sat Dharma. According to legend, the town and kingdom owed their origins to hermits, sons of a Hindu king, who had come to settle in the country when the sea still occupied the land that has since become rice fields. They are said to have found very savage inhabitants in the region, to whom they imparted their own civilisation, while it was by Aryans that the brothers of these same savages were civilised in the regions to the north. There is a list of 29 more or less fabulous kings from the origins of Thaton to the foundation in the 6th century by a son of the king of Thaton of the city of Hangsawadi, also known as Pegu.

The oldest known indigenous inhabitants of this whole region were the Taungthus, whose descendants still survive and who appear to be of Mongoloid race. Their language is somewhere between that of the Shans, i.e. Thai, and that of the Karen, according to Mr W. Abbey, who has visited them. They occupied the country between Sittang and the Salween and were good farmers.

In the 11th century, a powerful prince arose in Pagan, on the Irrawaddy in the country north of Prome, who appears to have been of Burmese race and who re-established, for the benefit of his compatriots from the north, the domination of the former kings of Tharekkettara over this kingdom of Thaton and the neighbouring territory of Hangsawadi where the Hindu princes had established their power.

It was in 1010 CE that the Pagan king Anuratha, the hero of Burmese legends, carried out this conquest and seized everything that had remained of the ancient Hindu kingdom of Thaton since the foundation of Hangsawadi. Hangsawadi also succumbed and all the chronicles were destroyed or taken away by the Burmese to erase even the memory of the past.

The Mon or Peguan, also known as Talaing and who made up the population of Hangsawadi, never forgave the Burmese for this attack on their history. They were not the only ones to suffer under the tyranny of the conquerors: in the 13th century, following another Burmese victory, the Taungthu farmers were forced to leave the region near the sea and migrate north and east to the Shan areas, where they are still to be found.

Anuratha, the great patron of Buddhism in his kingdom of Pagan, had been lured to Thaton by the fame of a famous collection of the Tripitaka, which the king of that country had refused him. After the capture of the city, the king and his family were taken captive to Pagan along with the Buddhist books and images, and so Thaton came to an end.

Later, in the 14th century, the Peguans, who had long been subjugated by the Siamese and the Burmese, regained their independence, but their written traditions were lost. They only remembered the past greatness of Thaton, the kingdom and capital whose kings had given birth to the founders of their own capital Hangsawadi, and they confused many things.

This is how they ended up imagining that Thaton, the ancient capital of the kingdom, had been the landing point for the first hermits who founded the kingdom, whereas other, more precise legends reserve this honour for Golanagara, today's Ayetthima, which lies around twenty miles north of Thaton.

This town, which in the 16th century was known as Takkala and whose ruins can still be found between Ayetthima and Kinywa, is said to have been isolated from the rivers and the sea by the gradual rise in the ground over the last two or three centuries.

Takkala or Taikkala, the Kulataik of the Burmese, first mentioned by Ptolemy, is thought to be none other than the Tegala or Tagala of Mendes Pinto in the 16th century. But for Indochinese, Siamese, Cambodian and other historians, it is Kalah or Kuleh, sometimes Kola or Kulanagara, the crossing point for emigrants and pilgrims between Siam and the sacred cities of India. It was here that the first Buddhist mission landed in the land of Ramanadesa, and it was from here that the founders of Thaton came.

In Hindu geography, the name Ramanadesa was originally used to designate the region between the river Sittang and the Salween. It was not until much later, in the 14th century, under the predecessor of the Peguan king Dhammaceti, that the collective name of Ramanadesa was given to the three provinces of Ukkala, Kusima and Muttima, the first of which stretched from Rangoon to Hangsawadi, the second towards Bassein and the third towards Martaban.

After the 14th century, the names Rammavati are applied to the region to the east of the holy mountain of Shwé Dagon, Dhammavati to the region to the south, Adhipaccaya to the west and Ukkala to the north.

Before the end of the 13th century, there is no mention of Adhipaccaya in Burmese history. It was the capital of Dala, also known as Pokkhara, the lower region between the Rangoon river and Bassein. The name Pokkhara is also found in the kingdom of Bacala mentioned by ancient European travellers.

Ukkalanagara was located on the Kokain hills, while Rammavati, not far from Rangoon, was founded in the 13th century by a successor of Anuratha.

The name Suvannabhumi has often been used to designate the country where southern Buddhism was introduced by Sona and Uttara. The Peguan inscriptions of Kalyani tell us that Sona and Utttara were sent to Ramanna, which is part of Suvannabhumi, to propagate the faith. This was at a time when King Siri Dhammasoka ruled the country, whose capital was Golamattikanagara (Kola = Tokkala) near the sea. This was 236 years after Buddha's entry into nirvana. After years of great prosperity, the country of Ramanna fell into great decline at the time of King Manohari, under whose reign religion suffered greatly.

In the 15th century, at a time of a Buddhist renaissance, King Dhammaceti had inscriptions engraved to commemorate these events. These inscriptions have been found not only at Kalyani but also at Shwe Dagon, Lekkaik, Kelasa and Tanut. Forchhammer used the Kalyani inscriptions to pinpoint the location of the town of Kola, visited by Sona and Uttara. It is 22 miles north-west of Thaton and today twelve miles from the sea in the Kelasa mountains. The pagoda we see today on the site of Kola, or rather Golanagara (Takkala), was built by King Dhammaceti.

Suvannabhumi, although used exclusively by works such as the *Dipavamsa*, *Mahavamsa* and *Samantapasadika* as referring to the Buddhist mission of Sona and Uttara, has a much wider meaning than any of the others. Lassen identified it with the present-day Pegu, i.e. the Irrawaddy delta. Colonel Yule tried to apply it to a promontory on the coast of the Gulf of Martaban. Other writers have thought that this name should be attributed either to Burma as a whole, or to the large islands of the Straits. In modern Burmese, it is only used to refer to Upper and Lower Burma. In reality, it belongs to the whole of Indochina, to the land of gold called Chersonese or Khrysé by the peoples of the West.

Unable to explore Takkala, whose ruins lost in the bush are said to be insignificant, I was at least keen to visit Thaton, which lies on the line from Martaban to Rangoon.

Mr Dawson had done things well. He had telegraphed to Major W. Abbey, Thaton District Commander, who was waiting for me at the station at 2 o'clock with his car and who took me home to rest until 4.30 pm. He has been in the Shan States Service, where he knew Scott, Stirling, Lloyd, Woodthorpe and some of my old companions from 1894. So when he heard that I was on the 1894 commission he gave me the warmest welcome. His district is very large, and to the east of the Salween he is in charge of fairly sparsely inhabited Shan and Karen territories lost in the forest and mountains, which he rarely visits. Dawson, like the Commissioner of Moulmein, is his direct chief.

The part of his district which stretches between Moulmein and Pegu, is one of the most densely populated and richest in the region. All along the railway, at the foot of the hills, there are nothing but villages. When I expressed surprise at the considerable number of Hindus I had met since I landed at Mergui, he told me that except in the towns and along the railway, there were hardly any. Almost all the villages are inhabited by Burmese, Peguan or Taungthu, who all speak Burmese. The Peguan women differ from the Burmese, however, in the shape of their *sin* or sarong, which is similar to that of the Shan women, and in the bun they wear at the back rather than on top of their heads like the Burmese.

At 4.30 we set off with a Burmese attendant in charge of antiquities to visit the main pagoda of Thaton, which is vast, and accompanied by large pyramids and many small aediculae. But restoration has piled on restoration, and the present style, where painted or plain zinc struggles with mirrorwork more suited to a music hall, is totally deplorable.

Some of the pyramids are very old, but it's hard to tell with the brick cladding that tends to hide the ancient limonite foundations. One of them, however, shows significant traces of primitive work. The staircases and walls are made of limonite, on which some remains of ornamentation can still be seen.

At the base of the bell, there were also terracotta metopes that had been whitewashed more than once. Unfortunately, most of these have now disappeared, but the surviving elements reveal rather graceful subjects in which the Hindu costume and the attributes of the figures have a distinctly foreign style.

The same traces can be found on a number of stone stelae, which have been badly mutilated and have illegible inscriptions. They still retain some interesting sculptural details, but do not seem to have been treated with sufficient care.

In the neighbouring pagodas, we were also shown some debris of the same origin, but this is all that can be found of interest in Thaton, unless the pagoda built on the summit of the mountain, to which access seems very difficult, contains some special elements that I am told do not exist.

All in all, the archaeological interest of my visit was mediocre, but I was satisfied to have a topographical and geographical idea of the place, and the hints of Hindu art that I found are not to be sneezed at either. The village is large and pretty, with its streets disappearing under the trees and laid out with precision. A small club serves as a meeting place for the few Europeans living in Thaton. At 6 pm, there were four of them there today, which is a lot for the village.

Before taking me back to the station, where the train was waiting with a berth reserved for me to Rangoon, Mr Abbey invited me to his house for dinner. Two details struck me in his conversation. Firstly, he thought it would be in Burma's interest to be a separate and independent colony from India. I would gladly believe him. What I have seen of it makes me realise that it is a country administered and run from afar by authorities who know little about it and have no direct interest in it. Mr Abbey cites the fine initiatives of the Straits, who in their prosperity and independence find themselves in a position to offer a dreadnought to the mother country. It is true that the Straits have superior resources with their rubber and tin. Mr Abbey is obliged to admit that the Burmese mining companies have caused more than one misfortune. Timber is disappearing, although they hope to succeed with wolfram. As for rubber, it is far from being a production area as concentrated and as close to the main trade routes as the Straits are.

He gave me the very interesting example of a French missionary from the French Missions who had settled in Zingyaik between Martaban and Thaton, and who was highly skilled in botany and agriculture, and had set up a rubber plantation near his Christian home. If I had stayed longer, he would have told me moved.

15 November 1912

It was a night without sleep because of mosquitoes, frequent stops and infernal noise at each station. At 6.30 am we arrived in Rangoon and I moved into the Strand hotel. The Bibby line boat due to bring Henriette and the Vilmorins from Colombo is expected here tomorrow morning at 9 o'clock.

After freshening up, I set off on various errands around the city, such as to the National Bank of India, which put me in touch with its Martaban branch and with the Bengal Bank in Moulmein. The absence of commercial relations with Siam is even more evident in the impossibility of obtaining a tical from the Bank of India and, above all, in the naivety of the manager who advised me to take English gold with me to change at the border. He must not have the slightest idea of what a gold coin means to a Siamese from the interior. I believe, however, that if I take a sufficient quantity of rupees to Moulmein, I will be able to do my business.

At Cook's, I had to deal with people who were obliging but so entrenched in their routine that any suggestions for an itinerary that I offered was met with the reply that it's not worth doing because the place isn't worth visiting. This was the opinion they had of the famous ruins of Pagan and of Lashio, the capital of the Northern Shan States. The latter now has a railway and a visit their would give an insight into the Thai part of Burmese territory.

It is my old companion from 1894, Stirling, who is now High Commissioner in Lashio and I would have some pleasure in seeing him again. In addition, it would have been interesting for me to see the future of this railway line which has started heading east, towards Yunnan, and which will probably one day be extended as far as Kunlong and the Upper Salween ferry.

Abbey does not believe in the future of railway lines in this direction, any more than he does in that of Mogaung or an extension of the main line beyond Bhamo. He believes, not without reason, that Yunnan is too poor a country to pay for such expensive and difficult construction, and he thinks, having lived in Assam, that there are far greater advantages in linking Sichuan to India from this side, both countries being much more worthwhile than Yunnan and Burma. It is true that the mountains are very high in Assam, but we would be facing a large plateau that is easy enough to reach by winding roads and we would not have to cross all the deep valleys that the Irrawaddy, the Salween and the Mekong have to offer.

As all in all I only have too few days from the 18th to the 29th to attempt the excursion to Lashio, I gave it up but I was holding out for the one to Pagan. But then I came up against the difficulties of combining boats and railways which would make the visit to Pagan possible only with means other than those that Cook can put at my disposal. So why not take advantage of the goodwill of the English authorities, as Abbey suggested to me yesterday. A government rowboat would easily allow me, after the visit to Bhamo and Mandalay, to push a point of Mandalay as far as Pagan on the way back and return to Rangoon in time to catch the evening train on the 29th which would take me back to Moulmein on the 30th.

Armed with these instructions, I went to the Government Office, a huge Renaissance-style quadrangle where I found the Secretary General of the Government of Burma, Mr Tonkinson, who in the absence of the Lieutenant Governor was busy organising my affairs with the authorities in Moulmein. He is a very amiable young man to whom I reported on the arrangements made with Dawson and the difficulties I had encountered with Cook in organising the excursion to Pagan. On his own initiative, he proposed the solution I wanted. He is going to telegraph Mandalay to find out if on the morning of the 26th we can get a boat from Bhamo to Mandalay, which will take us to Pagan and then back to Myingyan on the morning of the 28th, from where we will reach Rangoon by rail on the 29th, so that we still have a whole day to rest before leaving for Moulmein. The Lieutenant Governor is away until the 28th and has expressed a desire to see us on his return to Rangoon.

It all worked out well and all I had to do was get my companions' approval. Rangoon is a big city, but it's ordinary, not very picturesque and doesn't seem very well maintained. The city, which today has a population of 2,500,000, was built around the Shwé Dagon pagoda and was once the residence of the regents of Pegou, before falling definitively into Burmese hands in 1763. Its indigenous name is Dagohn or Yangohn and its classical name is Tikumbanagara. It was surrounded by walls when it was conquered by the British in 1824, but it has long since spread outside these walls. The capital of Lower Burma after the first British war, which established the centre of their administration there, it has remained the seat of government since the fall of the Burmese monarchy. However, the Lieutenant Governor of Burma does not have his usual residence here, which is in Remyo in the upper region.

The Shwé Dagon pagoda is an important place of pilgrimage for Buddhists because of the relics it is supposed to contain. Rebuilt in the 17th century, it was only restored to its current state around 1770 by King Alompra's successor. However, the inscriptions it contains date from 1485 and are Peguan. They therefore date back to an earlier period in the pagoda's history.

It's a truly remarkable place that I went to visit at the end of the day. I've rarely ever seen anything quite like it, as it's quite a summary of Burmese life and I don't think there's any place where the local picturesque can be better displayed.

The area around the pagoda, which stands on a slight rise, is crowded with merchants selling flowers, candles, images, food and refreshments. Pilgrims in groups or on their own stop in unexpected places to say

Shwedagon pagoda. (Thweep Rittinaphakorn Collection)

their prayers. And there's no stopping them, from the outer portico at the bottom of one of the covered staircases, to the top and all the way up to the platform where the gigantic golden pyramid rests.

The eye is diverted but also grows weary of the profusion of forms, ornaments, sculptures, gilding and mirrors in which the native taste manifests itself with unparalleled variety. In fact, around the main pyramid, there are so many chapels, rest rooms, mats of fantastic animals and isolated statues of Buddha that the imagination of the artists has been given free rein. There are pavilions and wooden roofs marvellously carved and gilded, but there are also horrors. Nevertheless, the overall effect is most attractive, perhaps mainly because the monuments are interspersed with beautiful trees and coconut palms, and also because of the indigenous life that is evident on all sides: worshippers in prayer, with their candles lit in front of the chapels, merchants and buyers in the small shops, families in festive clothes and with flowers gathered on platforms and chatting, pretty Burmese girls adorned and mincing about, circulating with friends on the temple platform; black Hindus in prayer before the Buddha and old Burmese monks in devotion. It's all very curious and picturesque.

16 November 1912

Walking around the city this morning, I pushed my way up to the Catholic cathedral, a vast brick edifice built in the last ten years. It's neat, very neat, and clean, although the style is a bit indecisive, it's a monument that does honour to the French missionary who built it.

Many French memories are depicted in the stained glass windows and statues of French saints, Joan of Arc, J-B. de la Salle, and recent martyrs from the Far East.

This church belongs to the Foreign Missions, who have spent a million on it, and it is said to be worth two or three million. At least that's what the Bishop told me, surrounded by his missionaries, whom I met at the door of his cathedral when, at the end of the retreat, he was having his photo taken with all his clergy.

I don't think there are many French people other than them in Rangoon. I saw them all at once. They seem to be thriving and, like their brothers, have very well-developed establishments.

The Bibby Line *Worcestershire* bringing Henriette and the de Vilmorins arrived at the quay at 10 o'clock. I was delighted to welcome them in good health and satisfied with their stay in Ceylon.

As they had sent a wire from the ship to reserve accommodation at Minto Mansions, I left the Strand and we moved to this other hotel in the middle of the English Quarter, surrounded by bungalows but a long way from the business district, which is not very convenient.

Vilmorin's travel plans didn't quite coincide with mine, so we spent a good while together at Cook's, but still didn't decide anything. Vilmorin doesn't care about Pagan, whereas Henriette and I do, and he is much more interested in nature, forests and botany. I'll probably let him go along the Lashio road, although he doesn't even care to go as far as this interesting centre of Shan country where a railway now ends. It is also likely that Henriette and I will be satisfied with the express boat trip to Bhamo, while Vilmorin wants to take the slower cargo boat. But to reconcile Pagan, Mandalay and Bhamo, we cannot do otherwise, given the short time available.

At the end of the day, the four of us went together by car for the pretty walk around the lakes and climbed up to Shwé Dagon, where my companions were completely surprised and amazed.

17 November 1912

There was an excellent high mass in Rangoon's beautiful French cathedral. Then a few strolls and purchases in the shops and back to Minto at 11 am for an appointment with Mr Tonkinson, whose house I discovered was right next to the hotel.

Our decision has been made. Bored with the Vilmorins going their own way, Henriette and I will first go straight from Mandalay to Bhamo on Wednesday, and on the way back to Mandalay we'll take a government rowboat on an excursion to Pagan.

I even hoped at one point that the same boat could take us as far as Prome, from where we would return by rail to Rangoon. This additional journey had been suggested to us by Major Des Voeux, who seems to be in the same service as Tonkinson. But at the end of the day, he came to tell me that for service reasons, the longboat would not be able to take us back to Prome until around 3rd December, which would be much too late.

I have agreed to extend our stay in Burma by a few days to fit in with the Vilmorins' plans, but on condition that I arrive in Moulmein on the 4th so that we can start our return journey on the 5th, thus forgoing the trip to Sukhothai. I had been planning to do this for a long time, and it upsets me somewhat, but I am not prepared to be delayed in Burma, to the point of arriving in Bangkok later than the date of the 20th that I have long set for myself.

According to the latest combinations, we will be leaving Mandalay on the 27th and returning on the 30th after visiting Pagan, but without pushing on to Prome, which I would certainly have liked to see, but whose visit is not vital.

Earlier, in front of the hotel lobby, we had an amusing display by a Hindu snake charmer with his pythons, cobras and mongoose. At any moment in the street, amidst the coolies, the mosques and the painted multi-storey houses, you could have imagined yourself much more in India than in Burma. But then Shwé Dagon, with its purely indigenous appearance and the exquisite charm of the shapes, colours and flowers presented by its Burmese visitors, brought us back to reality. We did not exhaust the charm of the pagoda during our visit, which we repeated once more. Before returning to the hotel, we took a rather nice drive through the woods north of Rangoon.

18 November 1912

An unbearably hot morning spent shopping in town and dealing with the authorities, banks and so on. Our meeting with Cook was very long. As for Tonkinson, Secretary to the Government of Burma, he was extremely obliging and eagerly helped Vilmorin obtain his arms licence and buy his ammunition.

Henriette and I went to visit Mrs Tonkinson. Then, at the hotel, we had to take delivery of the purchased items, divide them up and sort out what we were leaving in Rangoon under the maid's supervision and what we were taking with us.

The question of sleeping arrangements is fairly straightforward for us, as is that of cooking, as it seems that everywhere we go we will be accommodated either in bungalows or on well-equipped rowboats, but we may need a cook for part of the journey or for some of our stays.

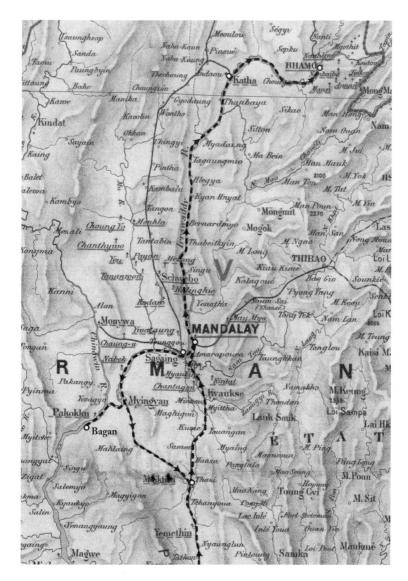

Itinerary from 19th November to 2nd December. Adaptation of the Map of the Catholic Missions of Siam, Burma and Laos drawn and engraved by R. Hausermann. Missions étrangères de Paris/IRFA.

So, we are taking Patte with us to Mandalay. As for sleeping, at least for the railway, mattresses and mosquito nets can be useful.

We left at 5.25 am on the railway for Mandalay, tired enough to sleep peacefully, as each of our households had reserved an entire compartment with four places and bunks. It was in ours that the Vilmorins came to spend the rest of the day and share the dinner prepared by the French chef from Minto Mansions, whose cooking had delighted us during our stay in Rangoon.

The area around Rangoon lacks interest, but the sight of Shwé Dagon at sunset was not without its charms.

19 November 1912

The night was cool and good; the mattress was a bit hard, but protected from insects by my mosquito net, I slept, happier than Henriette who felt her ribs crack and didn't sleep a wink.

For the second time I spent the night in Pegu without being able to stop to visit the ruins of the ancient capital Hangsawadi. I hope to be luckier on my return to Rangoon.

The ancient city is said to be completely in ruins, and the overgrown jungle area, with its dilapidated pagodas, old moats and crumbling walls, is a desolate sight. However, you can visit the remains of the Kalyanisima pagoda, whose inscriptions are Peguan and whose founder was the Peguan king Dhammaceti in the 15th century, the Shway Gyeen pagoda and the Shui Madu pagoda, which has lost all its cladding but contains a beautiful marble inscription recounting the deeds of the Burmese king Alompra in the 18th century. That's enough to try and make the excursion to Pegu by car, if possible, on the way back from the north.

The railway also passes through Toungoo, but as the stop there was also at night, I regretted not being able to see anything. Like Prome and Pegu, Toungoo played an important role in Burmese history. It is the main centre of the Sittang valley, which became the meeting point and point of conflict for the Burmese and Mon, or Peguan, populations when the oldest inhabitants, the Karen, who had long remained savage, were expelled. Today, a large number of Karen are concentrated to the east of the Paunglaung valley in a district under the jurisdiction of Toungoo.

The history of Toungoo is not known until the 12th century. For four centuries, the fate of this region depended on the respective degree of influence of the neighbouring princes. Pegu had difficulty establishing its supremacy. Later Wareru, King of Martaban, took control. The first city was built on high ground, then the inhabitants moved down to the plain.

After the fall of Pagan, the Shan dominated Toungoo for some time. Then it was the nominal turn of Ava, but as the power of Ava declined, that of Toungoo increased, although its territory was not very large. It was in 1426 that Toungoo's importance began to grow. From being a simple provincial chief, its governor became more or less the equal of the King of Ava and it was not long before he entered into an alliance with the King of Pegu, who by chance happened to be Burmese, whereas it was a Shan prince who reigned in Ava. Under these conditions, Toungoo became a concentration and retreat point for the Burmese. This situation continued into the 17th century as the Shan continued to rule Ava. The Burmese from Toungoo also tried to make common cause with their brothers from Prome.

The most brilliant period in the history of Toungoo was around 1530, when Tabeng Shwehti, son of Meng Kyinia, reigned. He was the champion of the Burmese race and the predecessor of the famous Bureng Naung, who had been the best of his generals. He himself established his supremacy over Pegu and Prome. As for Bureng Naung, it was at Toungoo in 1548 that he gathered his loyal Burmese, before setting out to conquer Chiang Mai.

I woke up on the outskirts of Yamethin. On the right, the high mountain range that borders the Sittang valley marked the beginning of the Shan country. The valley was cultivated with rice fields, but in many places there is already a shortage of water, and so a dry land with the most meagre vegetation appears, reminding Philippe de Vilmorin of certain parts of Sudan. Elsewhere, where irrigation is better ensured by water coming down from the mountains, the rice fields were beautiful and the future harvest looked superb. The villages are generally indicated by clumps of sugar palms, which are much more abundant than coconut trees in these parts.

Along the route, there were many colourful Burmese men and

women at the stations, but even more Hindus of all races and origins, who seem to have made this their home. Many have their own villages with considerable herds of cattle or goats.

We stopped for breakfast at Thazi, the junction of a line heading towards Myingyan. At several points, the Shan mountain range came closer, and on more than one knoll, we had fun counting the pyramids and white dagobas, brilliantly situated in highly picturesque locations.

The rice fields and crops are becoming more and more beautiful and it's a pleasure to follow with one's eyes the considerable number of fishing or foraging birds who spy out the fish in the swamp or the grain from the harvest. There are egrets, cranes, jays, kingfishers, delightful fig-bills and species of small green parakeets in abundance. Many are perched on the telegraph wire.

The approach to Mandalay is marked by a few larger pyramids along the track, then a few native dwellings and wide, dry avenues perpendicular to the railway, with no striking buildings.

We arrived at Mandalay station at around 2 pm, where the District Commissioner, Mr Saunders, had taken the trouble to come and meet us himself, accompanied by Mr Duroiselle, a Frenchman in charge of the archaeological service in Burma, whose work I know well. A superb crew, with Hindu footmen in the back, had been graciously placed at our disposal by one of the local notables, and the English authorities were kind enough to offer us the hospitality of the Circuit house, which is very welcome in a place like Mandalay where there are only miserable inns. At the station buffet, where we stopped for lunch before heading into town, we had great difficulty finding any food. Mr Saunders very kindly invited us to dinner this evening and Mr Duroiselle was kind enough to wait until we had had our lunch and had a wash and changed at the Circuit house, which was extremely comfortable, before taking us to the famous palace of Mindon (Lefèvre-Pontalis has Myndoon) and King Thibaw.

Apart from the life that they have taken from it and the damage that the lack of use and the fatal inadequacy of repairs inevitably cause, the English have preserved all the character and interest of the former royal city. After the conquest, they and their administration settled inside the city, but during a visit to Mandalay, the Viceroy Curzon dislodged them, and the royal city has become a sort of relic of the past.

It's not as powerful an effect as the sacred city of Peking, but in its own way, it's prodigiously curious and evocative. These wide ditches, filled to the brim with water and covered with lotuses, which surround the enclosure, the crenellated brick enclosure, long and flat, with gates surmounted by multi-storey wooden pavilions, are perfect specimens of Indochinese art, more slender and less powerful than that of China, but no less curious.

This vast quadrangle, which once constituted the city reserved for the King, princes and mandarins, has gradually been emptied of buildings and is now just a vast park with beautiful trees and open land, with no attempt at European-style design, in the middle of which the Thibaw palace remains uninhabited. Although the decorative effect is very powerful, I was rather struck by the somewhat mean buildings. Almost all of them are made of wood, but the carving is mediocre; the rooms are not very numerous, they are dark and for the most part very low and very stuffy. The gilding on the columns, which is tending to fade, does not appear to have ever been extremely well cared for. However, the whole is very interesting and some of the details are very amusing. Naturally, there are more ceremonial and reception rooms than actual dwellings: isolated open-air pavilions with red and gold wooden roofs adorned with stylised sculptures; the throne room with its prodigious teak columns, the height of which corresponds to the different levels of the roofs, half-open rooms where the King appeared behind a gilded shuttered window like the Siamese kings at Lopburi and Ayutthaya, with a room reserved for the sovereign alone. At the back there were the King's and women's apartments, with gilded woodwork that was ugly to look at but beautifully designed, walls lined with carved mirror fragments, some of them to good effect, and highly ornate doors in the same spirit. The famous multi-storey tower, known as the centre of the world, must have been very elegant when its red and gold panelling was still fresh. It ends at the top with a mirrored point and a golden crown. This tower rose above one of the King's thrones, on which he appeared behind gilded shutters and under an ornamentation of *nagas* whose scrolls bore images of the various Brahman gods, with the hieratic signs of the sun and moon represented by the peacock and the rabbit. A cruciform room supported by red columns but without walls, a sort of verandah where the mandarins used to meet, is still intact in front of this throne, which the Burmese must have found sublime because it symbolised the glory and power of their kings. Still, it lacks a touch of the grandiose and is more decorative, like all things Burmese. With life now absent, all the glitz and glamour loses a little of its effect, whereas at the Shwé Dagon pagoda in Rangoon, you get the opposite impression. There, life, colour and movement take precedence over the sometimes dubious taste of the decor. It is worth noting that there, as here, there is not a single decorative detail whose artistic character or the intrinsic value of the materials could tempt the greed of a collector. And yet, it must have been an important and sumptuous residence at a time when the Queen's bloodthirsty intrigues gave rise to so many notorious crimes, the memory of which has stayed with the present generation. The last King and his wife still live on an English pension in southern India, and some of the ministers of the former regime have not disappeared. Those who took part in the treason that delivered the King and his family to the British were rewarded with money, but above all with titles. We met one of them at the Gymkhana, a gathering of English society, where we were taken to the exit of the palace.

It was in a delightful location, a huge square lawn, bordered by tall trees with the mountains to the east as a backdrop. I've never seen a more striking effect of light and colour than the brown, mauve, straw and greenish tones of this sporting landscape, enough to tempt many a watercolourist.

This series of gymkhanas, races and horse shows brought all the English from the region to Mandalay for several days. Some of them were charming and we were introduced. But unfortunately, we had no time to linger at the racecourse. Before sunset, we still had to see the tomb of King Mindon, the founder of Mandalay. It's not far from there, near the enclosure, and with the marvellous colouring of the late day, it and the white tower next to it, from which the hours were announced by striking a gong, are a truly attractive sight.

It is a dagoba like any other, but of very elegant shape and proportions. It's just brick covered in mirrors, but fortunately the

King Mindon's Tomb. (© Thweep Rittinaphakorn)

mirrors are colourless and create a silvery effect. At this point, in fact, all the tones are delicious. The Centre of the Universe is set against a backdrop of dull gold, and the rising moon shines over Mindon's tomb and the multi-storey golden pavilions that surround it.

All these memories commemorate a past that is very close to home, yet quite extinct. Mandalay was only the capital of Burma from 1857 to 1884, namely during the British conquest. It's hard to believe when you see all these abandoned monuments, which would be completely crumbling if the English authorities hadn't tried to preserve them.

When we return from Bhamo, we'll have to visit a few pagodas and monasteries. There is apparently a great abundance of them, and it is estimated that there are 30,000 monks in the capital.

For the moment, we were in a hurry to get back to the Circuit house, to close our bags before going to dine at Commissioner Saunders's, because we were to go from there to our boat, which was due to leave at 8 o'clock tomorrow morning, and where my boy had already gone on ahead of us. As for the Vilmorins, they're staying here tomorrow and leaving for Gothek the day after tomorrow. They will make the trip to Bhamo without us and more slowly with a cargo ship. As they don't have to go to Pagan, we'll meet up in Rangoon on 2nd or 3rd December.

Navigation on the Irrawaddy. (Lefèvre-Pontalis Archive)

Before leaving I wrote two telegrams to Moulmein and Bangkok. To Dawson, I advised him of our arrival in Moulmein on the 4th and asked that our departure for the frontier be set for the 5th. To Maugras, I telegraphed that we will be at Myawadi on the border on the 8th, that we are giving up the excursion to Sukhothai and that, as we must return directly from Raheng to Bangkok, we want boats at Raheng to go down to Paknampho.

These was a warm welcome at the Saunders', where there were two Englishmen plus a lady and a young girl for dinner. But we didn't prolong the evening, as everyone was exhausted. In the moonlight along the lotus ponds, the Vilmorins took us back to the Irrawaddy flotilla boat on which we embarked, which was a long way off.

20 November 1912

After an excellent, cool night's sleep, which gave Henriette and me a good night's rest, we left Mandalay at 8 am on the Irrawaddy Flotilla's Mogaung express, which will take us to Bhamo in two and a half days and back to Mandalay in less than two days.

We were very pleased with the first day of the trip, which was truly fresh. The light was superb and the colour everywhere so beautiful and varied that it seemed made for watercolours.

As for the landscape, it is nothing extraordinary, but it changes continually and is pleasant. Leaving Mandalay, the Irrawaddy valley is very wide and, to the east, it is clearly delimited by the Shan Mountains. To the west, slight knolls border the Irrawaddy, where there is no alluvium. Very soon you come across extensive sandbanks that divide the river into many arms. The charm of this navigation lies in the innumerable pagodas to be found in the most varied of sites. Almost always it is the white pyramid that dominates, sometimes on the lower bank, sometimes on the bank, under the trees of a village, sometimes on a wooded summit. Sometimes it is gilded. Its shape varies frequently, and very often it is accompanied by other buildings: Hindu-style housing for the monks, in rectangular buildings of whitewashed brick, or towers with several storeys of superimposed roofs, made of carved wood. The effect is always extremely decorative.

One of the most important monuments is the famous Mingun pagoda, which stands a short distance above Mandalay on the right bank. It was never finished. What remains is the unfinished base of an immense brick pyramid, whose construction was interrupted in 1839 by an earthquake that toppled part of what had already been built. Next to the Mingun pyramid, there is apparently an enormous bronze bell, but I didn't see it as the boat didn't stop.

It is a disadvantage of this system of express navigation that the boat rarely stops along the way. Nearly all these pagodas that look so good when seen from the river, there are often villages more or less hidden in the greenery, whose inhabitants approach the cargo boat as it stops for a while in important places and tows barges loaded with goods. In this way, small momentary markets are formed, which must be very picturesque, with the population wearing such colourful clothes.

This can be seen in the interesting groups of Burmese at more than one point of the riverbank. However, high banks with villages overlooking the river without trees are rarer than on the Mekong, although one encounters them sometimes. It was only after a few hours' navigation that you start to see them. Shortly afterwards, the river narrowed so much that it ended up forming a relatively thinner and probably deeper channel between two low wooded hills, as it is no longer necessary to probe and navigate in zigzags. The forest came close to the river and on a sandbank we could clearly see, to Henriette's great delight, a whole gang of monkeys frolicking about.

Before the end of the day we reached Thabeikhyin on the left bank of the Irrawaddy. This is the port for the Mogok ruby mines, which have an automobile service to communicate with the river. It was still light enough to make out the groups on the slopes of the riverbank.

Beautiful finery and brilliant colours. A few Yunnanese in dark indigo clothes and yellow waxed hats climbed aboard. They carried leather bags like those used in Yunnan on horses and mules. They are probably people from the mines. I'm told on board that some of them are Shans. The fact is that their appearance is identical to that of the Thai from the Black River and especially from Lai Châu.

It gets dark early at this time of year. After stopping for a quarter of an hour at Thabeikhyin, we could see nothing. As the Irrawaddy boats do not operate at night, we stopped off opposite Male, which is a landmark in the ancient history of Burma. It was almost cold in these already somewhat northerly parts, and after the heat we suffered in Mandalay we were not sure how to protect ourselves. In any case, it was very refreshing. It's worth noting that, as in Tonkin, some trees lose their leaves in this climate, and in the afternoon we saw many clumps of bamboo in the forest, completely grey and bare.

21 November 1912

At dawn, our boat set off again. The river valley widened once more. It is bounded on both sides by wooded hills. The alluvial deposits on both banks are also wooded. But often one of them is formed by a large sandbank, while the other is a more or less sheer or sloping bank with villages under the trees from time to time. We made a short stop at one of these villages on the left bank, Myngoon, a little above Kyanhyat.

An English colonel on board said to me: "It's amazing how similar

Navigation on the Irrawaddy. (Lefèvre-Pontalis Archive)

all the world's rivers are." "This one," I replied, "bears little resemblance to the Nile. In any case, it is fairly similar to the Mekong, except that its course is straight and not very turbulent."

I was surprised to see so few villages on the banks of the Irrawaddy, as the alluvium and flat terrain would seem to be extensive and suitable enough for cultivation to tempt the Burmese peasant. There is almost no movement either on this great river, which runs so smoothly. The depth must be less here than a little further down, because we have started to probe again. Sometimes, in fact, there are very large sandbanks in the middle of the river.

The river and the valley have a similar colouring to that which struck us so much the day before yesterday at the Mandalay racecourse. It is a superimposition of beige, white, brown and dark green with a slight hint of blue, which produces a singular effect of distinction.

We came across a fair number of wooden rafts. Some are made from bamboo, but others from teak harvested from the tributaries of the Irrawaddy. As on the Mekong, the rafts are steered by four helmsmen, two at the front and two at the back. They all have a small hut which serves as a dwelling for those who are in charge and who often seem to stop en route to fish in the river. On the other hand, there is hardly a sandbank, especially if it is only separated from the mainland by a small arm, that does not serve as a permanent settlement for the fishermen who set up dams there.

We stopped at around 10.30 am at Tagaung, a town on the left bank of the river at the confluence of a small river whose fairly wide valley must have attracted the Burmese in the past, when they arrived on the Irrawaddy in search of new lands.

Burmese historians trace the origins of their country back to the creation of the town of Tagaung, whose name is now remembered only by a small village. The city is said to have been built by a Sakya Hindu prince living in northern India, who left the Kapilavistu region following wars with his neighbours. Some traces of the ruins of the ancient city are said to remain, but they are not visible from the river.

The newcomers would have had to fight to establish themselves in the country, against the old inhabitants and against the Yunnanese, who put the first dynasty of Tagaung princes to flight.

It was replaced by Khsatryas from India, who built a town next to the old Tagaung, now called Old Pagan. Later they returned to Tagaung, where sixteen kings of the second dynasty reigned. It is from here that the blind prince who first ruled the southern kingdom of Prome is said to have set out in 483 BC.

It seems that the surviving ruins of Tagaung clearly indicate an Indo-Burmese origin. The Shans, or Tai, had nothing to do with the construction of this city, which they do not claim as their own. Buddhist images with Pali inscriptions in Devanagari script have been found here. The bricks found in the ruins are thought to have been made by workers from India. In the past, the Tagaung region had far more communications with the Ganges valley and northern India via Manipur than with Pegou and Thaton, which had regular links with southern India. Although the influence of the south eventually prevailed by means of writing applied to Buddhist texts, it had already been a long time, when this effect occurred, that northern India was exerting its influence on the Tagaung region and working to transform the savage tribes who inhabited it into a civilised people.

At 2.30 pm, in the radiant light that illuminated so brilliantly the sandy beach, the market houses on stilts, and the white and golden pyramids on top of three wooded mounds, we stopped for a few minutes in front of the village of Tigyaing situated on the right bank of the river. Here, as everywhere, we were extremely interested in the arrival and departure of the Burmese travellers in their turbans and *panungs* coloured in all shades of pink.

The sandbanks are as numerous and as treacherous as ever. Some time ago, one of the Irrawaddy flotilla's liners ran aground on one of them just as the water began to recede. That evening the captain had dropped anchor in a place where he thought there would be enough water. But during the night there was a drop of two inches which was enough to put the boat on the sand, where she will remain until next year. As a punishment, the captain had to retain command and custody of his sunken ship, where he is a sort of captive with a crew reduced to only four men. This says a lot about the character of the Irrawaddy, which, although more navigable than most Indochinese rivers, is no less subject to the vagaries of flooding.

As the day progressed, the light became purer and more radiant. The sky was completely clear of clouds before sunset and the landscape was increasingly seductive with the charm and variety of its subtle colours. The sunset was magical. At this point we were lucky enough to be stopped in the vicinity of a village, and the boats loaded with passengers moving around the boat on all sides presented a charming picture.

At 8 o'clock in the evening, we anchored at Khata on the right bank of the river. The moon was shining brightly. Henriette and I got off and went for a walk along the riverbank and through the village. The effects of the moon on the tall, isolated trees overlooking the river and on the elaborately designed white pyramids and wooden spires of the pagoda pavilions with their overlapping roofs were quite striking, as were the silver reflections on the plumes of the coconut and sugar palms.

I noticed Hindus selling fabrics and Yunnanese in dark indigo clothes and turbans, selling iron tools, under the lampposts of the few half-open shops. Coastal Chinese are a rarity here. On board we have a few Yunnanese who also no longer wear the plait, but my boy Ahine, who is from Hainan, cannot converse with them. The only compatriot he has found on the boat is the Captain's boy.

Katha is linked by rail to the Mandalay to Myitkyina line, which serves the region west of the Irrawaddy. On examining the map, it seems that the English intended, by choosing this starting point on the river, to make it the point of departure for a line to Manipur, which would in the future link up via Cachar and Katigara with the already existing main line to East Bengal and Assam. The choice of Katha also seems to indicate a possible extension of the railway to the east towards Bhamo, which lies at about the same latitude and is one of the gateways to China. In this way, China would be linked by railway in these parts to the great line which already serves the whole of Burma from north to south as far as Rangoon and Moulmein. I know of nothing more intelligent than this English railway plan.

Further down towards Monywa, another branch line running directly from Mandalay currently stops at Ahlone beyond Monywa on the Chindwin. It is likely to be extended along this valley, also to Manipur via Mindat.

Finally, there is reason to suppose that the line which at Thazi, south of Mandalay, splits off from the central artery to join the Myingyan point on the left bank of the Irrawaddy, opposite the confluence of the Chindwin, will one day be extended to Chittagong, the first port in India proper when coming up the Bay of Bengal, which is currently linked to the entire Indian railway network.

In the east, the British seem to be in less haste to act than in the past. It seems that with their Mandalay-Lashio railway, they were in more of a hurry. Will they ever extend it into China, via Kunlong on the Salween, and Meng Ting on the other side of the border? This is doubtful, because the difficulties of building in this steep country are as unattractive as the few advantages offered to trade by a country as poor and as sparsely populated as this entire region. Nearly all the English today agree on this and consider that with our Haiphong-Yunnan Sen line we have taken the lead in economic conditions that are far preferable to those they would encounter on their side.

I regret that I don't have the time to go and see for myself. In any case, the Lashio line is of the greatest local interest, for it has opened up the northern Shan region, one of the most turbulent in Burma. The British are now in a position to exercise serious surveillance there and to control the intrigues of influential chiefs such as Theinni with his neighbours of the same race on the other side of the Chinese border.

The history of Indochina is full of accounts of the internal struggles of these Shan princes and their intrigues with or against the Chinese, the Burmese and the Shan or Thai of northern Siam.

Theinni, which is not very far from Bhamo in the east, and whose territory is very extensive along the Yunnan border, (Tsen-vi = Hsen-wi) is the largest Shan principality, dependent on Burma. It once paid tribute to China. When Burmese influence became preponderant, its Sawbwa was obliged to pay tribute twice a year to the sovereign of Ava.

The English do not appear to have been involved until 1892, when they explored and took possession of this territory, which was then exactly bounded by the Shweli and Salween rivers and bordered the Chinese frontier to the north. In 1892-93, it was Georges Scott, the same man who in 1894 came temporarily as England's minister to Bangkok and at the end of the same year was the head of the English group of the Franco-English commission of the Buffer State, of which I was a member, who proceeded, as Superintendent of the Northern Shan States, to organise this territory.

The natives call Hsen-wi what the Burmese call Theinni. It should also be noted that the name Hsen-wi also applies to the principality of Chiang Hung, situated much further south-east on the Mekong and which, in the final arrangements of 1895, ended up remaining part of China.

The Chinese call Chiang Hung, Tcheli, but they distinguish between a Greater Tcheli and a Lesser Tcheli. According to their historians, the greater Tcheli obeyed a Burmese vassal prince in the 16th century, while the latter's younger brother was the chief of the lesser Tcheli and in this capacity a vassal of China. This seems to me to explain the name Hsen-wi, applied to two localities, for it is certain that in 1556 Bureng Naung, the first Burmese conqueror who had set his capital at Hangsawady, went north to conquer Muong Mau and Theinni, which he confirmed in 1559 and 1561 with two new expeditions against the Shan states in the north. He even went as far as Sanda and Muong La in Chinese territory, but Chiang Hung seems to have escaped him, if I am to judge by a list of princes that was sent to me in 1891 and which begins precisely in 1565, a time slightly earlier than that when the little Tcheli would no longer have been tributary to China. In 1895 we ourselves made a major contribution to maintaining Chinese suzerainty there, so that the English would not establish theirs. But it seems from an allusion made to me the other day in Thaton by Mr Abbey, that the people of Chiang Hung are now fed up with Chinese domination and are making serious efforts to escape it. I don't know whether the General Government in Hanoi attaches any real importance to these issues. What is certain is that in 1583, under the reign of Nanda Bureng, the son and successor of Bureng Naung, the Burmese Empire broke up, and China, like Siam, took advantage of the situation to resume the offensive and force the dismembered Burma to pay tribute. It was probably at this point that the destinies of the princes of Theinni and Chiang Hung became quite distinct, Chiang Hung only remaining a vassal of Burma from 1522 to 1566.

Yunnan is largely inhabited by the Tai, who were for a long time the undisputed masters of the whole region during the flourishing Nanzhao kingdom.

In western Yunnan, in the rounded territory to the east of the Irrawaddy and to the north of the Burmese Shan territories, there was an early confederation of small Shan (Tai) principalities which China and Burma fought over for a long time and which ended up in Chinese hands. This was the Ko Shan Pri, or the nine Shan states, also known as Koshambi, Kosambi or Kopyidoung, regardless of the meaning of the words. Burney, Yule and MacLeod agree on the names of the principalities that formed part of this confederation. According to them, they were Muong Mau, Tsiguen, Hotha, Latha, Mona, Tsanta also called Santafau and Thanta, Mowun also called Muong Woun and Long Chuen, Kaing Ma i.e. Chiang Ma and Maing Lyin which is none other than Maing leng Gyi, Mong Lien and Muong Lam.

Hannay's list is slightly different. In reality, the confederation of which Muong Mau, close to Bhamo, seems to have been the main centre in the past, often varied in its composition and extent. Ney Elias estimates that the number of states that formed it was more often ten than nine. At the time of its greatest expansion, Ko Shan Pri would, according to him, have included: Mogaung, Monyin, Khamti, Mong Nai, Theinni, Kaing Ma, Maing Maing, Maing Lung, Maing Lem, Chiang-hung, Chiang Tung and Momiet. Although its boundaries are difficult to define, the same author believes it is likely that it extended eastwards, further than the present-day Chinese Shan states on the Salween side.

In a list published in the *Peking Gazette* on 30 August 1873, the Chinese Shan states are listed as dependencies of the Yung Chang prefecture. These were Meng Ting, Wan Tien and Chen Kang, which were transformed into Chinese territories, and the principalities of Tsien Jai, Lung Chwan, Thei Fang, Sanda, Lu Kiang, Mang Shé, Mantien and Meng Mau.

This is what remains of the old Ko Shan Pri. Their acquisition by the English would not add much to the value of the Indian Empire, as they are mountainous territories like the Burmese Shan states, and from an economic point of view the Shan population is meagre. By being able to group these fairly turbulent populations into a single block,

England's only gain would be to be in a position to trace new and safer access routes to China proper through their territory. But as Mr Abbey said, would it not be much more in her interest to open up this route between Assam, in India, and Sichuan, in one of the richest and most populous parts of China, which would be easier to use?

If this is the case, the field remains open for our initiative and our activity in Tonkin. We have taken the lead near Yunnanfou, we must continue at least as far as Dali. Then, by tracing from the centre of Yunnan towards Muong Ou or Muong Sing, the railway line that will link the Indochinese network to the main lines of southern China, we can take the lead in economic movement and rail transport in the whole of the part of Far Asia that normally comes under our influence.

If we let the British take our place, the Yunnan railways will, despite the geographical difficulties, head for Bhamo or Lashio or Chiang Tung with a connection to the Siamese railways at Chiang Saen. It is important that the Chinese routes into Indochina should be extended not to the English right bank of the Mekong but to the French left bank.

22 November 1912

The magic of the colours continued, but not as intensely as yesterday, because the air is less clear. The landscape is also a little less varied. The hills are further away and the sandbanks less complicated; they don't block the route as much. The riverbank continues to be frequently ravaged, with trees toppled or about to be swept away along with the clods of earth supporting them.

We passed a few small villages and several fisheries. Large teak trains belonging to the Bombay Burmah, recognisable by their red and white flags, were traveling down the river. A little further up the river, we came across trains with blue and white flags belonging to the Steel Brothers of Mandalay and Rangoon. An agent from the latter company came on board this morning at our first stop after leaving Katha. He is young, open and friendly, and the passengers are interested in what he has to say about his life in the forest and the charms of bush life.

Around 11.30 we stopped at Shwé Gu on the right bank. These stops are always very short, but enough to note the picturesque colours

Navigation on the Irrawaddy. (Lefèvre-Pontalis Archive)

and shapes in the groups crouching or standing on the bank, and in those of the passengers arriving and leaving in boats. There are dugouts with the long proportions of a needle case, where the rows of figures create a most graceful effect on the water.

Above Shwé Gu, the river narrows and an hour or so beyond this village, it forms a sort of defile where the wooded hills descend directly to the water. Strictly speaking, this is not a gorge, as the Irrawaddy does not yet have rapids as in the part of its course above Bhamo, but it resembles the Black River in the parts where it does not have the appearance of a torrent. The vegetation is also much the same as in our Upper Tonkin. It's not a big forest, but a rather pleasant scrub with bamboo of the lightest species. One of the rocks on the river bank is shaped like an ogre, so the Burmese have crowned it with a small pyramid and decorated it with white banners.

The air is exquisite and the scents of the forest waft through this passage, where a few dugout canoes with monks and Burmese in coloured turbans circulate and fishermen's nets are strung across the rocks. Unfortunately, this passage, the only narrow one on the whole route, is a bit short. It doesn't even last an hour. On leaving it, we found again the Irrawaddy valley at its full extent, with sandbanks and woods, although it seemed curtailed in the distance by the mountains on the left bank, which form a long straight line and are considerably higher than any we had seen. It is clear that this is the barrier that separates China from Burma, although behind this line of high mountains, there are fairly important rivers in Chinese territory, such as the Taping near Bhamo and the Shweli, which are tributaries of the Irrawaddy. When the Shan and Chinese invaders emerged from these mountains and saw the great valley, there is no doubt that they must have had the feeling that they were arriving in a new country. This landscape has a truly historical character.

We did not reach the Bhamo riverbank until about 4.30 pm, at an hour when the light is exquisite but when, at this time of year, the daylight doesn't last long. There was nothing so strange as the effect of the whole band of Yunnanese muleteers with their golden-brown faces, yellow waxed hats and blue clothes grouped together on the sloping bank when the boat arrived. Among them were a few Burmese with bright, clear tones, and also a Kachin woman from the mountains in blue, embroidered clothes and silver bracelets. Her husband, a very handsome man with a pleasant face, wore a superb red turban.

The District Commissioner, who had been informed of our visit but was on an inspection tour, had sent us an English-speaking Burmese to guide us, so we hurried into town before sunset to have a little look around. We stopped at two caravan camps, one of Shans with oxen, the other of Yunnanese Chinese with mules. We also visited a Chinese pagoda, which didn't seem out of place at one of the busiest gateways to the Great Empire, where so many Yunnanese have been coming for centuries to make contact with Indochina. It seemed more at home than this singular little Hindu temple where blacks from Hindustan took turns striking a gong, blowing shells and waving a flame in front of the faces of their strange gods. But, being so close to India and China, don't they all belong? And when the railway is built, how much more will the mix of races that already makes Bhamo such a curious place increase?

A short stroll along the only street in Bhamo, which follows the course of the riverbank, was enough to show that there is nothing to see here but the gathering of people of different races. Burmese, Chinese, Hindus, Shans, and various Khas from the mountain where their paths and their clearings attract the eyes of all sides, meet in this market, in this street and especially in this grassy plain where the pack animals of the caravans can graze in peace, at the end of their journey on the banks of the river.

The Irrawaddy is truly majestic, forming a lake of calm water that extends into an open plain on the other bank. As it is on this side that the sun sets, we witnessed a fantastic display of colours, on the water and in the sky ablaze with gold and red. Then, in the orange light of the almost full moon, a shadow play of a few tall trees, muleteers at rest and mules quietly eating and falling asleep as the day fades, stood out against the river.

A telegram from the Commissioner of Moulmein, Mr Dawson, forwarded to me from Mandalay by Vilmorin, was waiting for me when I got back on board. Unfortunately, it was very disappointing, as Dawson told me that he had definitely been unable to obtain elephants to go from Kokarit to Myawadi, and suggested ox carts for lack of any other means of transport.

It's all very annoying, but what can we do? If Dawson has come to this last resort, it's because there was nothing he could do regarding the elephants, and he also knows how complicated, time-consuming and expensive it would be to get horses from a local dealer in Moulmein. The best thing is therefore to leave it to him and by adding a note to the telegram, the Vilmorins leave me free to do what is best. I wrote to Dawson to tell him that while I regret these difficulties, I'm relying on him to adopt the best solution. Henriette and I are both equally upset by this setback.

23 November 1912

In the morning, Shan merchants were on deck. They offered us woven and embroidered dresses, scarves, bags, jackets, turbans, sabres, and silver chains, but nothing really appealing, as I've seen better from the Chinese Shan of southern Yunnan. However, I was tempted by two enormous silver bracelets that are like shackles. They'll make a nice addition to my collection of Thai silver objects and can easily be turned into vases. I also bought some small green jade discs used as earrings by Burmese women and one of those triangular bronze gongs sometimes used by caravan drivers.

Here in Bhamo, at the early hour when we were walking along the main street, these little gongs were being used by the young monks who were seeking alms followed by two porters who were going from door to door begging for food. In all the years I've been travelling in Indochina, I've rarely had the opportunity to witness this scene, so often described

Bhamo market. (Lefèvre-Pontalis Archive)

and so picturesque. Henriette captured it with her Kodak, as well as various scenes in the Shan camp, so curious for their tattoos, their big straw hats, their set ups under bamboo huts sheltered by the sacks of their oxen. The brown and yellow tones of the oxen went very well with the general colour of the plain and the mountains in the background.

The market was also bright and lively. It was a competition between the most varied races, as was the case throughout the town, and you were spoilt for choice between the Burmese woman, the Chinese woman with small feet, the Shan woman with her dark clothes embellished with coloured embroidery and the Kachin women so strange with their belts of lacquered rattan threaded around their waists and ankles. On the banks of the river we witnessed a curious scene, when the muleteers of a Chinese caravan called their animals down to the riverbank to water them. It was a piquant picture of this ever-paced, ever-active and ever-trading China, whose caravans have been coming to this very Bhamo for centuries, where they will continue to load and unload their goods in the same way until the railway comes to replace them.

The wife of the Commissioner of Bhamo came on board this morning, in her husband's absence, to tell us that she would have been happy to welcome us both to her home and that her husband had the rest house at our disposal, as well as a government boat to take us up the rapids of the upper Irrawaddy if we so wished. The English authorities have definitely thought of everything, and with as much simplicity as good grace. This very pleasant lady told us how much she was enjoying her stay in this interesting district with such a varied population. In her opinion, Bhamo is much less interesting than the inland towns and especially the mountain villages. Her husband is frequently on the road and she often accompanies him on horseback on his rounds. She herself has only had one opportunity to cross the Chinese border to visit a market, but her husband went as far as Dali and returned via Tonkin. At the moment, we're avoiding any risky excursions to Yunnan, because of the political unrest that followed the revolution. As for the local populations, the Burmese are few in number in the Bhamo district, but so much more cultivated and civilised than the Shan! The Shan are more picturesque, as are the Kachin, to whose education the Missions are devoting serious efforts and who are gradually being transformed to their advantage. Many serve in the local militia and do well. Not everyone is as indulgent towards the Kachin, and the Burmese who acted as my guide last night told me that they were a very unintelligent people who understood nothing of what they wanted to teach them.

We left Bhamo around midday. The descent is considerably faster than the ascent. So we quickly crossed the pass, which, if I'm not mistaken, has been the scene of serious battles in times of war between the Burmese and the Chinese. By 3 o'clock we were already in Shwe Gu and by a quarter to 7 we were in Katha, where we spent the night before yesterday and where we will spend tonight.

It wasn't a particularly clear day, but the sunset was once again superb.

At Katha, another young Englishman who, like the previous one, belonged to one of the logging companies, came on board. He said that teak was plentiful in the region at only a few miles from Khata. Elephants are used to haul the logs to the small rivers nearby, but this year the water has been so low due to lack of rain that, apart from the month of October, almost nothing has been done. There is no shortage of big game either. My Englishman said he had two tigers on his conscience.

With the full moon in full bloom, we let ourselves be tempted, as we were the day before, to take a stroll under the coconut palms and along the white pagodas of Khata. Some passengers, who had discovered a funfair the other day, took us to a pagoda on this side of the road, beyond the railway. For several hundred metres, the road was illuminated by lanterns hanging from bent bamboo, the fringed white paper enhancing their golden effect.

The festival was taking place in a pagoda. The pyramid itself was adorned with lanterns, as were the roofs of the pavilions, the restaurants and improvised shops around which the crowd strolled, wrapped in scarves and turbans.

The main attractions were an open-air puppet theatre with an orchestra very similar to those in the Bangkok theatres, a bamboo labyrinth where people who are unwise enough to enter get lost and finally the exhibition of gifts offered to the neighbouring monastery where, under the watchful eye of young monks and brilliantly illuminated, all the offerings of food, clothing, golden beakers and other essential items from the generosity of the faithful were arranged on tiers with great order and care.

The whole festival had the appearance of a sort of fair, deliciously oriental and without any hustle and bustle. The light effects and the crowds were charming and the setting itself was remarkable, with beautiful teak buildings on stilts, with overlapping roofs, multiple spires and staircases in the style of monastic buildings, surrounded by coconut palms and sugar palms, all deliciously lit by the moon.

We were delighted to be able to take advantage of this opportunity to see a completely Burmese folk festival in such a remote location.

24 November 1912

If the Irrawaddy itself, whose upper part is encumbered by rapids, was the natural route of Burmese immigrants, whose point of departure was close to Tibet, the Taping and the Bhamo route giving access to the Irrawaddy below the rapids was the historic choice for the Chinese invasions of Burma, just as it is still the trade route today.

As for the Tai or Shan, accustomed to small valleys and mountainous lands, but quick to insinuate themselves wherever they found space more or less free, they were not content with the limits of the narrow, incised basin of the Salween that they had made their own. Like the

Burmese and the Chinese, they were drawn to the great valley of the Irrawaddy, where they could have found all the room they needed to expand. Although they overflowed on all sides, as far as beyond the Irrawaddy, they pushed themselves as far as Assam and, in the very basin of the great river, they made a Shan country out of the entire mountainous region which forms the eastern part. There the Burmese, more domesticated and much more accustomed to comfort, have never settled, and it seems that in their advance towards the Irrawaddy, the Tai made the most of the easy access offered by the valley of the Shweli.

Muong Mau, the most important point of their Yunnanese confederation of Ko Shan Pri, is just above the valley of this tributary of the Irrawaddy and from there commands the most accessible passage between the valleys of the Salween and the upper Irrawaddy. Nowadays, when the water is high enough, small steamers can serve the lower reaches of the Shweli, providing a service to the logging companies that exploit the abundant teak in its basin.

The Tai didn't ask for much. With their pirogues carved from these same teak trees, they quickly reached the Irrawaddy, whose waters are so calm, without rapids or whirlpools, and whose sandbanks, uncovered during the low-water season, make access even easier for the lightest pirogues.

We passed Inywa early this morning at the confluence of this river and the Irrawaddy, and around 9 o'clock we also stopped in grey and misty weather at Tigyaing on the opposite bank, in front of this pretty village with its houses squeezed in a row on the beach and its white pagodas amongst the greenery, where the pink-skirted inhabitants make brilliant spots on the shore.

It is likely that when the first invaders from the Shweli appeared in this region, they already came up against a number of fixed settlements belonging to the Tagaung masters, and from then on their eyes and ambitions turned in this direction.

The people of Tagaung no longer felt safe, and it was no doubt as much to protect themselves from invasion as to follow the natural law that leads populations along the valleys until they have reached the large fertile alluvial deposits, that they descended as far as Prome, neglecting in the process the important part of the valley near the mouths of the

Chindwin that the Burmese kings, who later became more powerful, chose as the best location for their successive capitals.

Prome preceded the capitals of Pagan and Ava in Burmese history, and even more so those of Amarapura and Mandalay. According to legend, the town was founded by a group of blind princes from the ruling Tagaung family, who, because of their infirmity, were carried away on a raft by the current of the Irrawaddy and landed at a place where they had been preceded by a member of their family who lived there as a hermit and whose daughter one of the young princes later married. This is the origin of the first dynasty of the famous kingdom of Tharekkettara, whose capital was Prome.

According to Burmese historians, the first dynasty came to an end in 110 BC, which would place the founding of Prome shortly after the first appearance of the Tai in northern Indochina, since it was in the 1st century AD that Chinese historians report the presence and activity of the Ai-Lao on the southern borders of Yunnan.

In reality, the offensive action of the Tai against the Burmese only became truly formidable many centuries later, when the Mughal invasion had wiped out the Burmese empire of Pagan after the battle of Male in 1286, and all the ambitions of the petty Shan princes were given free rein from the north to the south of the Irrawaddy basin. It was then that Ava became the Burmese's main centre of influence, but the Burmese suffered more than once on the river during the period that followed the domination of the Shan, masters of Panya and Sagaing in the second half of the 14th century. In the 16th century, the struggle continued between the Burmese on the Irrawaddy and the Shan from the eastern mountains, who were trying to establish themselves in the valley and become its masters. Without the support they found in Toungoo and Prome among the people of their race, the Burmese, placed between the Peguan of the south and the Shan of the east, would never have had the last word. It was the great kings Tabeng Shwehti and Bureng Naung who, in the second half of the 16th century, restored the authority of the Burmese over the entire course of the Irrawaddy and put an end for ever to the claims of the Shan in this region.

Below Male we were surprised to find the river much narrower than it had seemed to us on the way up. This proves how much the Irrawaddy, with its winding course through the sandbanks, has a wider valley in the upper part of its course than we had realised. The officers on board call the stretch between Male and Kyauk Myaung a defile. This is perhaps a bit of an exaggeration, as although the river is fairly narrow between its wooded banks and has no sandbanks, it has no real gorge to cross. It is nevertheless certain that the valley is narrow enough for the course of the river to have been easily controlled by military posts. This undoubtedly explains the decisive battle of Male, fought above the gorge by the Mongols at the end of the 13th century. Hence also the importance of the post of Kyauk Myaung in the last English war against Burma, which was apparently vigorously defended by the Burmese under the leadership of a patriotic monk, who had erected fortifications there.

On the left bank, the last foothills of the small Mogok massif reach the Irrawaddy. In the afternoon we stopped for a while at the Thabeikhyin station, where we saw the beginning of the road on which a daily bus service connects the ruby mines of Mogok with the river. It seems that rubies are not the only product of the district, as the Bombay Burmah operates teak concessions there, and we took on board a young inspector from the Burma Forest Service who, following an inspection, was going down to Mandalay, accompanied by the Deputy Commissioner of Mogok.

He has studied the history and archaeology of Burma and likes to talk about these subjects which interest him and about which he has very strong ideas. He believes in the Hindu origin of the Pyus from whom the Burmese are descended and in the very great antiquity of Prome as one of their foundations, which seems to me to be rather questionable.

Just as at about 6.30 pm our boat came to moor at the bank of Kyauk Myaung, the boat bringing the Vilmorins from Mandalay appeared in the other direction. It came to stop for the night next to ours, and we were able to have dinner and spend part of the evening together. They are delighted with what they saw in Mandalay and with the harvest they made in Gothek for their herbarium.

The Cargo on which they sailed was very amusing, as it was lined with two covered two-storey barges, one occupied by cloth and fancy goods merchants and the other by merchants selling food who were squeezed together as in a market. There are Burmese and Hindus among these merchants, who pay for their space and rent the location of their stalls. At each port of call, the locals come on board and, day or night, they do their shopping. It's a singularly ingenious system that the Messageries fluviales de Cochinchine, so backward and so solely concerned with their subsidies, have been careful not to imitate on the Mekong. Yet it would be the best way of securing for us the commercial advantages that only Bangkok merchants still enjoy in our Indochinese waters.

From a picturesque point of view, the spectacle is amusing, as is that of our boat's warehouse, where Burmese families sleep, eat, chat and smoke cheroots sitting on the floor, next to Yunnanese Shans dressed in blue cloth with yellow hats, who float down the river with their double bamboo baskets where green tea for chewing is carefully wrapped in banana leaves.

There are also Hindus smoking their *chibouk* (a long pipe), and a Chinese woman with small feet who is travelling alone and yet doesn't look like it is her first trip, because she has beautiful earrings of the best green jade and a Burmese amber charm of a beautiful golden yellow dangling from her silver chain.

The boat's crew is made up of Chittagong people with fairly dark skins and cropped hair, and the domestic staff are handsome dark Hindus who look much better than the Malabars.

All these people feel at home on the Irrawaddy. Some have their wives in villages along the way. The English have succeeded in turning this beautiful river into the great highway for which it was intended.

25 November 1912

Fog delayed our walk this morning. Along the sandbanks we could see lots of waders and egrets pecking at their morning breakfast.

It is now easy to see how much more inhabited and lively this part of the river becomes the closer we get to Mandalay.

The white pyramids are more numerous and we were delighted to see again those of Sheinmaga, one of the most beautiful villages on the right bank. Opposite, at some distance, the valley is encircled on the left bank by fairly high hills with noble lines. Madaya lies at the foot of these hills. It is surprising to note how rarely, during our entire journey, we came across any crops on the banks of the river. It seems that from here we will enter the beautiful agricultural region that we found on our way from Rangoon to Mandalay.

We disembarked at 11 am on the dusty riverbank. At the height of the dry season, Mandalay must be uninhabitable with its wide, white, powdery avenues and sparse vegetation, judging by what we can see now. The distances are so great with these sparsely inhabited suburbs spread out around the enormous quadrilateral of the royal city, that it took us almost half an hour by car to get from the landing stage to the circuit house, which is at the south-east corner of the royal city outside the moat. There we found our things in order and our cook Patte, who had prepared the meals for the Vilmorins during their two stays and who was ready to make us lunch.

But before lunch I had to run down to the river again to make arrangements with the navy, which is providing us with the longboat that will take us to Pagan. It was decided that we would leave Mandalay on the 27th at 8 am to be in Pagan the next day around the same time, and that if the captain of the longboat thought it possible, instead of returning to Mandalay we would take the train to Rangoon on the 30th in the morning at Myingyan, which would extend our stay in Pagan long enough to visit the ruins. The train times lend themselves so well to this combination that it would be unfortunate not to take advantage of it. As the early hour of our departure on the 27th has reduced our stay in Mandalay to a strict minimum, I have decided not to visit Ava and Amarapura, the remains of which our boat will take us past anyway.

The trip I made in search of the Marine office led me back into the royal city where my guide had mistakenly led me. I was very happy about this, as I was able to judge much better, by taking a tour of the palace buildings, their external appearance as well as the effect that the royal majesty must have produced, when on any of its four faces, the King of Kings appeared either on a glittering throne or under a gilded pavilion before the crowds massed under the verandahs or in the gardens. These gardens, which today are rather poorly maintained, contain small ponds and some rather amusing fake rocks, on which the Burmese kings are said to have enjoyed boating.

Mandalay has a French bishop, a cathedral next to the market and the palace of the missionaries of the Missions Etrangères and French Franciscan nuns who look after lepers. After lunch, we were visited by two of the latter, who told us about their charitable work.

At 3.15 pm Mr Duroiselle came to collect us and with him we visited the pagodas to the north-east of the town, beginning at Kyauk Taw at the foot of Mandalay Hill. This is a mongrel-style pagoda with a stepped white pyramid surrounded by golden zinc crowns. The cloister galleries are all in zinc. Unfortunately, this deplorable taste is the one in ascendant throughout Burma at the moment. The main attraction of this pagoda is the alabaster statues of all the disciples of Buddha, each in a different attitude, above which small brick and plaster domes have been erected all around the area of the great pyramid. As everywhere around the pagodas, there are merchants selling offerings and food. Under a separate small aedicula, the isolated figures in painted wood, treated realistically and not without some talent, depict in Burmese costumes a scene from the life of a Buddhist saint who, having left

A corner of the moat around the Royal Palace Mandalay.
(© Thweep Rittinaphakorn)

his robes to go hunting, returned to the monastic life when his wife's insults had made him realise how much he had lost. These wooden statues are almost as interesting as the three ascetics I admired in one of Moulmein's pagodas.

A whole series of religious monuments, pavilions for the Buddha footprint, terraces and covered staircases are being built on Mandalay Hill, a hill that rises behind the royal city, where zinc and sheet metal unfortunately play a considerable role. It is a hermit living on this hill who, it seems, has enough prestige over the otherwise not very wealthy inhabitants of Mandalay to induce them to make very considerable financial sacrifices in favour of these very ugly constructions. It was the pious people of Mandalay who carried on their backs all the bricks demanded by the holy man. A gigantic statue of Buddha standing with his finger pointing towards the palace occupies one of the terraces. But the whole decorative ensemble needs to be completed, and work is being carried out on all parts of the hill.

The view from here is of course very beautiful, since in addition to Mandalay, its palace and pagodas, a large part of the Irrawaddy valley can be seen. The bend in the river, in the region of Sagaing and Ava, is particularly eye-catching, as are the picturesque heights that demarcate the valley on the left bank in this direction.

Panoramic View of Kuthodaw Pagoda. (© Thweep Rittinaphakorn)

View over Sutaungpyei Pagoda on Mandalay Hill. (Lefèvre-Pontalis Archive)

For several centuries this was the centre par excellence of Burmese power, and this is understandable because it was the geographical centre of the country, where, blocking the road to invasions from the north, it could effectively watch over the Chindwin valley in the west and the Shan territories in the east, and collect the tribute from their rice paddies from the countries as far south as the sea, without being hindered by its neighbours.

Alongside Kyauk Taw, a number of pagodas and convents can be found at the foot of the hill.

The largest of these all-white groups is the 450 pagodas, where King Mindon Min surrounded a central golden pyramid copied from an ancient Pagan monument with a multitude of small domes. Each of these buildings, which resemble Arab or Hindu fountains, although decorated in pure Indochinese style with white plaster nagas and peacocks, houses an alabaster table on which is engraved a text from the Buddhist canon in Pali. The entire *Tripitaka* collection is housed here, making it a unique and precious sanctuary that would undoubtedly have grown in importance had the monarchy lasted.

Opposite the 450 pagodas is the Glass Monastery, famous for its mirrored decorations. We didn't visit it, but close by, next to Mindon's tomb, the tower of the hours and the eastern gate, we saw a small ruined convent located inside the palace. It is a perfect model of these wooden buildings on stilts, with carved roofs, multi-storey bell towers and balustrades. Fortunately, there is not a single piece of sheet metal in the building, and the mirrors are faded enough to produce the decorative effect of mother-of-pearl mosaics.

These wooden buildings are one of the most remarkable features of Burmese architecture, and at Kyauk Taw, the most interesting remains from the royal era are the beautiful conference or rest rooms with large teak casks, stacked in decreasing progression.

Before heading back to the Circuit house, we drove through the royal city again, then went to the District Commissioner's office to drop off some maps. Early in the morning, the full moon illuminated the lotus-covered ponds with their greenish-blue foliage and the red brick walls of the royal city, topped by seven-storey wooden pavilions. It was a most evocative sight, as we were staying in the south-east corner of the city and could enjoy the spectacle at our leisure.

The weather was conducive to walking and although we were tired, we left after dinner to go and see a festival similar to the one in Katha at the monastery of Shwé Gyi Bié. The crowds were much larger and consequently livelier. It was also noisier and brighter. All the little chapels and rest rooms were filled with food and offerings to the monks, luxuriously displayed and illuminated as in daylight, as are the Buddha statues, of which there are many. The corridors are bustling with activity, with people praying, smoking, chatting and eating on carpets in front of the altars. In one of the courtyards, there is a historical theatre, elsewhere a puppet theatre, in a third place acrobats, in a fourth comic actors with a young girl with somewhat suggestive figures and dancers who contemplates in expressive silence, in silhouette, a whole grimp of young and old monks wrapped in their yellow robes sitting on a while wall against the dark blue sky illuminated by the moon, whose gaze I could not make out in the low light. This was one of the most bizarre and strange impressions I got from this very Burmese festival, which we were delighted to have had the opportunity to see and which only Mandalay could have given such a complete spectacle.

26 November 1912

At 8 o'clock in the morning the ever-obliging M. Duroiselle, came to find us. He brought me three delightful Buddhist ex-votos from his excavations in Prome, where he found nearly 700 of them, which are not yet in any museum but which the English authorities, not without reason, forbid to be dispersed.

These, which Duroiselle had chosen with care and which he believes date from the period between the 6th and 7th centuries, come from the Baw Baw Gyi stupa in ancient Prome.

According to him, Prome is not so much the oldest town as the one where the most indisputable traces of ancient monuments have been discovered to date. There are inscriptions in Prome that are said to date from the 6th century. Duroiselle does not at all agree with G. Scott and the Commissioner of Mogok on the origin of the Burmese. They are obviously not Buddhist Hindus representing, according to this thesis, the ancient state of the populations of India at the time of their emigration, but they are indeed Tibetans or at least people of the same origin as the Tibetans who became civilised as they travelled down the Irrawaddy. But then, is the Hindu civilisation that Indochina has benefited from to be attributed to the Blacks of southern India? This is what many people are reluctant to admit. Not only must and could India, according to them, at the time of the creation of its colonies in Indochina, have had, even in the south, masters of a different race from today's Blacks, but moreover, relying on the Burmese's pretentious traditions of a superior Hindu origin (since, according to them, it came from North India), they want to see in the Burmese of today the exact image of the ancient civilisation of India deformed for centuries by revolutions, wars and racial conflicts.

In the morning, Mr Duroiselle showed us the famous Arakan pagoda on the road to Amarapura, whose style, inspired by the monuments of Pagan, differs slightly from that of ordinary pyramids. The pagoda is rectangular, with processional paths at various levels, and the covered galleries surround it so closely at the base that they form a sort of body with the monument and constitute a type of temple in the true sense of the word. Overall the flattened temple plans of the Angkor Wat type can be recognised.

This pagoda was built around 1780 to house the statues removed by the Burmese during their conquest of Arakan. In a central cell, enclosed by iron gates and on view for worship by the faithful who throng the galleries, there is an immense bronze Buddha brought from Arakan and which has been unceasingly covered every day with new gold leaf by the devout pilgrims who visit it. We ourselves saw Burmese people climb up to the statue amidst the candles and flowers and in front of the praying women, and make their pious offering with their hands. It's easy to see how much gold has accumulated on this statue, which has become very rough.

In one of the courtyards, also venerated by devotees who rub them as they pass by and make wishes in front of them, are two magnificent bronze statues of men, unfortunately very mutilated, three bronze lions, one of which is superb in its entirety and the head of another intact, and a beautifully worked three-headed elephant. All these ancient bronzes were brought back from Arakan and are considered by the Burmese to be war trophies. Duroiselle, seeing them deteriorating in the rain, has not dared hope to obtain them for the Rangoon Museum. But at least he is currently trying to interest devotees in their conservation and to raise money to have shelters built for the statues. He doubts he will be successful because nothing matches the prodigality of the Burmese when it comes to religious expenditure, and since we have been in this country, we have noticed this at every moment.

The particular glory and interest of the Arakan pagoda is the famous collection of copies of inscriptions that King Bodawpaya assembled here. These copies, engraved on stone in modern Burmese characters, are the most admirable archaeological collection that a professional amateur could have assembled. It seems that when studied closely, many errors of date or transcription appear, but this collection is no less a credit to its creator and, as it stands, can be of great service.

Bodawpaya had collected these texts, without paying particular attention to their content, from a wide variety of pagodas, but especially from religious monuments in neighbouring towns. Duroiselle found some of the originals at the spot where they had been copied. He also found some in Amarapura itself, collected by Bodawpaya in a pagoda where he had built up a collection almost as large as that in

Mandalay. He was therefore able to compare the original texts with those from Arakan, which had been published in Rangoon in two volumes in 1897. He has also been able to identify unpublished texts and is currently preparing their publication. He kindly told me that his volume will be sent to me shortly, along with the other volume and those of Forchhammer and Tan Nyen on the inscriptions of Pagan, Pinya and Ava. This archaeological knowledge touches me to the core, and it gave me particular pleasure to visit the Arakan steles under their low roofs, which occupy the outer gallery of one of the courtyards of the famous Arakan pagoda and are not the least of its treasures.

On the other side of the pagoda, two sacred ponds line the avenue, as if to complete the resemblance with Khmer temples and no doubt with ancient Hindu temples. Turtles are kept in one of them and we witnessed an extremely picturesque scene when, surrounded by young Burmese women with Bengal roses in their hair offering us meatballs for the turtles, we saw other young elegant women bending over the green water where the swimmers were showing their heads and snapping the food that flights of eaglets flapping around the edges of the pond in all directions were trying to snatch from them. Not far away, merchants were selling live fish to devotees willing to throw them into the pond to keep them alive. I have heard about all such Buddhist practices so many times and yet, neither in Siam nor in Laos, have I ever been able to observe them in person.

It is in the pagodas that you'll find the picturesque and the life. In the market, a large brick building constructed by the French, such things are absent. The shopkeepers are indifferent and don't seem to be used to selling goods that in themselves are of little interest. I didn't see any fine jewellery, just a few interesting Shan silver objects, a few common lacquer pieces that weren't very original and silks that were more attractive for their soft colours than for their quality. I did, however, buy two head scarves to complete the prince's costume that I had brought back from Muong Sing and which Jean will be able to use at a fancy dress ball.

We found silks of superior quality at the home of Mlle Denegui, an old lady who has lived in Mandalay for at least forty years and who, because of her dual Italian and Lyonnais origins, has always been involved in the world of silk.

She knew the regime before the conquest, because her brother, a silk supplier to the Court, had regular access to it, and she herself was often admitted to the Queen, a great lady and benefactor at times, she says, but incapable of restraining a fit of anger. Along with a French architect, Mr Duroiselle, the brothers and the nuns, Mlle Denegui made up the entire French colony in Mandalay. There are not many Europeans here. The city was designed on a large scale by French engineers who laid out immense avenues in the style of Versailles and Washington. Life has never circulated there and probably never will, because it was in Rangoon that the British concentrated all their efforts. They did not destroy anything in Mandalay, but time is their accomplice, as is the climate, in erasing the traces of the past.

In the afternoon, Duroiselle came back to pick us up to go and see the famous Golden Monastery, built by the last queen, the cruel and beautiful one who died a few months ago in the residence in southern India where she had lived with her husband King Thibaw since the events of 1884.

When this monastery, all carved wood painted red and gold, was shining in all its splendour, it was probably striking above all for its overabundance and its flashiness. As it stands, it is a marvel of its kind, and, if we we allow for that, there are very few faults of taste to criticise. The golds and reds are muted, and the rather too numerous wood carvings have taken on an old-fashioned look that makes them resemble work from the Middle Ages. The only thing that is a little shocking is the warped metal sheeting that has replaced the wooden tiles on the top floors of the roofs. As for the glasswork, it is not overdone, and that inside the main hall and on the doors of the seven-storey pavilion is as sober as it is elegant.

The overall tone is as attractive in the double pavilions with carvings at each entrance to the monastery courtyard as it is in the central building. Coconut, sugar palm and tamarind trees complete the decorative effect of this monastery, which is truly one of the most unusual things you can see in Burma. The great chief of the Burmese monks lives in the small golden room in the seven-storey pavilion. He was ill and apologised for not being able to grace us with his presence. The movable carved wooden shutters that allow the different rooms to be ventilated or completely closed are very practical and change the appearance of the monument depending on how they are used.

From the Golden Monastery, we moved on to the Aindaw Pagoda, one of the capital's most popular places of prayer. The paved courtyard is the largest in Mandalay, with a large golden pyramid guarded by four lions at its centre. Around the courtyard are pavilions of various styles, some with multi-storey roofs painted red and gold. A number of other beautiful pavilions along the walls and the four aisles leading to the pagoda are the main feature of this pleasant place, which is less smothered in zinc corridors and rest rooms than some of the other pagodas in the city. In one of the four aisles, at the entrance to which are two large white elephants made of brick and plaster, there are a number of vendors selling those delicious little light-coloured oiled parasols that Burmese women use so charmingly. We made some purchases here.

27 November 1912

If one has to be ready for anything with boats and be patient with them, I have to admit that ours was put to a severe test this morning. Having organised with great difficulty and precision our departure for today at 8 am with the Commander of the Navy, when I arrived in Mandalay the other day, I had every right to hope that our early rising, the rapid transport of our luggage and people through this immense city and the sacrifice of a last morning of strolling through the palaces and pagodas of Mandalay would be of some benefit to us. However, at 3 o'clock in the afternoon, we were barely on our way. From 8 in the morning until midday, we had to wait for the arrival of the *Bhamo*, which had been delayed by the fog. Cdr Balfour and his wife very kindly offered us hospitality and breakfast in their house. But from midday to 3 pm, we had to moor up, unload the *Bhamo* and go to the market to stock up on provisions for the road. If, with all that, we have a few hours to devote to visiting Pagan, we'll be very lucky.

Fortunately, we were dealing with English naval officers who were as obliging and courteous as any of the Englishmen we have had to deal with since our arrival in Burma. As the telegram summoning them to Mandalay for our service had not informed them of what they had to do, they were caught unawares and were a little surprised to learn that this time they would have to transport, instead of food, a household of French diplomats.

The *Bhamo* made fast work of the descent and tried to make up for lost time. In a few minutes we passed the golden dome of Amarapura's main pagoda on the left bank. It was here, just a few miles from present-day Mandalay, that the capital of Burma was moved from Ava at the end of the 18th century. It was the fourth son of Alaungpra (also Alaungpaya) who carried out this transfer in 1783. This city was still the capital in 1855 when Yule visited it. It was surrounded by a brick wall with three gates on each side. The palace was in the centre, with its walls parallel to those of the city. All the buildings were made of wood and there was a spire at the centre of the palace. All these features were reproduced in the construction of Mandalay, where the wooden materials from the Amarapura palace were apparently used.

There was a temple in every corner of the city. The streets were rectangular and the princes' wooden houses were distinguished by their triple roofs.

The most curious pagodas were those of Naga Yon Phya and Pato-Daugyi. Outside the city, to the north, i.e. in present-day Mandalay, was the King's water palace, built on wooden stilts in the style of a monastery, and known as Ye-Nan Dau.

Two miles to the east is the temple of Maha Myet Muni, the Arakan pagoda that we visited yesterday and which contained the famous bronze statue of Buddha that the Burmese had brought back as a victory trophy.

Some pretty lakes still exist to the south-west of Mandalay, in the vicinity of the town of Amarapura. On the banks of one of these lakes, close to the river, is the house where the naval commander received us this morning.

You can't see much of the Amarapura ruins from the river. All you can see are a few more or less dilapidated pyramids lost in the scrub that covers part of the left bank in front of the superb rice fields that stretch away towards the mountains.

On the other side of the Irrawaddy, the hills hug the shore. They are green, but the soil is poor and the vegetation mediocre. I am told that these hills are full of fossils and contain the remains of important animals, including elephants.

You wouldn't believe the extent to which the Burmese have given themselves over to piety on these heights. From Myngoon onwards, pyramids and monasteries begin to proliferate, but as you advance towards the spur formed by the Irrawaddy, behind which lies Sagaing, these monuments multiply to such an extent, on the shore, on every hill, and in every fold of land, that you would think you were in a dream city. I hadn't been told about this particular feature of the Sagaing mountain just opposite Amarapura.

In the 14th century, Sagaing had its moment of glory as the capital of one of the small states that had sprung up following the destruction of the kingdom of Pagan. The prince who reigned there extended his domination as far north as Manipur and came into conflict with the Shan prince of Pinya, who had established his capital in the same part of the Irrawaddy but on the left bank and a little inland from what later became the Burmese capital of Ava.

Under British rule, Sagaing strove to take on the economic importance in the region stretching northwards between the Irrawaddy and the Chindwin that the kingdom of Sagaing would undoubtedly have acquired if it had been extended, since it is from here that the main railway line serving central Burma starts. Because there is no bridge over the river, Sagaing is not directly linked to Mandalay, but a ferry boat carries trains from the north across the Irrawaddy to a station on the left bank just below Mandalay.

What prevented Sagaing from prospering was its rivalry with Panya, the capital of the Shan kingdom on the left bank, which itself only lasted 54 years. Panya had been founded in 1310 by the third of the Shan brothers who had put an end to the Pagan monarchy. From 1313 onwards, Panya was at war with Sagaing, whose conquest it attempted again in 1342, but in vain.

In 1364, Panya was absorbed into the kingdom of Ava, whose ruined capital can still be recognised today from the brick wall ending in an unfinished conical pyramid that can be seen on the left bank of the river, immediately after passing the evocative point of Sagaing that lies opposite it.

Ava, which for 400 years was the capital of Burma, owes its foundation in 1364 to Thado Men Bya, Prince of Tagaung, who seized the kingdoms of Panya and Sagaing, between which the country was then divided. He gave his capital the grandiloquent name of Ratnapura, the City of Light.

The first European to mention having visited it was Nicolo di Conti, who passed through in 1440.

In 1526, the Shan of Mogaung and Monyin, who had not forgotten the domination of Panya by princes of their race, tried to regain a foothold in the Irrawaddy valley and came to attack Ava. They took the city and ravaged the country until 1554, when the king of Pegu also took Ava and destroyed it.

It was not until 1601, when Pegu had also succumbed, that Ava once again became the capital under King Nyoung Men Tara, who reconstituted the ancient Burmese kingdom.

Later, from 1752 to 1763, Ava was once again eclipsed as the capital, before becoming the royal city again for 20 years until 1783.

In 1855, Yule went from Amarapura to visit the ruins of Ava. At the time, he found the city's ancient ramparts quite dilapidated. Where, in the middle of the second wall, the palace of the kings had once stood, he noted the remains of an interesting belvedere. In another part of the city, he also visited the very shining pagoda of Shwé Kyet Yet situated on a summit. Since then, the ruins have only become more pronounced, and if we recommend a visit to Sagaing, it is for the monuments that Buddhist fervour has created and maintained there, which are still so interesting. If an excursion to Amarapura, whose remains are more recent and therefore a little better preserved, is made easier, very few people today will remember the ruins of Ava. And yet how many memories do they evoke since the time of its founder Thadomeng-bya in 1364. He, who claimed to have all the more right to reign alone over the Irrawaddy valley as he was descended from both the kings of Sagaing and those of Tagaung on the upper river, the undisputed ancestors of the Burmese monarchy. His aim was nothing other than to reconstitute the ancient Burmese kingdom of Pagan, which had left such deep memories among the Burmese, who had almost always been enslaved since the great Mongol invasion.

The Chinese, who had destroyed Pagan and tolerated the existence of small kingdoms in this part of Indochina, were not prepared to accept the reconstitution of large monarchies. In 1418, they led one of their armies against Ava.

The Burmese then had to fight other enemies of their race to maintain their domination of the central Irrawaddy, because in 1426, the Shan chief of Monyin succeeded in seizing the crown of Ava and joined forces with the Pegu against the Burmese of Toungoo to keep it. This alliance also benefited the Peguans of Hangsawadi and the Shans. Until 1543, it was the Shan influence that prevailed in Ava and in this part of the Irrawaddy basin.

But in 1554, the Burmese began to take serious revenge. With the Prince of Toungoo and Bureng Naung (Bayinnaung), his successor, the Burmese took Pegu, then Ava, then the Shan countries and finally a large part of Indochina. But it was not Ava that benefited as a capital, either because he was seduced by the past glory of Hangsawadi, or because he found it preferable to confirm his conquest by his presence in the midst of the Talaing in order to put an end to them once and for all, or because the extent of his conquests to the east and southeast meant that he had to keep a closer eye on his new possessions. He simply entrusted the supervision of the Burmese domain itself to the prince of his family who was closest to him and who, under the title of King of Ava, obeyed him as if he were the King of Kings.

Bureng Naung established his court and capital at Hangsawadi, but he was often absent, travelling all over Indochina, from Chiang Mai to Lan Chang, Ayutthaya and the Shan countries of the north.

Ava was not to become the Burmese capital again until 1634, when, after the complete collapse of the Bureng Naung kingdom, it was a question of reassembling its remnants and fortifying the Burmese idea by re-establishing the centre of action at the point historically best suited for this purpose. There, at least, the Shans and the Chinese could be confronted and fought against effectively to maintain Burmese influence over the entire Irrawaddy.

In 1752, however, the eternal enemy, the Talaing (Mon), felt strong enough to once again take the offensive against the Burmese. The Peguans took Ava, which they ransacked and burnt. But the Burmese

Alaungpra emerged and revived the prestige of his race. In 1753 he reoccupied Ava.

But despite everything, as a capital city, Ava has lost its raison d'être. Through various alternatives and from siege to siege, its importance diminished and its masters grew sick of it. Except in 1823, when the whim of a Burmese king of the Alaungpra dynasty temporarily restored the capital to Ava, the seat of the royal residence was moved several miles further north, first to Amarapura, then to Mandalay, which in 1884 saw the end of both the dynasty and Burmese kingship.

Seen remotely in books and even on close examination of maps, one is tempted to exaggerate the distances separating all these famous sites from Sagaing, Panya, Ava, Amarapura and Mandalay. In reality, all these points touch each other, and in the vast valley of the river formed on the opposite bank by the spur of Sagaing, there is behind all these names nothing but a unique geographical situation whose influence has not ceased to exert itself on the historical destinies of the country, as the conflict of the races has proved that for the Shan, as for the Burmese and the Peguan, possession of this corner of land meant domination of the river and all the territory that its waters irrigate.

In this respect, an examination of the site proves the importance of Sagaing, which was, after all, the first capital in this region and which seems to have remained, down the centuries, the site most revered by the tradition-loving natives. I would never have understood this, if I hadn't seen it. What's more, the sight of all these Buddhist buildings on the hillsides of Sagaing is one of the most beautiful and curious that I have yet seen in Indochina, and I am delighted that my river trip this evening has enabled me to admire it, at the same time as explaining to me the main problems of Burmese history.

When the Pyu from Tagaung came down the river in search of a permanent settlement, they did not stop on the plain opposite Sagaing, probably because they found the way clear before them and at Prome, which can be considered the beginning of the Irrawaddy delta, they found a much larger area of land suitable for cultivation.

According to General de Beylié, who described its ruins, Prome, which successively bore the names Srikshetra and Pissanumyo, the city of Vishnu, and then Prome, the city of Brahma, was never the splendid city it is thought to have been. According to the same author, this capital of the Pyu of the kingdom of Tarekkatara, as described by Ptolemy, was an agglomeration of villages whose very modest temples and dwellings were built, as they are today, from light and not very durable materials.

What seems to distinguish the stupas of old Prome are the *linga*-shaped protuberances on top, in the same style as the Brahman towers of Nha Trang in Annam. These stupas are thought to belong to the oldest and most prosperous period of this ancient city, which should not be confused with modern Prome, which contains no monuments dating from before the 17th century.

Burmese tradition has it that old Prome, whose remains lie near Hmanza station on the Rangoon to Prome railway, was founded in 454 BC by Hindus who first settled in Tagaung and belonged to the Kapilavastu dynasty, a kingdom located in the Ganges valley. This dynasty is said to have lasted until 110 BC and then continued by adoption until AD 84, with a series of 27 kings, in the chronological list, for a period of 578 years. It was from Prome that, following conflicts with other inhabitants of the kingdom, the Pyu tribe left to found Pagan, in fact the new Pagan, as the old Pagan was none other than Tagaung on the upper river.

This tradition is generally disputed, particularly by Beylié, who points out that it was only in the 11th century, under King Anuratha, that the Burmese nation was definitively constituted and the capital established in the hitherto secondary city of Pagan. It was this same prince who subsequently conquered the whole of the Talaing country, Martaban, Tavoy and Tenasserim and destroyed the city of Prome.

From the 7th to the 11th century, Prome continued to be a very lively town, judging by the three Buddhist chapels of Lahandakon, Bebegyi and Lemietna, which still exist and date from this period. It should be noted that these monuments have vaults built according to Persian and Mongolian methods. The three pretty terracotta medallions given to me by Duroiselle come from Bebegyi (alias Baw Baw Gyi).

It is likely that long before the foundation of Hangsawadi by the Talaing or Peguan, the Burmese kingdom of Prome was under attack from these rivals, whose main centre was Thaton. Anuratha moved his capital further north to Pagan in order to be able to withstand the attacks of the invaders from the north as well as those of the Peguan.

Under the Burmese kings of Pagan and Ava, Prome was often the seat of viceroyalties dependent on neighbouring kingdoms. In the 15th century in particular, these viceroys conquered the territories of these kingdoms on more than one occasion. Prome, like Toungoo, was also more than once a place of refuge for Burmese who were being bullied by rival races. It was a stronghold which, in 1539, successfully resisted the attacks of King Tabeng Shwehti. He didn't take it until 1541, but he proved to be a vigorous defender of the Burmese cause, preventing the Shan from taking control. Lost and recaptured several times by the Burmese, Prome was not dominated by the Shan, but had to withstand more than one siege by the Peguans. It was perhaps during one of these sieges that the town was moved. Until 1755, when the Burmese Alaungpra definitively repulsed the Peguans from Prome, the struggle continued between the two races in this part of the Irrawaddy basin. The English occupied Prome during their Burmese war of 1825, but surrendered it in 1826.

It is unfortunate that the needs of the service do not allow the military transport *Bhamo* to take us to Prome.

The two officers on board, who belong to the Royal Navy, are very well-mannered and well-spoken people whose conversation is most pleasant. At 6 o'clock, after an admirable sunset, the boat stopped for the night, and our hosts were all ours. The food and table were impeccable.

The oldest took part in the campaign against the Boxers. In these seas, he knows the Tenasserim coast well and visited Victoria Point at the mouth of the Pak Chan River. He found that the bridge was good, but that the river was hardly navigable due to its lack of depth, which made it less interesting as a route to Bangkok and the Gulf of Siam. Generally speaking, he says that the Government of India does not encourage private initiative in this part of the Empire, finding that the time has not yet come for this. But like all the English officials with whom I have discussed the matter, he feels that the Government of India is not qualified to deal with Burmese matters of which it is ignorant. Burma is a very different country from India and cannot be administered from afar by offices and would gain much from being more independent.

It is true that Burma's resources are insufficient to administer it and that India, which is paying, is not letting go.

Moreover, by his indolence and indulgent laissez faire, the Burmese have allowed the Hindu to take root. Burmese women do not reject the idea of a union with a Hindu, however black he may be. "What will it be like", says our lieutenant, "when the railways of India are linked to those of this country?". On that day the Burmese will disappear and merge with the invader from the west.

28 November 1912

The insects attracted by the lights were such a nuisance on the *Bhamo* last night that we were only able to have dinner under a mosquito net, and after that we didn't stay out much longer. The first mate showed us a very beautiful, huge butterfly with pearly wings that had been caught on board a few weeks ago and which he is trying to keep. He has only been in Burma since spring, and the first time he went into the jungle to look for wild chickens, he came face to face with a gigantic cobra over seven feet tall, which stood menacingly in front of him and which he killed with a shotgun blast. He showed us the skin, which he dried very well. That was all it took to renew Henriette's terror of snakes, which my stories from Bangkok had ignited in her imagination. These are terrible encounters that I too would like to avoid.

The English certainly do things admirably. The lieutenant found a way to make up two hours by realising that he didn't need to make any wood for his boat this morning. Instead of arriving in Pagan at the end of the day, we can disembark perhaps in the early afternoon and reach the ruins an hour away by oxcart. He will give us some food. We can sleep at the bungalow, take a walk around the ruins this evening and a longer one tomorrow morning and get back to *Bhamo* in time to head back to Myingian at midday and be there the next morning in time to catch the Rangoon train. There was no fog on the river this morning either, which made our navigation much easier.

Around 10.15 am we were at the first arm of the Chindwin, but it was lost amidst so many sandbanks that it was difficult to distinguish the main arm amidst the small streams that make their way through. The river is navigable, however, by flat boats specially designed for the purpose. It flows down from strange countries neighbouring Manipur, where the Naga people worship spirits and demons, adore snakes and practice human sacrifice to obtain favourable harvests. These people have a certain influence on the practices of the Burmese, who may originally have been more or less related to them before their descent to the south. Be that as it may, shamanism and the worship of spirits still hold a considerable place in Burmese religion, despite Buddhist prohibitions.

In Mandalay, there is a whole district inhabited by Naga people. Duroiselle, who showed us some, said that the women of this race, with their pointed noses and snake-like eyes, gave off an appalling smell and were odious.

At 11 o'clock we passed Myingian, where our journey is due to end the day after tomorrow. From here, the Irrawaddy valley looks like a vast plain with few trees, and the sandbanks along the river are very extensive. A few sugar palm trees standing out against the horizon give the occasional impression of the Nile. The villages are more visible but less picturesque than on the upper river. Despite the width of the Irrawaddy, it is still possible to make out what is happening on both banks at the moment, but at high water, the river must be a veritable lake whose limits cannot be seen.

At one o'clock we passed the confluence of the main mouth of the Chindwin. This one at least is recognisable.

On the other side of the river, on the left bank, the riverbank finally appeared a little higher and lightly wooded, with the great isolated peak of Poppa in the distance, which resembles Vesuvius and is said to be volcanic. As far as this mountain, the country appears flat with lightly wooded scrub in the middle of which clearings can be seen in the distance. A little further down, this plain ends in a sort of cliff overlooking the river. This is where Pagan is located.

At 3 am we arrived at our destination, not Pagan itself, but four or five miles further up, where Lieutenant Wisch, for that was the Commander's name, had decided to take on his wood, in order to avoid a sandbank. But there must have been a misunderstanding with the locals, because they were waiting for us at the Pagan ruins. We lost quite a bit of time before we had two ox carts and could set off. It was only at

Pagan. (Photograph: Olivier Évrard)

4 o'clock that we left the banks of the Irrawaddy with our boys, sleeping gear and provisions. But the route we had to take had the advantage of passing through most of the ruins and showing us some pagodas that we would probably not have seen otherwise. What's more, the path under the tall tamarind and sugar palm trees is not lacking in character, and Henriette is having a lot of fun on this oxcart ride, despite the dust.

We stopped at Shwe Sigon, a golden pyramid in the shape of a squashed bell, surrounded by many small pagodas. This pagoda is quite different from the most beautiful ones in Mandalay. The cult has continued here and is maintained. A few painted and carved wooden figures around a pavilion attracted our attention. But this pagoda was not within the walls of the ancient city, and although it is highly renowned and commendable for the glazed terracotta metopes embedded in its base, it did not yet give the impression of the unique city that is Pagan.

A little after leaving Shwe Sigon, when the tamarind trees and houses ceased, we found ourselves in the middle of the low scrub, whose extent in clearly visible. One is deeply surprised to encounter, as far as the eye can see, rising up in the middle of this greenery, red brick monuments whose colour takes on a particular hue in the setting sun, and which, although all in ruins, have remained sufficiently intact for their architecture to be clearly distinguished.

This architecture is new to me, in that there is not a single pyramid that is not preceded by a porch that forms one with it and is of such dimensions that the whole edifice appears not as a stupa but as a chapel. Almost always, from the large to the small, the impressions are harmonious. This is architecture at its best. The materials themselves, albeit brick, have proved their worth, since some of these monuments are almost 900 years old.

The domes also vary quite frequently, but most often take the form of a long, toothed gourd.

The foundations are almost always magnificent and imposing because of the height of their walls, which is repeated on the second floor, after the processional terrace and above the tiers adorned with staircases and doors on each side leading up to the dome. It is easy to imagine the priests and offering bearers moving around on these terraces and staircases in front of the crowds below when, by chance, the sacred chapel was above the first floor instead of on the ground floor.

We arrived at the famous Ananda pagoda just as the day was drawing to a close and the sun was setting with a brilliance that strangely illuminated the whole setting. We had just been joined a few moments earlier by a cavalcade of Pagan notables in pink turbans, led by the village chief in his carved oxcart, covered with a blanket on which he sat like a prince of old, his driver seated cross legged in front.

They had come to apologise for not having met us earlier, believing that our boat would stop at the bottom of the ruins, where they had prepared everything to receive us and where young Burmese dancers had been waiting for us all day.

They brought us two oxcarts covered in green gauze where we could sit perfectly on fixed chairs with pink cushions.

Nothing could be more curious than this meeting and the polite and deferential gestures of welcome from all these people who had received the most careful instructions about us from Rangoon and who carried them out with great eagerness.

They began by showing us the interior of the Ananda pagoda, so unusual with its four deep, ogival-vaulted niches built of stone, which form veritable chapels on each side of the quadrilateral to which they give a rational meaning. Large standing golden Buddhas occupy these high niches. And from these chapels emerge large, high, half-vaulted corridors with windows facing outwards, which go all the way round the inside of the building. One could quibble that the outside is made of brick, but nevertheless this is still really good architecture.

The walls of these corridors themselves contain a number of niches in which stone stelae, almost all intact, recount in an archaic but striking style the main features of the Buddha's life, in a variety of attitudes.

These stelae are covered in gold, with red and green backgrounds, but they are not damaged for this reason. In addition, in one of the four chapels, in an attitude of adoration, there are two other interesting sculptures representing the founding king Alaungsithu and the head of the monks at that time.

But it was getting dark and we had nothing better to do than to go and find the comfortable circuit house a mile away, and while the boys prepared dinner for us with the eggs and superb fish offered by the notables, to watch below our verandah dances by the eleven little local girls who have been brought in for our enchantment. They ranged in age from 6 to 12, were dressed in pink with white jackets and wings, metal necklaces and bracelets, and gracefully danced in the Indochinese style, under the direction of two horrible matrons and a dancing master who watched over them on one side, while on the other a five-piece Burmese band accompanied them with the flute, xylophone, drums, cymbals and bamboo sticks, which were beaten against each other.

At 9 o'clock we said goodbye to all these interesting people, because we needed to rest and tomorrow morning we have a lot to do.

The foundation of Pagan is attributed to Thamuradit, chief of a Pyu tribe who, following internal dissension, left Prome, capital of the kingdom of Tharekkettara.

Thamuradit was not of royal descent, but it seems that he was later given an ancestry and linked to the Khsatrya princes of Tharekkettara.

In the 4th century, did Pagan participate in the benefits of Buddhist propaganda that Buddhagosa brought to Thaton? This is a controversial point. In any case, some of these monuments bear traces of South Indian influence. In terms of both its plan and its sculptures, it seems that the Ananda pagoda is reminiscent of more than one temple in Ceylon and southern India. It is said to have been altered from one repair to another, but it is perfectly recognisable as a smaller and more compact version of the Angkor plan. It has the same system of rectangular terraces rising gradually to the final dome or lantern. The domes here are not phallic like those in Cambodia. These temples have never been anything but Buddhist. The monuments end more like gourds or spires. When the gourd dominates, we are reminded of India, or even the Arab domes. When it is a spire, the appearance is quite special, above these high bases, and what these monuments evoke is more a Christian church or an enchanted palace.

George Scott observed that although Pagan is a dead city, it is perhaps from a religious point of view the most interesting city in the world, not excepting Mecca or Benares. "For eight miles," he says, "along the river, there are nothing but ruins of pagodas, so much so that a Burmese proverb speaks of 9,999 temples. The sight of these ruins on the river, which is very wide at this point, gives rise to the idea of a religious metropolis devoted to solitude."

To whom did Pagan owe this religious character, as its origins do not seem to assign it particularly well to the period when the Pyu of Prome came to settle there between 107 and 152 CE? Its names were Pyugama, Pugama, Pugam and Pagan. These do not recall a religious idea but rather a racial one.

The kingdom's beginnings were modest for 200 years. Towards the end of the 2nd century or the beginning of the 3rd, the Chinese became aware of its existence and wanted to claim tribute, but they were refused and the matter seems to have had no follow-up. The location of the capital varied more than once during these early years. Initially fixed at Yonhlutgyun, also known as Arimaddana, it was transferred in the 4th century to Thiripitsaya, still within the same radius in the region of present-day Pagan. So it was from the outset in this corner of the Irrawaddy, as later in the area where Sagaing is located. The place is imposing, with this vast expanse of river in front of the cliffs and behind it a plain that goes all the way up to Poppa mountain. This plain is not very fertile. Sesame, corn and tamarind are its only products, but were the Pyu great farmers? What were they in fact? A very small tribe, and it wasn't until the 11th century that they came out of their obscurity with King Anuratha. Twice again, the location of the capital was changed. It had moved from Thiripitsaya to Tampawadi, and in 850 it was finally moved to Pagan.

Anuratha is the great Burmese king of legend and history. He reigned from 1017 to 1059 and is remembered for the role he played in protecting religion, literature and the arts, and in leading armies.

An enemy of shamanism and Lamaism, which had distorted the purity of his people's Buddhist beliefs, he attacked above all the diabolical snake cult introduced by the Naga of Assam and Manipur. To counter their priests, the impure Ayis, he called on the renowned monks of Thaton, who represented the unblemished Buddhism of the south. He tried to obtain relics from the Talaing king, Manuha, but when Manuha refused, he attacked Thaton. His victory was complete. He took the relics, books and images of Thaton to Pagan, having also taken the king and his family prisoner.

With the King of Ceylon, Anuratha settled for less. Without a fleet to back up his claims, he was offered fake relics and accepted them. It was admitted that Buddha had performed a miracle by splitting them in two.

In his relations with China, the facts attributed to Anuratha are pure fantasy and intimidation, like those attributed in the same circumstances to Ramkhamhaeng, the traditional hero of Siamese history.

With regard to Pegu, his role was much more precise and continuous. But he also seems to have had relations with Arakan, Assam and the Shan lands.

He died on an elephant torn apart by a raging buffalo.

It was Anuratha's Buddhist fervour that was responsible for the religious development of Pagan, and yet there is very little in the ruins of present-day Pagan to recall his name. It was during the reign of his second successor Alaungsithu that the Thatbyinnyu pagoda was built in 1160, while the Ananda pagoda was built in 1085 under Kyansittha, Anuratha's immediate successor. Gawdawpallin dates from 1190 and Mahabodhi from 1198.

Temples continued to be built from the end of the 11th century until the beginning of the 13th. The last great temple to be built in Pagan, that of Boadi, dates from around 1227 and was the work of King Zeyathinkha, who is said to have had golden statues of himself and various members of his family erected there. But this was already a time of decadent architecture in Pagan. Marco Polo left us a description of Pagan, capital of the Mien kingdom, which he visited at that time. The Mongol expeditions, which undermined all the Indochinese dynasties prior to their emergence and, on the contrary, consolidated some of the new monarchies, were a great encouragement to the enemies of Burmese Pagan. The Shan on the one hand, with Wareru in Martaban, and the Peguans of Hangsawadi on the other, had their eyes on this kingdom, which had already passed the time of its apogee.

The Mongols came down the Irrawaddy, winning victory at Male. The king of Pagan fled his capital and Pagan suffered the pain of devastation and fire. However, the general opinion is that the Mongols did not descend that far and that it was Pagan's other enemies who caused its destruction.

Nominally, the kingdom continued to exist until 1368, when Zo Moun Nit, son of Zonit, died. But in reality Kyoaewa was the last true king of Pagan under the protection of the Mongols, who were unable even to defend him, for it was during the reign of this prince that the three famous Shan brothers arose, deposed him and themselves settled in Panya, a little further up the Irrawaddy. The last three kings of Pagan had shown themselves to be completely incapable and instead of keeping the same friendly relations with the Mongols that their predecessors had always endeavoured to maintain with the Chinese, King Tayokpyi (1250-1286) had their ambassador assassinated. This provoked the anger of Kublai Khan.

Huber, a member of the École française d'archéologie in Hanoi, has worked hard to reconstruct this period of Burmese history. He translated the fifth book of the Hman Nan Yazawin Royal Chronicle, which deals with the end of the Pagan monarchy (Volume n°9 of the *Bulletin de l'École française*, 1909). He also looked at Chinese sources for confirmation and found a great deal of information in the Yuan *Tchao Tcheng Mien Lou*, a contemporary Chinese account of the Mongol expeditions to Burma. This document is apparently far more authentic than the official *Annals of the Yuan* or *Mongols*.

There is also a whole special Burmese literature on the history of Pagan. It consists of the *Pagan Yazawin* in Burmese, the *Pakkam Maharajawamsa* in Pali and the *Rajavamsajalini in Burmese*, a good study on the history of Pagan, accompanied by maps and plans and giving copies of some inscriptions unknown elsewhere. This work appears to be the work of a government epigraphist.

Low tells us in his history of Tenasserim that when, in 1826-27, an English embassy was sent to Ava, i.e. Amarapura, it discovered 60 ancient inscriptions in Pagan and assumed that copies of these inscriptions were to be found in the Arakan pagoda among the 596 collected by King Bodawpaya. This may well be the case. In any case, a collection of inscriptions from Ava and Pagan was published in 1892 and translated in 1899. This is an interesting mine of useful information.

29 November 1912

It would be impossible to visit all the pagodas of Pagan in a single day. The area covered by ruins is too large. Moreover, although many of the buildings are more or less intact, a large number have in some way become tumuli, and apart from a few minor details, the type of most of them is more or less the same, namely the chapel stupa, gradually rising to the proportions of a temple with superimposed terraces ending in tiers topped by a point or a dome.

Having little time in the morning, from 7-10.30 am, I had the satisfaction of noticing from the outset that all the main pagodas, or those at least whose fame had led the piety of the faithful to maintain them, were grouped within a radius limited enough to be able to visit them easily. The most interesting pagodas are grouped around the King's palace, which was fairly close to the river, but of which only the probable location can now be made out, as the buildings must have been made of wood.

The head of the village and the notables had worked together well by building a bamboo *sala* decorated with carpets and poles with banners on the banks of the river below the Bupaya pagoda, as this is the first nucleus of Pagan. A gourd-shaped aedicula supported by tiers of lime-covered bricks that slope down to the river, together with a small cell for the *phya*, commemorates King Yathegyaung, who reigned from 152 to 167, and Pyuzawdi, his successor from 167 to 242. The aedicula is shaped like a gourd because Pyuzawdi succeeded in ridding the country of the wild gourds that infested the soil there. The genies' niche and the proximity of the river also recall the memory of the *Nats*, masters of this part of the Irrawaddy, who made navigation so difficult in these parts that you could only pass through after offering them sacrifices. All this happened long before Pagan became the great and famous capital of Anuratha. Since Bupaya is the oldest temple, it seemed the right place to start.

The Palace of the Kings was built very close to here, along with the pretty Hindu-style Mahabodhi pagoda with its four-sided, mitre-shaped dome that forms almost the entire edifice, with the statue of Buddha in a niche below.

The entire upper structure is inlaid with small Buddha statues. As for the different sides of the base, they are very carefully decorated. There are fine sculpted Buddhas, jagged arabesques in plaster in the Angkor style and celestial bayadere dances. This charming, well-maintained temple is an imitation of the Gaya Buddha (Bodhgaya) temple in Bengal and was built in 1198 by King Nandaungmya.

Not far from there, in the vicinity of the river and the circuit house where we spent the night, is the temple of Gawdawpallin, which in my opinion is the finest and best proportioned of those in Pagan. It falls into the category of those with superimposed terraces and is crowned by a very harmoniously constructed dome. It dates back to 1190 and was erected by King Narapatisithu, who was robbed of his pride by the loss of his sight and only regained it after erecting this very pretty edifice to Buddha.

The vaulted corridors that run around the inside of the monument are beautifully structured. The Buddha chapel is on the ground floor, and the windows and stairway vaults are ogival. One would hardly say one was in Indochina.

I climbed up to the first and second terraces and from there the view was truly admirable in the morning sun over the whole panorama of low greenery and innumerable red-brick monuments, in the midst of which the temple of Ananda, with its whitewashed appearance and the lightness of an airy, jagged pyramid, shone with all its brilliance. The isolated mountain of Poppa in the distance, and a smaller, less elevated range closer by, embellish the landscape. Among the most important monuments pointed out nearby, were two fairly heavy bell-shaped pyramids, both of which appear to be very old. They are Shwé Sigon, the prototype of the pagoda of the same name that we visited yesterday, and Mingla Sedi, which dates from the time of the Mongol war and was barely finished when the kingdom of Pagan was destroyed.

Thatbyinnyu temple, built under Alaungsithu in 1160, is the largest of the series. Its base is incomparable in size and grace. The terraces are also very beautiful and provide wonderful access to the sanctuary, which unusually is on a higher floor in the central part of the building. It is unfortunate that this beautiful ensemble is slightly marred by the crown, as the dome is too small.

It is said that this 5-storey temple was built on the model of those in North India, with the lower storey reserved for the bonzes, the central storey for Buddha worship and the two upper storeys for relics and sacred books.

The temple of Shwe Gu Gyi, smaller than the previous two and designed in the same style, is very close by. Like them, it adjoined the royal residence. Its inscriptions are still intact. On the first floor in front of the sanctuary is a beautiful open terrace. The sanctuary itself and the interior corridors that surround it are well constructed.

From the terrace, as from Thatbyinnyu, there is an extensive view, and before leaving this temple, the last one I was to climb, I asked for the names of the half-ruined buildings that attracted my attention most by their shapes and dimensions, and which were too far away in the direction of Poppa for us to visit them. I was told of Sudha Muni, Dhamayangee and Shwé San Dau. The last would have been interesting to see, as it was built by Anuratha to house the Buddha's hair he brought back from Thaton. It seems that the statues of Brahman gods that guard this monument must be attributed to the Hindu workers that Anuratha brought as prisoners from Thaton at the same time as King Manuha.

It was actually the only temple I regret not having been able to visit. The panorama of the city is so distinct that the location of each monument is easy to remember.

We ended our visit to Pagan with a final walk around the base of the Ananda. The base and that of one of the upper terraces are decorated with greenish-blue glazed terracotta tiles that are extremely interesting, not because the work is refined, but because their age and the naivety of their subjects add a curious element to the decoration. There are series of offering bearers, elephants, birds, etc., which deserve a great deal of attention from the point of view of ceramic documentation.

Some of them can be examined more closely, along with other ceramic fragments, in the small museum that has been built near the Ananda pagoda, where, along with some fairly ordinary objects of worship, are also grouped together the stelae with inscriptions and the terracotta

ex-votos of which Duroiselle provided me with such lovely specimens.
In the corridors leading to the Ananda, lacquer merchants offered their wares. Pagan is renowned for the quality of its lacquerware, but I found them very ugly, especially since the use of aniline-based greens, reds and yellows has brought disgrace on the industry. In spite of everything, we did a bit of shopping and went to see some of their manufacturers, whose patience, if better directed, could lead to much finer results. But the Burmese are so reluctant to work and produce, that we should acknowledge the serious effort that the people of Pagan are making to improve their lot.

Throughout our walk, the village chief in his covered cart and the notables on horseback never stopped accompanying us. We were royally content in our green muslin-covered cart, which took us back to our boat in just over an hour, very bumpily and at the slow pace of our oxen. It was a quarter to twelve when we arrived, and Commander Wisch complimented us on our punctuality. At a quarter past twelve, the *Bhamo* was on the move again until 5.30 pm when we stopped for the night along one of the vast sandbanks at the confluence of the Shweli. Burmese men with their oxen were ploughing and sowing this very fertile soil.

I asked one of my Chinese boys what he thought of Pagan. He travelled with Petithuguenin in Cambodia and prides himself on knowing what's good. He replied with a shrug of his shoulders: "Angkor Wat yes, very good! This is not good!"

It was a categoric answer. He likes stone better than brick. And so do I. But as far as brick goes, it was very good.

30 November 1912

Lieutenant Wisch was a punctual man who told us that we would be in Myingyan at 8 am. At 8 o'clock precisely we boarded and until his last command was given, the lieutenant didn't bother with us for even a quarter of a second, even to give us a little morning greeting. But the next thing we knew, he was the most polite, attentive and friendly man imaginable.

Before leaving, he made us have a substantial breakfast. On the riverbank, he had cut steps out of the sand, laid out a carpet, and handed us over to the Commissioner of Myingyan himself, whom he had informed of our arrival by telegraph and who was waiting for us with saddled horses, ox carts filled with carpets and cushions, and an escort of Burmese police riders. Myingyan is now quite a distance from the Irrawaddy, which until a few years ago flowed at the foot of its bank but now is separated from it by an immense sandbank. Driving around on this sunny morning, you'd think you were in the desert, and it's a very curious sight.

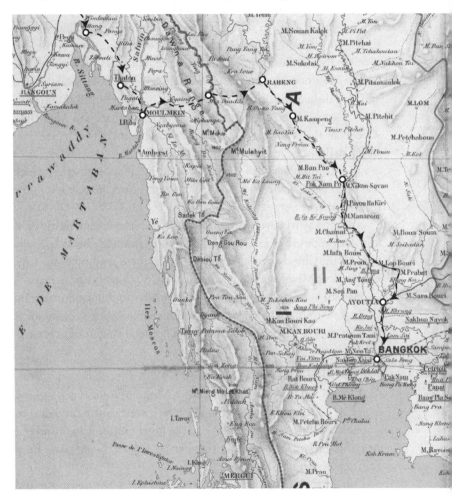

Itinerary from 3rd December to return to Bangkok. Adaptation of the Map of the Catholic Missions of Siam, Burma and Laos drawn and engraved by R. Hausermann. Missions étrangères de Paris/IRFA

Our train didn't leave until 10.55 am, so we paid an early morning visit to the Commissioner's wife before locking ourselves in our rolling cage, which took over six hours to cover the 70 miles to Thazi.

It was impossible to have any meals en route. Fortunately, it wasn't hot. But the country for two thirds of the way was very ugly, dry, and arid, producing little more than meagre maize and sugar palms where the unusable scrub does not dominate. The sugar palm grows in abundance. It is from its sap that the palm wine so highly prized throughout the country is made. I tasted both sweet and fermented wines in Pagan. The former seemed insipid, but the latter was a bit like beer and was not unpleasant. Around Meiktila, the rice fields appeared and quickly become superb. We were back in the beautiful countryside we had seen on the outward journey, between Thazi and Mandalay, watered by rivers flowing down from the mountains of the Shan region, which delimit the horizon in superb fashion.

The Commissioner of Myingyan told me that his district, which includes Pagan, is the driest in the whole of Burma because it is in the region where it rains least often.

The railway which crosses this country therefore seems destined, if it is not proposed to extend it, to serve the Irrawaddy boats specially built for the Chindwin via Myingyan. Under these conditions, the large sandbank at Myingyan has become a cause of great embarrassment.

Half an hour late, we reached the Mandalay to Rangoon mail train at Thazi, with the carriage reserved for the night, and the restaurant at the next station, Yamethin. We had been fasting for about eight hours.

1 December 1912

At 8.15 am in Rangoon, the man from Minto Mansions was waiting for us to collect our luggage, and while I went to the cathedral to attend mass, Henriette went back to the hotel to have a wash and put everything in order. I met her there at 10 o'clock. Good news from France was waiting for us there.

Our morning and afternoon were devoted to tidying up and correspondence. A letter from the Commissioner of Moulmein, Mr Dawson, confirmed what I had already learned from his telegram from Mandalay, that after some difficulty in finding elephants, he has finally got some for our journey from Kokarit to the border. This was a great satisfaction for us all.

At 4.30 pm we went out for a drive. We went to Government House to try to meet the Lieutenant-Governor and Lady Adamson, who arrived from Maymyo several days ago for the winter season. Their dwelling is a fine old English-style castle of several storeys, very near our hotel and surrounded by parkland enclosed by handsome gates with the arms of England.

As it is customary to register indicating the probable date of departure, I have complied by giving the date of the 3rd. It is to be hoped that, with the usual English discretion, the Lieutenant-Governor will not disturb us in the execution of our plans by an untimely invitation.

We finished our day with a sunset tour of the lakes. Shwé Dagon, like a spot of amber, looked very good, surrounded by an immense expanse of blazing sky, above the lake criss-crossed by English boats. The clubs were full on this Sunday evening.

2 December 1912

A particularly long, boring day of shopping, arranging things and correspondence. Around 5.30 pm, we drove around the lakes in a beautiful sunset. I have received another letter from Dawson telling us that our delay from 1st to 5th may cause us to lose a day on the way to Kokarit, as the water has dropped considerably and is making navigation more difficult.

Henriette and I were rather surprised that given all the attention the English have shown us in Burma, on the orders of Lieutenant-Governor Adamson, he and his wife ignored the approach we made to them yesterday. We were expecting an introduciton, a tea or at least something. I went to Major Des Voeux's house and wrote him a note on my card, but he too did not make a move.

3 December 1912

The Vilmorins arrived from Mandalay on the morning train and we agreed to take the train to Moulmein this evening instead of going there by boat tomorrow.

The whole of our morning was again spent dealing with merchants and Cook arranging the passage of the chambermaid. She will leave Rangoon on Thursday by a British India ship, which will drop her off in Singapore on the 10th. She will be received and accommodated by the ladies of St Maur whom I have informed by cable, and will leave on the 13th for Bangkok where she will arrive on the 17th on a North German Lloyd ship. I have also written to Maugras to keep him informed of our movements and ask him to send us a special wagon to Paknampho.

I also telegraphed Commissioner Dawson that we would be arriving tomorrow morning in Moulmein, where he informed me that we would find the Government launch to take us across the Salween.

At the end of the day, Henriette and I went up to Shwé Dagon one last time and circled the lakes again. On the way, we passed Lady Adamson's carriage with the bright red livery of the Hindus on duty in front and behind. But just as yesterday we had not the slightest sign from either the Governor or Des Voeux, which is rather strange, unless English discretion consists in doing people a favour, without making contact with them or receiving thanks.

In my note to Des Voeux, I said all that I owed to the Governor and that I had no other way of making my feelings known to him to convey my most sincere thanks. I don't know what more I could have done. We are nonetheless extremely surprised by this way of acting which differs so much from our own customs and which contrasts so greatly with all the goodwill we continue to enjoy, by Adamson's order, from all the authorities.

While the authorities are perfect in their way, the Rangoon hoteliers, most of whom are Armenian, are brigands. They tried to make me stay a whole day again, counting four instead of three. And the Vilmorins, who only slept the night, were charged a whole day of 30 rupees at the hotel. We left the hotel around 8 o'clock in the evening, after a scene that I would have preferred to avoid, but really there was no other way.

It was another matter when we arrived at the station at about 8.10 pm, the train being at 8.30 pm, and found that everyone's luggage, which was considerable, had gone in a cart pulled by men and was still a long way from arriving. We spent a bad quarter of an hour there. The luggage didn't arrive until the signal for departure had been given. If it hadn't been for the intelligent and calm kindness of the stationmaster, who delayed the departure of the train and allowed our twenty coolies to arrive and throw everything they brought into our compartments, we would still be in Rangoon.

At last we were on the train. But it wasn't easy. From Moulmein on, the travel schedule should be more regular and easier to establish.

4 December 1912

I regret that none of the last three days spent in Rangoon could be devoted to visiting Pegu. I was about to leave at noon the day before yesterday, but I didn't have the courage at the last minute. I would have lacked food, a guide and a vehicle to get around in.

I should not regret it too much. Everyone agrees that the state of deterioration of the ruins is very marked and that, apart from the very well restored reclining Buddha, there are no remaining monuments to recall the great capital of Hangsawadi, founded in the 6th century by Thamala and Wimala, originally from Thaton.

Pegu or Hangsawadi, the city of the Sacred Goose, was known under the names of Bago, Ramanaya and Arramana.

Indebted to the Hindus of the south for their Buddhist civilisation, the inhabitants of Hangsawadi then passed on their civilisation to the Burmese, who more than once forgot everything they owed to the Peguans and even tried to supplant and annihilate them.

The destruction by the Burmese in the course of their various expeditions of all the existing Peguan chronicles has deprived us of an important part of the history of Hangsawadi during the 500 years preceding the conquest of the country by the Burmese of Anuratha, the famous king of Pagan. It seems that during this period there were conflicts between Brahmins and Buddhists in Pegu.

In the 13th century, the Tai Wareru, who had made himself king of Martaban, helped Pagan against Pegu, which eventually fell to him. This Wareru is a very interesting character whose destiny is singularly intertwined with the Siamese history of this period and whose biography is known to us from very ancient contemporary Peguan chronicles.

In the 15th century, Pegu successfully fought against the Burmese, whose main centre of activity was Pagan. In the 16th century, Pegu enjoyed a quiet period from time to time, but in 1551 Bureng Naung and his Burmese army set up their own capital there to put an end to the Talaing once and for all. In 1587, as the Burmese capital, Pegu fell into decline under the son of Bureng Naung. Finally, in 1740, a Peguan monarchy reappeared, which lasted until 1756, when it succumbed to the blows of Alompra.

Pegu, Hangsawadi never recovered from the destruction it suffered at the hands of the Burmese Alompra (Alaungpaya).

Since then the city has been in ruins. Apparently at the Shwe Madu pagoda there is a beautiful marble inscription recounting the deeds of the destroyer of Alompra city. So overall, I don't have many regrets about having missed a visit to the ruins of Hangsawadi.

We arrived at Martaban at 7.15 am, where a Burmese sent by Mr Dawson was waiting for us with the Government launch, which quickly removed all our baggage. In a quarter of an hour the longboat took us to the Moulmein wharf, where Commissioner Dawson, always so thoughtful, came to pick us up in a superb suspended landau belonging to some notable. He offered us every hospitality in his home and before treating us to a most comforting breakfast, took us for a short walk through the town.

We visited a very curious logging site, where the elephants performed all their usual exercises before our very eyes, carrying wood chips, planks and huge teak logs with their trunks and arranging them in piles, then moving other logs on the bank with their foreheads, trunks and tusks lined with iron and putting them in order in front of the assembly line that carries them to the saw.

One of these elephants, who is 50 years old and has been working for 30 years, seemed to us to be particularly skilful. He's one of the most beautiful animals of his kind I've ever seen. As a reward for his work, we gave him whole bunches of bananas and he thanked us by bowing deeply.

When we arrived at the police station, Mr Dawson introduced us to a Burmese interpreter who would accompany us to the border. We made arrangements for the transport of the luggage, the purchase of a supply of soda, petrol etc. and the crating of a thousand rupees in cash. What a bore all these preparations are, especially with boys who are not yet trained and who understand so little French! But Mr Dawson was untiringly helpful and the Vilmorins were delighted with the pretty specimens of orchids in flower that he gave them, including two Venus clogs orchids.

But now it was our turn to pay the price. Moulmein society had been on the lookout for us for three weeks, and it was essential that we introduced ourselves to them. We missed the ball which may have been organised in our honour and which took place yesterday, but we could not miss today's wedding, where our host, who disappeared very discreetly after breakfast to go about his business, had arranged to meet us at the end of the day. Henriette and Mélanie protested in the background, for lack of outfits and interest, but we had to go along with it nonetheless. And at 4 o'clock another carriage, just as sumptuous as this morning's, came to collect us and take us to the wedding and around the town.

I was delighted to see the main pagoda on the hill again, and the marvellous panorama it afforded. My companions were amazed at the extent and beauty of the landscape. Today, when I saw it at the end of the day, the view is better from the back than from the side of the river where the sun sets.

We made a vain attempt to meet the fathers and brothers at the French School, but we paid a brief visit to the Mother Superior. The works of both are numerous and flourishing, but they are aimed more at Hindus, Chinese and Eurasians than Burmese. There are two Catholic churches in Moulmein and a third under construction to which our compatriot Father de Chirac d'Apchier has devoted his life and fortune.

We met him at the house of Deputy Commissioner Frazer, where we ended our tour and where the wedding of the English delegate to Kokarit was taking place, a young man whose fiancée had arrived directly from England on the last liner. At the end of the day, the Deputy Commissioner's house, which has a view to the north and the Salween, is delightful. The whole house was decorated with roses and white orchids; an orchestra and young Burmese professional dancers brightened up the meeting. I made the acquaintance of a few Englishmen. One of them, Mac Nawght, is a member of the staff of the Siamese forestry service and is responsible for controlling the export to Burma of teak wood cut in the Siamese forests in the region. I also met up with Russel, the Bombay Burmah Company agent whom I met on my first visit and who had given me some information. We dined quite late after the party at Dawson's with the same Russel, Chirac's father, the bride's mother, Deputy Commander Frazer and another English lady. Father de Chirac, who is an excellent man but a little too laudatory, gave me a French speech in sonnets as a toast. None of the English understood, but we all drank to the Entente Cordiale, all the more willingly since Father de Chirac, whose community has many Eurasians who are part of the militia, has a British military chaplain's certificate.

We were falling asleep from exhaustion and as soon as possible begged to go to bed.

5 December 1912

One cannot imagine the kindness and eagerness of this excellent Dawson, who has paid us every attention. Lodged, housed, fed, transported and toasted by him and his brother, we spent a good night under this kindly hospitable roof.

At 9 am they took us to the boat that runs the regular daily service to Chandoo, where we occupied the bow reserved for Europeans, and where our boys served us lunch that the cook had prepared for us in the stern. Father de Chirac also came to say goodbye to us at the pier.

Like all the boats on the Irrawaddy Flotilla, our boat is extremely colourful and picturesque. The backdrop to the landscape is a number of small, jagged limestone massifs, which the winding course of the Attarang often skirts. The boat stopped at least a dozen times to drop off or pick up passengers.

We had been worried that the low water would prevent us from reaching Chandoo in time to push on to Kokarik that evening. Fortunately, this was not the case. We did touch the bottom for a moment, but we quickly freed ourselves and at 3.30 pm we arrived at the Kokarik landing stage. A pretty picture greeted our arrival with

Boats on the Moulmein river. (Lefèvre-Pontalis Archive)

Hindus, Chinese and Burmese in clusters near the jetty and several Burmese militia men in *panung* and amaranth turbans with swords in the air.

The main or only street of Chandoo is nicely shaded and the diversity of colourful merchants in the bazaar who thronged to see us was amusing. The English chief of police, Prinsep, has received instructions from Moulmein to facilitate our journey. He was waiting for us when we arrived with a rather dilapidated 5-seater car, a number of rickshaws and ox carts. We loaded our five people in the car, the boys and the luggage in several carts and at 4.30 we were off on a fairly good road that crosses a rather open forest where a few teak trees stand with beautiful straight trunks and give an English park air to these surroundings.

It was 15 miles from Chandoo to Kokarik. On reaching Kokarik, Captain Prinsep congratulated himself for having got us there safely, as four of the five cars belonging to the local private company that runs the service had broken down over the past month. It's true that where there's only room for four or five, the Burmese, like all Asians, cram in as many as 11 or 12.

So this is how far we've come on the first day, both on land and in the water, and the bungalow the Captain has put us up in is as comfortable as any we've seen before.

Like all the other difficulties, that of our mounts no longer exists. The perseverance and goodwill of the English authorities have triumphed. Not only do we have at our disposal four elephants that had to be brought from beyond Moulmein, 60 miles from Kokarik, but they also have four ponies with European saddles to offer us.

Prinsep made every effort to discourage us from taking the elephants. He is like the people of Moulmein who, despite their kindness, have always seemed a little afraid of taking on the responsibility for two foreign ladies on a trip. In reality, there is no serious reason to oppose us, but if Henriette and Mélanie were less determined to go through with what they wanted, there would certainly be things to discourage them.

As the Vilmorins want to keep as much freedom of movement as possible for plant collecting, they will be using two of the ponies tomorrow, while Henriette and I will take our first elephant ride.

We dined a little late at the bungalow because although the cook's carriage arrived very quickly in the evening, it's true, thanks to two relays en route, one should not be demanding on the first evening. The dinner was good, by the way.

Captain Prinsep, who dined with us, had a lot to say about the 24 years he has spent in Burma. He has travelled the length and breadth of the country and has had enough of the loneliness of the remote corners during the rainy season. He is retiring next year and, at the age of 50, will be making his home near Richmond in England.

He believes that Tavoy is a place in Tenasserim that is currently undergoing a certain amount of development, thanks to the rubber and wolfram mines that have been exploited there for some time. Kokarik is only a small centre with a population of 3,000, but it is very popular with caravans during the winter. He believes that we will meet some Yunnanese along the way. A number of them came here last month with their horses and mules. Among the products they bring is rice from Mae Sot in Siam, which sells here for twice as much as it does on the other side of the border. I'm very surprised by this because this country seems to lend itself much more to rice cultivation than the high valleys of Siam. It is an economic phenomenon that deserves further consideration.

According to Prinsep, teak has never been so abundant in Burma. This is what I heard from all sides. The Siamese are less happy on the Menam, he tells me, judging by the number of Bombay Burmah agents who now come to Burma because they have less to do in Siam.

Roads and railways are always on the agenda. He knows about the project I was told about the other day in Moulmein, which would consist of running a railway line towards the Three Pagodas route. This is not without interest, as such a line would obviously link up with the Malay Peninsula line without the Germans of the Central Railways of Siam having anything to do with it, whereas the Moulmein-Raheng line would undoubtedly come up against more than one opposition or foreign intervention.

As chief of police for this part of the border, the Captain is in close contact with his Siamese colleague Fabricius, who is Danish and whom we will no doubt meet in Mae Sot. Together they keep an eye on the comings and goings of suspicious people, and it seems that there is no shortage of them on the road. Prinsep showed us in the bungalow book the names of two English deserters who crossed into Siam after spending one night without paying in this official lodging. The regulations on the use of arms and ammunition are very strict in Burma and the most severe penalties are applied to natives carrying arms, while their ammunition is immediately burnt on the spot.

It is thanks to these strict and rigorous measures that the English are able to fight with some effectiveness against the old dacoity of the Shan and Burmese. There is a great abundance of cattle in all parts of the country, but especially in the frontier regions theft is easier and more common. The Hindus seem to be quite adept at it. There was one with handcuffs on the boat today and the Kokarik jail contains several black individuals accused of the same petty theft.

As long as it's just a question of cattle rustling, the police seem to be sufficient, but if, as happened two years ago, there is some sort of political insurrection, one wonders what resources could be counted on. There were about 200 fanatics in the region north of Sagaing who remembered the existence of King Thibaw near Bombay. They tried to revolt and raise the country. The Captain believes that the Burmese, who are very superstitious by nature although pleasant in their dealings with Europeans, are easy to draw into a movement of this kind.

The idea of the defence of the colony by the whites therefore sometimes arises among the less far-sighted, and this was a subject dear to the heart of Dawson's brother, the magistrate who played an important role in the militia and who seemed keen to rely on the Filipinos, the Eurasians and some of the clients of the Catholic Mission. Hence the excellent relations between the latter and the British authorities, even though it was run by French fathers.

As long as Thibaw and Myngoon live, there will still be many patriots in Burma. The English are letting Mandalay die its own death; they have reduced the garrison; they are not doing away with anything altogether, even pretending to respect the memories of the past and to show every form of consideration for the funeral of Thibaw's former queen wife, who died a few months ago and whose cremation took place in Mandalay. As for maintaining things that are falling into ruin more than they need to, that would be asking too much of them.

However, it is not so much in Mandalay as elsewhere that great memories can be evoked. Sagaing seems to mean much more to the Burmese soul. This is clearly evident as you pass this city of living temples overlooking the Irrawaddy. From his Indian exile, Thibaw finds it difficult to correspond with his friends in Burma. The Captain tells us that he is watched very closely, that a police officer is always at his side and that his entire correspondence is monitored. But basically, despite isolated expressions of loyalty to his homeland and the fallen dynasty, the Burmese do not seem to be on the verge of regaining the upper hand.

Gradually they are being submerged by the Hindus, who will feel more and more at home here once the railway networks have been joined together. Burmese women are already contributing to the suicide of the race by the ease with which they marry foreigners from India or China. As husbands, Burmese men are too lazy and too demanding. With any other man, the Burmese woman feels more at ease, and that's how things will gradually progress. The day will come when there will be no more Burmese. This is Prinsep's opinion, much less Dawson's, who insists to the contrary on the development of the Burmese race in the agricultural townships as shown by the latest statistics. They both agree in regretting anything that might contribute to the reduction of Burmese influence in this country, because the polite Burmese is a being that the English generally consider to be pleasant, intelligent and easy to live with, although far too lazy and short-sighted.

6 December 1912

Captain Prinsep, who does not seem to me to be in complete agreement with the Burmese chief of Kokarik on this subject, has changed our itinerary as follows. Tonight, we sleep eight miles away in Kokarik. Tomorrow in Sukli, 13 miles further on. The day after tomorrow, 18 miles further on, in Myawadi.

The Burmese interpreter we were given in Moulmein and the chief of Kokarik village both thought Sukli was a bad fevenish spot. Prinsep's impression of Misty Hollow caused him to advise as to avoid it as a stopping-off point. The Englishman also felt that we should stay as long as possible in Kokarik and use the car to go to tonight's stage, called Third Camp, which is only eight miles away.

Fortunately, the village authorities told us not to do anything. Experience in fact showed us that we would not have got a third of the way along this poorly maintained road without breaking our machine. What's more, this Englishman, used to living alone, is a gossip without judgement, the only one of his kind we met on our journey. We had him on our backs until 3 o'clock. The ox carts had preceded us by about an hour. Henriette and I each got on our elephant. The Vilmorins left a little later on horseback.

All this was not achieved without difficulty, with a gentle anarchy reigning in our group, where everyone had their own ideas and wanted to follow them, and where boys, mahouts and ox drivers did as they pleased or went their own way. This morning at the market, we accompanied the Chinese cook Patte so that he could make all the essential purchases for at least three days' walking. It was impossible to persuade him to buy enough. It is hard to imagine how unforgiving, demanding and difficult these people are. At a time when it is so difficult to get chickens, eggs and milk, Patte wants to choose and lets opportunities slip through his fingers. You have to think of everything for everyone, and you come up against all kinds of resistance. Fortunately, things will settle down on the way, but the beginnings were not perfect.

Elephant trip to Myawadi. (Lefèvre-Pontalis Archive)

Henriette enjoyed herself like a queen on her elephant, where she sat very comfortably, carrying a Burmese umbrella made of oiled paper for shelter and looking extremely appropriate for the occasion. One of the four animals has strong tusks and is said to be a little more skittish than the others. We perched Patte and his kitchen on it, but he was only partially reassured.

Our mahouts are Karen who have come a long way, having travelled some sixty miles to be at our disposal. They look gentle and, except for their cropped hair, are quite indistinguishable from Burmese of the humblest class. All in all, our four animals seem very quiet, but they hate to smell other animals in front of or behind them on the road, and will swerve or sniff loudly when close to an ox or a dog. All in all, I have never had to deal with such peaceful elephants.

The road was fairly ordinary for the eight miles between Kokarik and Third Camp. This is the end of the wooded plain, but the vegetation is mediocre, with clearings or rice fields and the occasional hut. The best thing is the beautiful wooded heights of the Dewana hills, which we are getting closer to all the time and can often be seen in the evening light.

We arrived at sunset at the Third Camp bungalow, which was well set up like the others but with only two beds, so in addition to our ordinary bedding, our camp beds were not useless this time. There was good, clear water from the nearby stream, which we certainly took advantage of. It's too rare everywhere else.

The Vilmorins arrived a few moments behind us and the carts very shortly afterwards. But the days are so short at this time of year and night falls so quickly that settling in at the stopping place is not made any easier. It's also very cool, but not cold. The boys do what they can, but it's not easy in the dark. Nevertheless, Patte's dinner was excellent.

7 December 1912

Third Camp is at the foot of the first slopes of the Dewana hills, about nine miles from Misty Hollow, where the Captain advised us to venture only for lunch, as the place is shrouded in unhealthy mists both in the morning and in the evening.

At daybreak Philippe de Vilmorin was on his feet, as was his wife, who was determined to follow him. She had given up riding one of our four ponies with her Chinese silk trousers, as she had done yesterday, and bravely set off on foot to climb the Dewana hills, green collecting boxes slung over her shoulder.

At 7.30 am Henriette and I, weighed down at least by hot chocolate, eggs and toast, took our turn following them on foot, as the weather is fine and cool. Our two elephants accompanied us closely, as well as the two others on which my two boys were perched with the interpreter and everything we needed for lunch. Biane, the Vilmorins' Chinese boy, stayed behind with the five carts of luggage.

Henriette and I walked up the mountainside for an hour and a half until 9 o'clock. The road was sometimes very bad and the oxen had a hard time of it. Such a road cannot be considered passable for carriages, as the English had proposed to make it a few years ago, at the time of the de la Jonquière voyage, but as it is, it is very practicable for elephants and horses.

The higher up you go, the more splendid the view becomes of the entire wooded plain that stretches between Moulmein and the mountains bordering the Salween basin. Between the tall tree trunks, the forest that stretches down into the plain, occasionally interspersed with clearings or rice fields, is as extensive as it is beautiful. Its beauty is enhanced by the few limestone boulders or massifs that emerge from the low forest in the direction of Moulmein.

By 11 o'clock we were at the summit and by midday we were at Misty Hollow, in one of those high clearings to which I am accustomed and where the air is so pure. At midday there was a delicious breeze. A few oxen were grazing on rare grass next to the tall trees and you could still see some of the limestone boulders in the distance. It was excellent.

We stayed there longer than we would have liked, however, as the elephants had been carelessly allowed to go into the jungle and the ox carts themselves did not arrive until 4 o'clock, without the boys having been able to have their lunch.

We had to talk somewhat forcefully to leave at 4.20, the latest possible so as not to arrive at the Sukli stage before nightfall. Our two wives travelled by elephant. As for me, I preferred to walk the four miles between Misty Hollow and Sukli with Philippe.

Sukli is on the opposite side of the plateau from Misty Hollow on the

Siamese side. The bungalow backs onto extremely cool ravines where the virgin forest reigns. I understand what the Burmese meant when they spoke of the excessive coolness of this place. Henriette understands it too, because either damp or tired, she feels uncomfortable enough to go to bed without dinner. Patte had 3 hours to prepare the said dinner, but at 9 o'clock it had not yet been served, and everyone, boys and people alike, was in a rather bad mood, even though this stage had been easy on the whole and the first part of the journey quite interesting.

In this dark brown bungalow, where we were only too happy to find everything we needed to spend a peaceful night, a bouquet of fresh roses brought by the caretaker surprised and delighted us. At an altitude of no more than 500 metres, as the Wat Doi pass is only 450 metres high, these roses, grown on the slopes of the Dewana hills, and the cool evening and night air gave a real illusion of France.

8 December 1912

Sunday and the feast of the Immaculate Conception. The marvels of Creation, glimpsed in one of the most beautiful virgin forests I have ever travelled through, enabled us to lift our souls to God with gratitude and admiration.

Between 5.30 and 7.30 am it was long and difficult to get going, but

Elephant trip to Myawadi. (Lefèvre-Pontalis Archive)

once we had set off, everything went like clockwork. Straight away we found ourselves in the virgin forest and the surprise for my companions was immense.

Philippe had gone ahead on foot, Henriette and Mélanie were leading the way with their elephants, mine following empty, as I was at the front of the convoy. The fourth elephant was occupied by my boy Ahine and the lunch. The wagons followed close behind, with the cook Patte on a pony. Under these conditions, and with the cart drivers having been ordered to take the lead during the lunch break, there was some chance that the convoy would be better organised than yesterday and that dinner would be ready on time, although the stage to Myawadi is 18 miles, five more than yesterday.

The not too humid fresh morning air, as we were for about two hours well below the fog, which forms like an immense lake with islands below the trees at our feet, seemed truly delicious. There was still no sun to bother us and until 9.30 we missed nothing of the unforgettable spectacle offered to us by the virgin forest.

The gibbons were calling to each other from the treetops with their long, sonorous, charming call. Squirrels leapt across the road. Several times I saw large birds that appeared to be jungle fowl, which would make delicious roast meat, fluttering along the path. I counted as many as five. Henriette and Mélanie said they saw a monkey.

It is difficult to describe the beauty of the forest. Gigantic ferns, sago and wild banana trees abound under the immense trees, some of which were over fifty metres tall. The flora was charming too, with violet-flowered lianas and species of periwinkle and begonias that grow in every cool corner. Every little nook and cranny from which a stream flowed with its pure waters aroused our admiration for the wealth of vegetation it concealed. Below us, when these was an opening towards the distant plain through the tall columns of trees, we could see the sea of white fog condensing, and we dreamt of fairy tales and fantastic landscapes. In the midst of all this, the majesty of our elephants advancing slowly with the foreign ladies who ride them, completed the impressive grandeur of the spectacle. The strangest moment was when our caravan came up against a large tree that the storm had brought down across the path. It was impossible to get round it, even though Melanie's mahout was preparing to bravely launch his elephant into the ravine to attack the top of the obstructing tree. So the elephants were unloaded and reloaded after passing through the arch. The movements of these beasts, their crouching in this magnificent place, was very evocative. It was a pity that the lack of sunlight prevented us from using our Kodak.

This incident took place at the 40th mile from Kokarik. My companions and I were thrilled, especially when it was over and the three of us were back on our mounts. It could have been worse, because just as the elephants were being unloaded, some Hindus arrived from the opposite direction with loaded horses. It took some effort to make them understand that they had to turn back at all costs, as the slopes were too narrow on both sides to allow the horses to hide from the cowardly elephants and or to face them without becoming terrified. Fortunately, our elephants kept quiet, but in the process of turning back, one of the Hindus' horses ran away.

You can't imagine how uncompromising our elephants are. I think they are more proud and authoritarian than cowardly. They want to have the road free and clear for themselves. They don't want to share it with anyone, but among themselves they are sensitive to rank. Henriette's intelligent, easy-going beast has the honour of leading the way. The handsome male with the long tusks, who is thought to be a bit of a handful and carries the kitchen, generally walks at the back. I'm convinced he doesn't like it. In any case, on the way he saw fit to overtake me and when my mahout tried to regain his position, the beautiful animal let out such a roar and lunged with such energy from his tusks at mine that we had a moment's concern.

Crossing the virgin forest lasted two whole hours and we were able to enjoy it in a relaxed fashion without getting bored. At 9.30 am the landscape became less beautiful. We were at the bottom of the descent. A few small Karen fields with tobacco, and papaya trees signalled we were near human habitation. We followed the clear little stream that la Jonquière called the Pakthang Kan, because that is the Thai name for the hamlet of Thinganniung that it waters and which we reached at 11 o'clock sharp after having travelled 8 ½ miles from Sukli.

There's an official English bungalow there, modelled on all the others we've seen. This easy half-stage was comfortably completed by all. Philippe was there waiting for us, Kodak in hand. Lunch arrived at the same time as we did. Luggage, boys and carts too. They didn't stop and pushed straight on to Myawadi, leaving us to have our lunch and rest behind until 2.30 pm.

Beyond Thinganniung, a small oasis with rice paddies at the foot of the Dewana hills, we came to the dry, white earth forest, all teak and dyptocarp trees with orchids, flowerless at this time of year, growing on the trunks or hanging from the trees. For the first time, all four of us were on elephants, but the nine miles that separated us from Myawadi seemed a little long and monotonous. A few hamlets with small rice fields, where parakeets and other scavenging birds have a field day at harvest time, broke the monotony.

The kitchen arrived ahead of us. By a quarter to 6 we were all in the stage bungalow which was a brilliant result and the excellent dinner was also on time.

I was given a telegram dated the 6th in which Maugras told me that the boats we requested will be waiting for us on the 12th at Raheng. As for our new convoy, having arrived at the border, we must change here according to what the village chief tells me. Captain Fabricius of the Siamese police came yesterday from Mae Sot with 150 men, thinking he would find us in Meerawaddi. He left with his people, but as Mae Sot is only three miles away, it's not difficult to get there. So I immediately wrote to Fabricius that I would wait here tomorrow for him to send us the necessary means of transport to reach Mae Sot as soon as possible and be able to leave this place on Tuesday to reach Raheng quickly.

We took advantage of the evening to catch up on our correspondence and send our New Year's Day mail by the Indian route. It was one last chance, because after that we'll only have the mail from Bangkok on the day we arrive.

It's cold and damp here. This evening the thermometer dropped to 16° and will probably fall further during the night.

According to Bastian, who took this information from the *Annals of Martaban*, this Meerawaddi was the capital of a Lawa kingdom whose western border was at Kokarik and which embraced the whole territory of Chiang Mai, Labong and Lakhon.

When Wareru, or Makatho or Farua, took possession of the crown of Martaban in 1287, he attacked the capital of this kingdom, which was called Kalamani and was not far from Martaban. In the king's absence, he kidnapped his wives and pillaged the city, then married his daughter. When the king came to attack him, he pretended to come to an understanding with him, and invited him to a feast where he poisoned him and his companions. This is the origin of the great successes of the famous Tai prince Wareru.

Bastian claims to have seen the ruins of Kalamani or Kaupalene in the forest near Thinganniung.

According to the chronicle, Wareru took his magic sword from the king of Meerawaddi, who was a Lawa prince. The fame of this sword spread as far as Tavoy, whose prince offered him a marvellous emerald in exchange. Instead of the magic sword, Wareru sent him a rusty old one and kept the emerald, which he hid in the pagoda of Mya Thein Dau.

The rusty sword was thrown into the sea, but as it worked miracles, attempts were made to catch it. Every swimmer who came near, was killed by a blow from its edge. So they gave up trying to pull it out of the sea, and where it fell, the waves have been bubbling ever since.

I asked one of the Meerawaddi notables about the location of Kaupalene. He replied that it was quite close to Thinganniung, but to the north and not in the direction we came here. The ruins of the old town are in the jungle. The pagodas are completely ruined, but apparently you can still make out some traces of the walls.

My informant, who is Burmese, told me that Kaupalene was an ancient Karen city. When I told him about the Lawa and asked him if these people were of the same race as the Karen, he said no; that the Lawa are further north, towards Mainlaunggyee; that the Karen, on the other hand, are people from this country. They rarely come to Meerawaddi and stay in the jungle. The nearest are about fifteen miles from here. There are none in the village. Both men and women are dressed in a long, drooping tunic. It seems that we will see them more easily in Mae Sot. However, the 150 men who came to meet us the day before yesterday were not Karen but Shan.

According to la Jonquière, Myawadi is none other than the ancient Amarapati, re-established on the site of the ancient city discovered some fifty years ago by Khamuk, who had come to settle there. It was in these parts that the famous king of Siam, Phra Naret, died in the 17th century during one of his campaigns against the Burmese who ruled at Hangsawadi. This is also where the famous Burmese king Alongpra died in the 18th century, pursued by the Siamese. This was in 1760, but it is true that five years later, in 1765, the situation changed in favour of the Burmese, who have never since lost the exercise of their authority in this extreme part of the Tenasserim territory. Since 1825, Meerawaddi, along with the rest of Tenasserim, has formed part of the British possessions and comes under the jurisdiction of the Commissioner of Moulmein.

9 December 1912

It's very pleasant after a hard stage to be able to laze around a bit the next morning. We had to spend the whole morning in Myawadi because we had to change staff and mounts to get to the border, and none of us complained.

Philippe went hunting to kill some turtle doves for dinner. We wandered around the merchants where we found some milk, candles and flour that we'd been missing. The Burmese-style pagoda, the last one we would see, was quite unusual if dilapidated, with its white pyramid with a golden crown and multi-storey wooden pavilions. We spent a few moments there Kodak in hand. Philippe walked as far as he could with the elephants, because to our great regret, that's the end of that kind of locomotion for the rest of our trip. I learned this morning from the Siamese who were sent to me from Mae Sot with a whole gang of coolies, that there are no elephants available on the Siamese border, as they are all currently being used for teak by the logging companies.

Nothing is stranger than this band of people, appearing from all sides of the village with their large bamboos to carry the luggage. There were already 150 of them the day before yesterday, and they had waited in vain for us with Major Fabricius on the other side of the Nam Meuy, which forms the border at this point. Today there are fewer of them, but still more than enough for our service.

They also brought from Mae Sot two sedan chairs made from rattan armchairs supported by two large wooden rods. They are very heavy

Coolies en route between Myawadi and Mae Sot. (Lefèvre-Pontalis Archive)

and as impractical as possible for the men of the gendarmerie whose job it is to carry our two wives.

They were somewhat annoyed, as they were used to their elephants and were ill-equipped to ride astride, as there were no ladies' saddles either.

Fortunately there was no shortage of ponies and the boys could be on horseback. Henriette and Mélanie decided to try the chair, but to be ready for anything, they put on the plum silk Chinese trousers they had bought for this purpose before leaving Kokarik and the red Karen belts they had also bought at the market. They look amusing so attired, and I think they're perfectly equipped for this kind of trip.

It was only after we had been assured of all this that we let the elephants go, after having paid them. To the mahouts I gave 60 rupees plus 10 as a tip because they had a long way to go to get home and two rupees a day is a singularly low price for the hire of an animal of this species. I only paid the agreed price of 48 rupees in all to the drivers of the five ox carts, who owned them themselves with 47 rupees to the drivers of the horses, including 15 as a tip.

The departure of the elephants one way and the coolies and chairs to the other gave rise to new photographs. We sealed our letters to France, Kokarik and Moulmein, which Baba, our Burmese interpreter, will post once he has taken us to Mae Sot. It's between three and four miles from Myawadi to Mae Sot. It took us almost three hours, between 2 and 5 pm, to reach there, but our gendarmes were so unaccustomed to carrying chairs that immediately after Nam Meuy Mélanie and Henriette decided to abandon this inconvenient means of transport and they finished the journey on foot in the fine sand of the road and in the mud of the small streams, a journey of little interest.

The most interesting part of the route was crossing the Nam Meuy in a hollow canoe. The river is shallow at this time of year and the coolies forded it, as did the horses. Beyond that, the road passes through bush that is less dry than that at Thinganniung, with bamboo and a few rice fields, but it's boring and monotonous to do on foot.

Philippe, who, along with the boys on horseback, had beaten us to Mae Sot, came to meet us as we left the village, with Captain Fabricius, one of the Danes who has reorganised the Siamese gendarmerie and who, with his chief Phra Tcha Koun, with the rank of Colonel, constituted the delegation of the metropolitan authority in this frontier region. Phra Tcha Koun received me a little further on, at the same time as the village *ampheu*.

I hardly concealed from Major Fabricius my annoyance at seeing things organised so differently from the way I would have liked. Without elephants, without ladies' saddles, without any facilities other than the general's tent sent from Bangkok by Prince Chakrabongse and which, in principle, was never intended for that purpose but for quite occasional use, our wives will be badly housed, and more often than not obliged to walk, as the chairs are worse than useless.

Fabricius was apologetic, but it's not his fault. He only learned of our forthcoming visit a few days ago, on his return from a two-month tour. Everything was arranged from afar by the Governor of Raheng Phra Sak Ta Ruong Lit, who no doubt misunderstood the orders from Bangkok.

Fabricius offered to make up for the inadequacy of these preparations as far as possible. He obtained the Colonel's authorisation to go and prepare, at least as far as Palot, the stage lodgings in the villages rather than in the forest clearings where no bamboo *sala* had been built for us. For this night, he put his own house at our disposal and improved the chairs by doubling the number of porters and substituting bamboo uprights for the heavy wooden ones.

Stopover lodge between Myawadi and Mae Sot. (Lefèvre-Pontalis Archive)

It is very cool in the evening here, as in the previous cottages. After dinner, however, we went to watch a Burmese dance in front of the Colonel's house, where two little girls and a very agile boy entertained us for half an hour, although their dances were less skilful than those of Pagan. What was most notable was the crowd, well lit by an acetylene lamp, with the men's faces shrivelled up in Burmese style, under red, green and yellow turbans, and the colourful blankets in which all those present, crouching or standing, are draped.

Mae Sot is a rather nice place with 300 houses, where the Hindu element is still represented and where the Burmese seem as numerous as the Yellows. There are many coconut trees in the gardens and the main street is lined with shops selling fabrics, knick-knacks, milk, tea, coffee, etc, where you can buy a few essential items. The hardest thing to get is Siamese money in exchange for Hindu rupees. However, I managed to collect 250.

Our boys who found a Chinese man from Hainan here were very struck by what they heard him say about the health conditions of the place. According to him, all the Chinese living in Mae Sot had recently been taken by an epidemic. So they had a lot to tell us about this. It's upsetting for the men who are a bit overstretched by the trek, the speed of the stages, the hasty work, the cold nights and the horses that make their behinds sore.

10 December 1912

In consultation with Major Fabricius, here are the places we have agreed for this part of our journey:

1° Mae Sot-Melamao = 16 miles with lunch stop at the Manola clearing.

2° Melamao-Palot = 10 miles with no stop en route.

3° Palot-Metok = 18 miles with lunch stop at Pang Nam Jai.

4° Métok to Raheng = 12 miles

I've heard that the penultimate stage is pretty tough. As for the last stage, it's not long, but we'll do well to cut it short and have lunch en route before arriving.

I was a little emotional to see Henriette astride her horse when we left Mae Sot at 8 o'clock this morning, but as she often alternated

Crossing the ford at Mae Sot. (Lefèvre-Pontalis Archive)

between her horse and her chair, it worked out well, albeit slowly. Leaving Mae Sot, we immediately entered the forest. It was quite green and fresh and became more beautiful as we approached the three curious limestone peaks of Paklène on the left and Khawa and Nak Boa on the right. These are three very high perpendicular blocks with such, marvellously jagged tops, that I have never seen a more unusual silhouette. Below one of them, along the road, the natives have erected a small bamboo altar dedicated to the local genie. As we passed, it was adorned with marigolds and our coolies knelt down to pray to the one who could guarantee them a happy journey.

Before reaching this spot we had stopped for two hours in the pretty Manola clearing, one where the Governor of Raheng had suggested us could spend the night.

The place was inviting, spacious and clean, and when Henriette and Mélanie saw the bathroom on the stream, the two toilets, the bamboo kitchen, and the poles set up at either end of the camp for the acetylene lamps, they almost regretted having rejected the night camp in the forest, but it's so cold and damp at this time of year that even the smallest roof of planks or straw is preferable.

The three limestone peaks we admired belong to the Phra Wa massif, which separates several tributaries of the Nam Meuy, which flows directly into the Salween. It is undoubtedly these famous peaks that gave rise to the legend of Wareru, who set off as a merchant from Martaban on his way to Sukhothai, his family's homeland. He followed the same route as us in the opposite direction and suddenly saw a dream palace standing out against the sky, which a soothsayer told him was the sign of his future kingship. Emboldened by this omen, he arrived in Sukhothai where he entered the service of the Siamese king. Having won the confidence of this prince, who was none other than the famous Phra Ruang, he took advantage of his absence to seduce one of his daughters with whose treasures he returned to Martaban, where his fortune, his audacity, favourable circumstances and the forgiveness of his father-in-law enabled him to carve out a principality for himself, which he soon transformed into a kingdom. This was a great event in the history of the Tai, for it meant that their race took possession of the mouths of the Salween and the east coast of the Bay of Bengal. if Phra Ruang was so indulgent towards the abductor of his daughter, it was because he appreciated that this bold move and this success was worthy of his own methods and efforts. From that moment on, the Siamese kings who succeeded him exercised their suzerainty over Martaban, Moulmein and the Tenasserim adjacent for centuries.

I knew this legend, which my friend Hardouin had extracted from the *Chronique des Môn*, and I had always found it evocative. The look of the place confirmed my opinion. Few rocks are more expressive and the poetry of the immense surrounding forest is very great.

The view is best appreciated when, coming from Raheng in the morning, you descend the slopes of Phra Wa and, amidst the gigantic bamboo that covers the sheer flanks, you catch a glimpse of the jagged peaks of the three rocks as you descend a steep path. In the afternoon, we turned our backs on this spectacle, while the rocks were against the light and our horses, panting and in a hurry, climbed the steep path as best they could.

As we climbed, a vast panorama of mountain slopes and wooded valleys appeared in every direction below or through the gigantic bamboo, magnificently lit, but without the slightest trace of human habitation. It was all very beautiful and grandiose. But the path got worse and worse; the stricken horses had two terrible ascents and descents to complete in succession, and on more than one occasion we were obliged to rid them of their burdens by dismounting. I greatly admired Henriette's energy, as this was her first serious ride. We were on the road from 8 am to 5 pm, stopping for just under two hours at the Manola clearing. And God knows what 'roads' these were for pedestrians and horsemen alike. At many points it was just the track of the telegraph line.

At 5 o'clock, however, we emerged at the bottom of the second descent into a small rice field where the only street in the village of Melamao begins. The notables who had been notified by Major Fabricius were there to receive us. They took us to the far end of the village, near the pagoda, to a house belonging to a notable of the village, where there were neither beds nor tables, but which Fabricius had had cleaned and where we could enjoy a fine view of the Melamao valley. The colonel and Fabricius came to have dinner with us and, as the coolies had arrived on time, we had a good evening to rest up.

The stage had perhaps been a little tiring because of the climbs and especially the difficult descents on foot, but it was the bush, the real bush in its wildest nature that my companions had just seen for the first time. They were delighted and the character of our camp, which was more primitive than the previous ones, did not displease them.

11 December 1912

Philippe and I slept on the boards with our thin mattress and pillows and our wives could see that we didn't sleep any the worse for it. As today's stage was to be very short we took advantage of that to sleep in a bit more and we didn't leave until 8.30 am – Fabricius did the stage in two hours as far as Palot. Henriette did it in a chair, so our journey took just over three hours, even though there are barely 10 miles between Melamao and Palot.

The village of Melamao lies on the river of the same name, much like Myawadi on the Nam Meuy. The Melamao is a pretty, fast-flowing river, but clear and shallow at this time of year. We forded it.

On the other side, the bamboo forest begins again, on slightly uneven and often even flat terrain, with two small villages with rice fields in the clearing. One is called Ban Huay Sak, the other Ban Chiang Khong, and it was near the latter, in a clearing as beautiful as yesterday's, that we were expected to stop, if not for the stage then at least for lunch. As it was about halfway along the road to Palot, we continued on our way, stopping only to admire the bamboo toilet, bath and kitchen facilities. The only thing missing was the main house.

About an hour before reaching Palot, the forest changed and became dry. The bamboo disappeared and the teak and dipterocarp trees took their place.

We ended up descending by means of a steep slope on the banks of the clear Huay Palot stream, in a clearing where Palot's few huts are shaded by a small number of coconut trees. Ducks were on the stream. On the other side of the water, a much steeper path than the one we followed today. It's the harbinger of tomorrow's troubles, when we'll have to climb the peaks from where we can see the promised land, the waters of the Menam basin.

The place is charming with its little green clearing on the bank of the stream where the first coolies to arrive washed off the dust from the road and rested. As the old wooden house we were offered was too small for our two households, Henriette found it was an excellent opportunity to make use of the beautiful general's tent that Prince Chakrabongse had put at our disposal. So, we pitched the tent on the banks of the stream and left the Vilmorins the use of the house. Henriette was thus able to add one more impression to all those that have captivated her during her journey.

Our camp was the most complete we have ever had. Our people rested and put things in order under our supervision. A lot of food has been lost or stolen along the way. We need to know what we still have until we arrive in a civilised country.

At about 3.30 pm, we were visited by a whole Karen family who live in the mountains nearby and who, at my request, Colonel Phra Tcha Kun brought down to Palot. There were two women, two children and four or five men. The men are distinguished by their necklaces of silver, small pearls or varnished rattan, and the bone or wooden earrings or the large yellow flowers in their earlobes. Their hair is cropped; they differ markedly from one another, but nothing definitively distinguished them from the mixed populations of Tai or Burmese origin who live in this region. It is rather in the two women with slanted eyes and thick lips that the distinctive racial type appeared. One was really pretty and the other ugly, but they were equally pleasing in their big white canvas shirts with a few sketchy designs in red thread running down to their feet. They too had flowers and scented herbs in their earlobes and wore a few silver bracelets. We photographed them and let them go fairly quickly under the guidance of an old man, the only one of them who knows how to speak Thai. They were all in a hurry to get back to their villages before dark.

For my part, I was delighted to have met these specimens of the old indigenous race that abounds in the region, as long as these wooded mountains, where fields are so rare, are really inhabited. In any case, these Karen live with extreme care as far away from the beaten track as possible. The path we are following may often be an appalling footpath, but it is one of the great roads of Indochina. The telegraph runs alongside it. The police stations at Mae Sot and Metok keep an eye on it and the foresters from the big teak companies have used it for a long time. However, it does not seem that they are very active there now. Forests that were logged too extensively have had to be abandoned, such as that of Mae Sot, which Bombay Burmah stopped exploiting 15 years ago. This allows young teak trees to develop, and there are quite a few of them.

As for the caravans, we hardly came across any pack oxen and no Yunnanese mules at all. A few groups of Shan or Laotian, with two bamboo baskets carefully covered with bark on their shoulders, were the only travellers we met whether walking or stopped in clearings around their fires and rice.

In Melamao last night, at the pagoda, there were two Yunnanese Chinese, good-looking, smiling young men whose braids had been cut and who had with them a wild-looking Chinese woman. As for the famous mule caravans, we didn't see a single one. The locals say it's still too early in the season. However, in Moulmein they told me they had already seen one of these caravans arrive at the end of last month. In any case, there don't seem to be many of them.

12 December 1912

The night went well in our little camp at Palot, which has quite a bad reputation and which, given its location at the bottom of a damp hole, must be very unhealthy indeed during the rainy season. It wasn't as cold as the previous nights, but because of the damp the boys had another very bad night and complained a lot when they woke up. The Vilmorins settled in the telegrapher's house and we in the general's tent sent by Prince Chakrabongse, which, equipped with everything we needed, seemed perfectly comfortable.

We went to bed at about 8.15 pm having finished our night early. By 4 am I was no longer asleep, and by 5.30 the whole camp was on its feet.

Fabricius left us here to return to Mae Sot, and we set off ourselves at a quarter to seven, as we were told that the route was long and difficult, about 18 miles, but with terrible neck-breakers on the way up and down.

When we arrived at 3.15 pm at the Metok stop, Henriette and Mélanie, who had nevertheless travelled the whole way on foot and on horseback without using the chair, said that it had seemed rather short to them. In fact, we didn't dawdle on the way, and it was a good thing we didn't, because if we had let ourselves go in the slightest, we'd have quickly become enervated on this difficult road and we wouldn't have arrived until nightfall.

The most dreadful climb began as soon as we left Palot. As we climbed and reached the summit, the view became magnificent. Like yesterday when we climbed Pa Wa, there was a sea of forest on all sides, on the slopes of the mountains, on the peaks and in the valleys. The fairly low Pa Wa range came into view with its three rocky peaks, which didn't seem to stand out from the rest of the massif.

The path, which is very poor, continued to follow the telegraph line, skirting the ridges of the high valleys covered with tall bamboo alternating with superb *mai yang* trees with such slender, powerful trunks. Every hour or so, we came across a vast clearing set up for caravans, with stakes that have been used to tether pack oxen and extinguished fireplaces. The first of these is called Pang Ma Kam Pone. We passed it at around 8.30 am, an hour and a half after leaving Palot and starting the ascent of this terrible Doi Tai Chan, which will take us the whole stage.

By 9.30 am, we were on the summit. Below us was spread out the double clearing of Pang Pong Long, surrounded by tall trees in the manner of a theatrical landscape. It is all the more beautiful because the background of this sloping landscape is formed by the rounded tops of fine trees reminiscent of an English park with blue-green heights in the background.

Little by little, the vegetation became more abundant, as water was nearby. We had reached the high valley of the Metok torrent, which cascades abruptly down below a forest which, although not as wonderful as that of Sukli, is truly worthy of admiration. The middle of the valley is clear of trees and the Metok descends in a clear stream. Perhaps that's why the virgin forest seemed a little less impressive to us, because we're just skimming the surface of its mysteries. But there were enough tall trees, enough lianas, enough ferns, sago palms and wild banana trees to make the whole valley extremely interesting. Its particular charm consists in these beautiful glades with their noble allure. At 10.15 am we reached the one at Pang Nam Yai, where travelling monks had stopped and the yellow of their robes and the red of their Shan bags mingled with the greenery.

It was in this clearing that our evening lodging had been prepared for us, and the place would have been attractive if we had had a dwelling or two tents, but here as elsewhere we had made the mistake of thinking that our single tent would suffice. We stayed there for two hours to have lunch and rest and at 12.30 we set off again. It was a bad time to be travelling, because after the great coolness of the morning, the sun began to heat up just as we left the most shaded part of the valley and had to climb up and down steep red slopes once again.

The path kept crossing the Metho, but between the rocks of the torrent, which often form a waterfall, parts of the track were sometimes terrible, so that this section of the route can be considered one of the worst.

However, at around 2.30 pm we arrived on relatively flat ground. At one of the difficult spots on the road, Mélanie fell off her horse. Fortunately she didn't hurt herself too badly, but her mood was a bit dampened.

At 3.15 we arrived in Metho. A little before the entrance to the hamlet a camping place had been prepared for us. We would have preferred to set up in the gendarmerie cleaned up for our use. But as it was completely open at the front, a room was made with fabrics for the Vilmorins and we had the tent pitched for us where we were very comfortable.

We had a good end to the day to clean up and rest.

13 December 1912

A short stage. As we would not have much to do in Raheng, we agreed to extend our rest this morning until 8.30. Everyone would be better off, although we would be more likely to suffer the midday heat en route.

Metho is a small hamlet of around ten huts situated on the river of the same name, just like Myawadi. We forded at the river after the last hut in the hamlet. On the other side, the bush began again. We followed the valley of the Metho, which flows at a gentle slope with many twists and turns. We crossed it eight times. Fortunately, the water was not too deep at this time of year. On the sandbanks, which were still damp, we found elephant tracks and perhaps a few claws.

By 10.15 we were in the Ta Chane clearing, the last on the water's edge. Although it was very early, the Colonel advised us to stop for lunch under the bamboo on the banks of the Metho. Mélanie was grumpy and Philippe took the rap.

At noon we were on the road again, but this time it was brutally hot in the dry forest full of oil trees without shade, where the horses refuse to advance. So at about 1.30 pm we were happy to come across the first crossing paths in the forest, which were an indication that inhabited places were nearby. Then came a few clearings and at a quarter to two we finally reached the top of the red ridge overlooking the Mae Ping valley, from where we could see on the left the fairly high peaks from which we had just descended. Yesterday, at about a thousand metres above sea level, we came across the headwaters of the Metho, but at the point where we reached the Mae Ping we couldn't see the confluence of this river, which was hidden in the forest.

We arrived at the Mae Ping at a brisk trot. We passed gardens shaded by coconut palms. The path had been swept for us, but not all the grey dust had been removed. The Laotians sat on their heels watching us pass in front of their houses. At 2 o'clock we reached the river, in a charming spot shaded by tall trees under which Burmese Shan are resting on their way to Paknampho. The light and colours were perfect and, especially after this long ride through the bush and mountains, we were quite seduced by the panorama of Raheng which appeared as a completely civilised place on the other side of the wide Mae Ping where dugout canoes are beached near the sandbanks.

It was not at this pretty spot that the authorities were waiting for us, but a little further up the river, at a sunny beach where shelters had been erected and we were offered refreshing coconuts.

Phra Sak Ta Ruong Lit, Governor of Raheng for the last ten years or so, was there to welcome us in his blue *sampot* and white jacket with gold buttons. At first glance he seemed extremely unintelligent, which is no doubt an excuse for the mistakes he made during our trip. There is no question that he has not been inactive, but he has misunderstood our needs and even though we have arrived and are happy, we still miss our temporary camps and our elephants.

Near the beach were a number of white-painted houseboats. These comfortable wooden boats were inspired by the native pirogues of Chiang Mai and Mae Ping, with their fortified cabins at the stern. Ours has a double cabin running the full width of the boat, with a middle section that can be closed off and turned into a toilet.

The Vilmorins' boat is a little smaller but just as comfortable. The boys and the kitchen have another. The Colonel and some of the civilian mandarins who are going back down to Paknampho or Nakon Sawan will also have two boats. They would have liked us to make the journey in five stages so that we could take advantage of the facilities prepared for us at the stopping places, but I stated very clearly that I intend to be able to catch the train to Bangkok at Paknampho on Wednesday at 10.30 am and they promised to make arrangements for that.

Boats borrowed by Pontalis and Vilmorin on the Mae Ping.
(Lefèvre-Pontalis Archive)

With all our luggage deposited in the boats, we got on board to cross the Mae Ping, which took at least 20 minutes, as the point where the Moulmein road ends on the right bank is a little above the official part of the town of Raheng, namely the group of huts which cover both banks of the river shaded by coconut palms and which are home to nearly 20,000 inhabitants under the authority of a Governor reporting to the Commissioner of the *monthon* of Nakhon Sawan. The bulk of the population is on the left bank, where pretty old-style wooden houses with pointed gables adorn the shore, behind which stretches the market street, well-stocked with shops where the Chinese are fairly numerous. Our boats moored at a covered pier behind which bamboo steps led to a chalet of the same construction, with pillars adorned with orchids, and where a reception room, dining room, toilet and bathroom had been prepared for each of our two households. It was all very nice, and had a good effect on Henriette and Mélanie, who hastened to get out of their riding clothes – their plum silk Chinese trousers. That was the end of the ride and we can thank Providence for allowing us to complete it so well and without the slightest accident. Our wives put a lot of energy into it, but they were worn out and we were right to abandon the whole part of the journey that was to be devoted to the Sukhothai region.

I went to the telegraph to inform Bangkok of our arrival. I told Maugras that we expect to be in Bangkok on Wednesday evening, that the maid will be there on the 17th and that we were very surprised not to have found any mail in Raheng as agreed. As it takes nearly eight days for a letter to reach Raheng from Bangkok in the season of low water, and as the post arrives tomorrow, it is likely that the letters, if there are any, will have been sent last week, and that such a long delay was not calculated. It was agreed that if they arrive tomorrow, which is mail day, an express will be sent to try and reach us. I also sent a telegram to Dawson in Moulmein to tell him of our happy arrival and to thank him one last time for all the invaluable services he has rendered us.

The Governor of Raheng doesn't know a word of English. Fortunately, he has at his side a young man from Luang Pitchak who belongs to the forestry service and spent eight years in Europe. He knows France and understands a little French, but doesn't speak it. In English he expresses himself very well and, as he is obliging and competent, he can help us. Vilmorin got forestry and botanical information from him and I settled with him the payment of our coolie expenses and the plans for the journey over the coming days. For 76 porters and seven horses, we have been asked to pay one tical per head per day, which makes 332 ticals over four days. I'm told that the government's custom is to pay coolies an extra three days for the return journey, but they didn't insist and seemed satisfied with the sum of 500 ticals that we paid in total. As for the food provided en route, the *ampheu* bill was not very high. It only amounted to 14 ticals. The government would not hear of any reimbursement for the bottles of soda that were served in profusion during our four days in the mountains.

As for the boats, one was hired for us at Raheng at a cost of 70 ticals for the trip down and the eight days it will take the boatmen to get back up from Paknampho. We will pay for the other two on arrival.

The most difficult thing in Raheng was to exchange some of the rupees we had in our pockets. A Chinese in the market offered an inflated exchange price. We were happier with one of the few Hindus in the locality, trading in Moulmein, who exchanged 50 rupees for 43 ticals at a more or less normal rate, and also accepted a few guineas from Vilmorin for a fairly large profit. This, like everything else, seems to indicate how limited business relations are between Siam and Burma via Moulmein.

We had fun visiting the market. It was no longer the bright colours of Burma, but the women had their striped *sin* with yellow backgrounds, Chiang Mai style. We bargained for silk ones in a shop. They also sell red and brown lacquerware from Chiang Mai, and red cotton bags from the Shan lands. A few Karen women in pretty costumes also appeared at the market.

From our chalet, where we then returned, the view of the river was superb, with the mountains of the left bank in the background; the greenery of the banks, the plumes of the coconut palms, the pretty lilac and slate blue hues of the setting sun. We had a quiet dinner in our dining room after saying goodbye to the authorities, whom we would not be seeing again, as departure is set for 6 am tomorrow.

We were delighted to find a few bottles of white wine that I had had sent from Bangkok and which the Bombay Burmah had been kind

On the Mae Ping between Kamphaeng Phet and Nakhon Sawan. (Lefèvre-Pontalis Archive)

enough to transport. Then we went to bed in our boats. The Siamese name for Raheng is Muong Tak.

14 December 1912

Our boats set off at 6 am, without us having a chance to go ashore again. We stopped at 7.30 am for breakfast. At 11 o'clock we stopped again for lunch. The Vilmorins came to take it on our boat. The sector ended at 6 pm on the right bank at Ban Dok Mai.

The water was low enough for us to get stuck on the sand more than once and our boatmen had to get into the water to pull our boats, but all in all navigation was still fairly quick and easy. It must be a lot more complicated when, a few months later, the sandbanks cover almost the entire river, leaving only a few thin trickles of water. Even so, we had to zigzag a lot to follow the channel indicated by reed stems.

Many of the pirogues travel up the river with the supple, agile and energetic gestures of the Laotians from Mae Ping, with their tattooed thighs, who run swiftly on the plank placed alongside their boats.

A number of teak rafts sometimes blocked the current, but generally they are stopped at the end of a sandbank and held back, until the next high water, by stakes fixed into the ground. Variously coloured pennants indicate the names of their owners, and the guardians of the timber trains have their little bamboo huts set up on the large logs. There are also some isolated logs on the sandbanks that have not yet been assembled into rafts. This must be the job of the elephants. Philippe saw some today working on the banks of the river. These are green from one end to the other, the forest alternating continuously with the villages, which can be recognised from afar by their coconut palms and the junks or pirogues moored at the foot of the low banks.

There were also fishermen drying their nets on the sandbanks, but there are fewer of them than on the Irrawaddy.

We came across only one steam boat, but it was very small and had difficulty making its way through the sandbanks. It was an amusing and picturesque sight, because in the background, sitting oriental style on carpets, we saw a Hindu with white clothes and a black beard, and next to him his wife, also Hindu, wrapped in yellow veils and sending us smiles, which seemed to annoy him. What are these people doing here?

At the end of this leg, our people looked a little tired. They had rowed for twelve hours straight without flinching. They looked like the dullards we are used to with our Laotians. I don't know why they've been dressed in a blue suit with white braid and a police cap, which makes them look grotesque. A local crew would have been much more interesting.

Henriette found the day long. She doesn't usually like slow river navigation, and here the changes of direction were so frequent that we had to close the shutters at all times to avoid the sun but lose part of the landscape. Behind us, the mountains we climbed continued to form a very impressive backdrop on the Raheng side, which was sometimes beautifully lit. Towards the descent, the hills drop away and are hardly visible from the forested river.

Philippe was overjoyed. He loves this life on the water and in the open air, and as soon as he sets foot on land, he starts botanising. His wife was paying for her fall and the fatigue of the previous days. She felt bilious and her complexion had suddenly turned a singular shade of brown. As for Henriette, she is already rested and in excellent health.

15 December 1912

The trip resumed as calmly as yesterday at 6 o'clock. At the 7.30 am stop for breakfast, I took a delightful bath in the Mae Ping, although I had to lie down flat to get enough water.

Before 10 o'clock we had already reached Kamphaeng Phet, which, according to the map, was more than a third of the way along the river. I thought we could stop there for several hours without any inconvenience, especially as the Commissioner and his interpreter, who were on the bank waiting for us, immediately told me that the ruins were only a mile away and that in a two-hour walk we could see a good part of them.

The idea of going ashore and seeing something pleased everyone. So, Patte having received orders to have lunch ready by noon, we set off nimbly along the shore, towards the ruins which are actually less than a mile away.

The paths had been carefully cleared for us, even the trees had been cut down, and nothing was easier than this walk, which it would have been a great shame to have missed.

The first step was to cross the ancient enclosure, which in this part now formed nothing more than a mound of earth, and then we were in the forest, which at the time we visited was so well illuminated that we were able to see the ruins in their best light and use the Kodaks.

The first pagoda we saw was Wat Phra Keo, with its laterite enclosure, its brick and laterite pillars, its *chedi* at the back and its three Buddhas at rest, utterly picturesque in the solitude of the forest. This must have been the main pagoda, as it is very close to the site of the royal palace, of which there are hardly any traces left, but near which there is still a *sra* or sacred pond.

The town does not appear to have been very large, by which I mean the royal town, as the exit gate is not far away. On this side, the wall is better preserved and still has a few battlements, and the moat covered by a long wooden bridge is filled with water.

The other two pagodas, those of Phra Non and Phra Nhiun, were therefore outside the royal city. They are of normal dimensions, the first formed by a regular pyramid preceded by a *bot* and the other by a quadrangular pyramid also preceded by its *bot*. This takes us away from Burmese temples, either of the Hindu type from Pagan, or of the later Burmese type where the pyramid merges with the dwelling of the *phra* (monks). Here, as in all Siamese temples, the main residence of the *phra* is in the *bot*, whose outer enclosure and main pillars have survived. The special thing about them is that they are all made of laterite, as are the pyramids. Stucco may have been used as a covering. Most of the time it has disappeared. There are a few stuccoed brick Buddhas along the paths. They are more or less dilapidated, but their type is more expressive than the Burmese Buddhas. There are remnants of a

In front of the ruins of Kamphaeng Phet. (Lefèvre-Pontalis Archive)

bronze Buddha in the *bot* of Phra Non, and the large pyramid behind it is said to contain one. I wasn't able to see it, but the laterite pyramid itself seemed marvellous, especially to my companions, because of the superb banyan tree that crowns it completely and embraces the whole monument with its powerful roots.

In this temple, as in the others, I noticed the use of laterite for the perpendicular bars of the *bot* windows and for some of the pillars inside, which have a massive structure with the locations of the transverse beams. The plan of these buildings is interesting, as are the materials used, but there are no details of terracotta, sandstone or sculpted stucco to attract the particular attention of the artist or archaeologist, as in Ayutthaya or Lopburi. What was particularly attractive, especially in the light that illuminated the ruins this morning, was the picturesque appearance of the monuments and especially the statues, in their intimate union with the forest.

Wat Phra Nhiun, with its four faces featuring gigantic Buddhas, sitting and standing, half ruined but surrounded by greenery and creepers, was particularly evocative. In Pagan, I saw monuments such as the Ananda, where the Buddhas were also housed, but they lacked the charm of ruins. What's more, I saw birds here like none I had seen elsewhere, birds from dreams or fairy tales, two sparkling red ones and two yellows birds playing on the banyan tree that crowns the pyramid.

On another branch of the tree, a gentle red-tailed squirrel was taking a leisurely stroll. I've never been so lucky as to see such unusual birds in the forest as on this trip. Burma was full of them and this morning's sighting was even more interesting. Perhaps this luck is due to the season.

We were escorted on our walk by the vice-commissioner, his interpreter, the colonel and some notables. They showed us an ancient well carved out of laterite and a strange image venerated by the locals as a local *phi*. They call it the Lak Muong. It's an ogre's head half sunk into the earth, probably the remains of a *yak* statue. A small shelter has been built and offerings of gold leaves, flowers, fruit and small statues are made; candles and incense sticks are burnt in front of him and all my officials took off their hats when they approached him.

By noon exactly we were back at our boats, delighted to have been able to make at least a short visit to one of the most interesting historical places in Siam. Our compatriot Fournereau, who was the first to study this dead city, which he confused with Sri Satchanalai, has drawn the plan of five of the Kamphaeng Phet temples, but he mentions a few others. We would have needed a day or two to visit Wat Xang Pheuk with its 28 lions surrounding the pyramid, the cloister of Phra Prathan and the colossal laterite elephant called Xang Phala, with the temple's bas-reliefs evoking memories of Angkor Wat. What I have seen of Kamphaeng Phet made me want to see it again in greater depth when I make my trip to the ruins of Sukhothai. However, if I don't get to see it again, I'm delighted to have caught a glimpse of it and, above all, to have been able to pinpoint certain important events in the history of the Tais as they migrated south.

A little upstream on the Mae Ping, on the right bank and opposite the ruins of the old *vieng,* stands a large white pyramid in Burmese style with a golden crown. It forms an attractive backdrop among the trees, with the Raheng mountains in the background. The best place to see it is from the quay, where the Kamphaeng Phet authorities had set up two bamboo pavilions for us in the same style as those at Raheng, and where we were very comfortable for lunch. Further up along the quay was the Commissioner's house, the government, the court, the prison and the gendarmerie. All of this is maintained with the greatest care and in the middle is a stele commemorating King Chulalongkorn's historic visit to the restored city of Kamphaeng Phet, which played such an important role in Siam's past.

According to tradition, it was here that the Tai from Chiang Rai, from where their princes had been driven out by the king of Thaton, found refuge on their way south. In the course of their migration, they reached the abandoned town of Pep, which, according to La Jonquière, was located at the spot marked today by the great pyramid on the right bank. A hermit appeared before the elephant of the king of Chiang Rai and advised him to build his new royal city there. This hermit was none other than Indra. His advice was followed and the city was built on the spot indicated. It was given the name Trai Trung, the city of the gods, because the god with a thousand eyes had indicated its location. The dethroned king of Chiang Rai reigned here until his death, and his family retained authority for four generations.

The fact that the city was soon moved to the other bank of the Mae Ping was due to the famous adventure of the daughter of the king of Trai Trung who, having had a son without having had any relations with anyone, realised that the father of this child was a man covered in tumours who was growing cucumbers in his garden on the left bank, watered with his urine. The princess ate one of these cucumbers, without knowing where it came from, and later it was recognised that this was how her son had been fathered. This young prince of such curious origin, whose father reigned after the death of the king of Trai Trung and transferred the capital to the left bank at Kamphaeng Phet, called Muong Thep, in 1319, was the famous Chao Uthong who himself emigrated southwards and is credited with founding Ayutthaya. This is why the Siamese are so interested in souvenirs from Kamphaeng Phet. They have taken the superb bronze statues of Hindu gods found there to the Bangkok Museum, and thanks to the interest shown in Siamese antiquities by the present King and Prince Damrong, the ruins are being maintained in a most satisfactory manner.

The conclusion to be drawn from the legend is that the march of the Tai Noi or Laotians from Chiang Rai towards the west and the Mae Ping valley was provoked by an attack from the kings of Thaton, the Hindu-Peguan town whose ruins I visited to the north of Martaban. Since the last traces of the Thaton kingship disappeared in the 11th century under the blows of Anuratha, King of Pagan, this war between Thaton and Chiang Rai must have taken place earlier. It would therefore indicate a very early contact between the Laotian and the Hindu populations of the Martaban region.

On the other hand, as the Laotian Tai Noi current flowed from the north-east to the south-west over the Sukhothai region, it must be concluded that the Menam Pho was not yet colonised at that time, as it was later by the Tai, unless the migration from Chiang Rai took place either via Chiang Mai or Lakhon, which is perfectly likely.

It is also very interesting to observe that if Sukhothai became an extremely powerful centre of Tai influence in the 13th century, there were also others no less lively on the Lower Mae Ping, unless we are to abandon the tradition of an ancient war of Thaton against Chiang-Hai and postpone all these events to the 14th century, thus conforming to the part of the legend which places the foundation of Kamphaeng Phet in 1319. In this case, the establishment of a Tai principality of this importance on the lower Mae Ping should be considered as confirmation of the conquests accomplished by the race in the course of the 13th century, and as a fact of the same kind as the hold of the Tai of Wareru on Martaban and the mouth of the Salween.

The vanguard of the Tai from Kamphaeng Phet to the west was active and perhaps had more influence than the Sukhothai group on the destiny of the Siamese people, if it is true that it was among them that the founders of the Siamese capital of Ayutthaya are to be found.

Ayutthaya already existed before the Siamese occupation, as Prince Damrong has shown, and Suphan Buri also existed before the Siamese took possession of it, as La Jonquière has shown. At the old Suphan Buri, there are still monuments of Hindu origin which seem to prove that a Hindu colony existed there when the Siamese took it over.

The fact that the Siamese were particularly active in the 13th century throughout the western part of the southern Menam basin cannot be disputed, since it was at this time that they established their influence as far afield as the Malay Peninsula.

Now that Prince Damrong's research seems to have shown that there never was a prince called Uthong, but a *chao* of Uthong, and that this Uthong was located west of the present Suphan Buri in the direction of ancient Kanburi, it must be admitted that it was definitely not the Siamese group of Sukhothai but that of Kamphaeng Phet, which had extended its domination beyond Suphan Buri at the beginning of the 14th century. To them should be attributed the installation of the capital of Ayutthaya and consequently the creation of the Siamese monarchy. It is therefore from the west that the race would have accomplished the turning and enveloping movement that ensured its possession of the Menam estuary. This can be explained all the better by the fact that in the east, where the Tai invasion was also successful, the preoccupation with the fight against the Cambodians diminished the power of action of the invaders, who seem to have finally had to give way to their cousins from Suphan Buri, who remained freer in their movements.

What is certain is that the hypothesis of a great Siamese kingdom growing steadily as it extended southwards must be abandoned. Nothing could be further from the Thai way of proceeding. The *muang* is essentially an individualistic concept susceptible to momentary aggregations. Under these conditions, Suphan Buri secured the domination of Ayutthaya, but Ayutthaya the capital then had to conquer the *muang* of the North. Phitsanulok, Kamphaeng Phet and Sukhothai, which had at times had an individual existence and whose *muang* had dominated others, were conquered and more than once lost. Their situation vis-à-vis Ayutthaya was similar to that of the Shan principalities vis-à-vis the Kingdom of Siam in the 19th century.

In the 17th century, European travellers still found vestiges of this state of affairs in the Siam of Phra Narai, which did not include Chiang Mai and where the *muang*, even the Siamese of the north, were far from being as centralised as they are today. According to Gervaise, if Phitsanulok, Tenasserim, Bangkok and Peply had viceroys, it is because in the past they obeyed independent princes, and he concludes that the king of Ayutthaya, who was the greatest landowner and the most powerful of all, gradually conquered all the principalities that eventually made up his kingdom.

As for the Laotian origin of the Siamese, this was also noted in the 17th century by La Loubère, who found it confirmed in the chronological compendium of Siamese history which was given to him in Ayutthaya by order of the king. This is also where he drew the information confirmed by all the indigenous documents that the Siamese are the Tai Noi, as opposed to the Tai Yai, and that the Tai Noi came from the east and the Tai Yai from the west, as can be seen from the comparison of the various Indochinese chronicles carried out in recent years.

Where La Loubère had the intuition of a genius is when he considered the Siamese of the 17th century as an amalgam of Tai, Laotians, whom he considered almost as one nation with the Siamese, Peguans and a large number of foreigners who had taken refuge in Siam because of the freedom of trade and because of the wars. Nothing is more accurate than this hypothesis. That the race which formed the Peguan kingdom, i.e. the Talaing, played a large part in the formation of the Siamese people, seems to be fully accepted today, when it is recognised that when the Siamese took possession of the lower Menam basin they found there a Mon-Khmer population civilised to varying degrees by Hinduism and whose half-civilisation they themselves adopted. Nowhere was the mixing of the two races more likely to have taken place than on the lower Mae Ping.

At one o'clock, having finished lunch, we left our chalet at Kamphaeng Phet without fanfare, having taken leave of the authorities before lunch.

The morning's expedition had prepared us for a siesta. In any case, there was nothing salient in this graceful but somewhat monotonous navigation. Until 6 o'clock in the evening our boatmen rowed in the sun and then we camped on a sandbank in the middle of the river, a little above the village of Ta Ka Lium, which is said to be the middle of the stretch of river between Raheng and Paknampho.

16 December 1912

We set off at the usual time and stopped at 7.30 am and noon as on previous days. The river remained the same, but the mountain cold was behind as and there were more beautiful *yang* trees with straight white trunks on the banks.

At 2 am a little above Ban Pha Nu, a village on the right bank where shelter had been prepared and where we stopped for a few minutes, we were joined by the small steam launch we had met the other day. In the absence of more important mail, it brought me a letter from Maugras dated December 5th, saying that all was well at the legation and that all the arrangements had been made to house the Vilmorins. Our change of itinerary made Petithuguenin decide to give up on Sukhothai and Kamphaeng Phet, but he may come and join us in Paknampho.

It was Prince Yugala who, in charge of Phya Maha Ammad's duties at the Ministry of the Interior, in the latter's absence, made the arrangements for our journey from the border and our descent of the Mae Ping by boat. As he was not there when I left Bangkok, it is not surprising that the orders given regarding our intentions were somewhat imprecise, but one can only pay tribute to the alacrity and care with which all the arrangements were made.

These chalets, installed at every half-stage, are perfect, and it was a shame not to be able to enjoy all the preparations made by these good people who are there waiting for us and in front of whom more than once we were forced to pass without stopping.

The stage ended at 5.20 pm on the right bank at the village of Ban Deng, not far from which stands a beautiful double-peaked limestone boulder known as Phu Khao Chang, Elephant Mountain, which looked quite impressive as we descended the river.

Here, as earlier, we found bamboo chalets with dining rooms and bathrooms. The district *ampheu* came with his little daughters adorned in gold jewellery to give us eggs and Henriette three pretty green and brown pigeons in their cage. We'll be taking them with us to Bangkok.

Mélanie was in a state because since this morning there had been a sick man among her boatmen. She spoke of plague, cholera, and every possible disease. I sent him ashore. On enquiry, I found that his feet were a little swollen from the perpetual dampness in which these people have to live. There's a lot of fog on the river at this time of year. At night, in the morning and in the evening, it's really annoying and unhealthy.

17 December 1912

The last stage was not long. We had lunch under the trees of a pagoda at Ban Deng on the right bank and around 3 o'clock we reached the first houses of Paknampho, then the confluence of the Mae Ping and Menam rivers. There are quite a few floating houses on the Menam, which is narrower than the Mae Ping.

The colonel of the gendarmerie had our convoy go as far as Nakhon Sawan, which is nothing more than an extension of Paknampho on the right bank of the Menam. Indeed the government is in Nakhon Sawan in its entirety and the governor's establishment with the gendarmerie and other official buildings is outside Paknampho, which is linked to it by a regular omnibus service.

We were towed there to find accommodation, as there was none available in the town of Paknampho. We were allocated a floating house, which serves as a rest house for official travellers. The current was so strong that we found it very difficult to land. There were countless insects and the noise of the violent current was hardly conducive to sleep. The Governor, who was ill, did not show up, and the interpreter provided for us spoke poor English.

We emptied all our boats, and were handed our correspondence sent from Bangkok at my request. Nothing very interesting, but everyone's news was good. Reading our letters absorbed us so much that in the coach, which we boarded to visit Paknampho and the market street, which is similar to all the others but where the Chinese are once again in the majority, we didn't pay much attention to anything.

As soon as we got back, we were in a hurry to finish our own letters so that we can take advantage of the mail that will probably leave Bangkok the day after tomorrow.

The Siamese authorities have done a good job. They refused payment for two of our three boats, which belong to the administration. We just got off with a tip.

18 December 1912

While our luggage was being loaded onto a longboat, we ourselves left on another for Paknampho, wishing to go up the Menam a little and see the floating houses in detail. These were of great interest to Henriette and the Vilmorins. Before reaching the confluence of the Mae Ping and Menam rivers, we passed the French Catholic mission on the right bank. It is a very modest church, attended almost exclusively by Chinese and served by a native priest. But the mission, which understands the importance of the Paknampho station on the road to the north and the western frontiers, intends, I know, to develop this small centre and

On the Chao Phraya near Ayutthaya. (Lefèvre-Pontalis Archive)

successively set up schools and a hospital there. I gave the bishop a lot of encouragement in this direction and I found him willing to act because the place has not yet been taken over, as in the north, by the Protestant missions. Paknampho will always remain a large market as well as a meeting point for different routes. Especially now that it is served by the railway, its development will not be long in coming and it is there for the taking by our French Catholic missions.

Almost the entire floating home population is Chinese. All the more reason to convert to them, as they are more easily approachable.

This is where my route intersected with the one I followed in 1894, when I travelled with Mr Panu up the Menam to Uttaradit. The railway did not exist at that time. It had already transformed the whole region, since we left at 10.30 in the morning and arrived in Bangkok at 6 in the evening.

On the way, I was struck by the dryness of the soil, which was already much more pronounced than in the north. The bamboo was yellowing and losing its leaves; the rice was ripe and in many places the harvest was already well advanced, although next to the bare fields there were rice fields that were still very green.

As we approached Lopburi and Ayutthaya the fields were better cultivated, but beyond that, as I've seen before, many fields lay fallow.

This seemed surprising, given the vastness and openness of the plain, but drainage and irrigation have been neglected, and perhaps the proximity of Bangkok and its pleasures has also contributed to the depopulation of an area that should be one of the most fertile in Siam. It seems that there is much to be done in this area.

Lopburi and Ayutthaya, with their ruins near the railway, seemed interesting to my companions. If they can, they will at least visit Ayutthaya in the next few days.

But for the moment we were in a hurry to arrive. Night was falling when at 6 o'clock we entered Bangkok station where Maugras, the Petithuguenins, Nothon and Bonnafons were waiting for us. Everything had gone well in our absence, with no incidents. The car took us quickly through the noise and lights of the big city to the Legation, where the chambermaid had arrived that very day from Rangoon and which, despite the pleasure of having arrived, Henriette considered to be nothing more than a large hall. It has been very hot for several days and it was rather unpleasant for settling in and our return.

But everything went so well during our trip that we can't thank Providence enough!

The Pontalis and Vilmorin families in front of Wat Pho. (Lefèvre-Pontalis Archive)

Acknowledgements

The publication of this book was made possible by the warm welcome and kindness of Patrick Pontalis, who gave us access to his great-grandfather's archives and authorized their digitization and publication. He welcomed us into his home and always supported us in this project, even when it turned out to take much longer than expected.

The transcription of the text was carried out partly by ourselves, partly with the help of Patrick Binot, with whom we came into contact on Gérard Fouquet's advice. For the iconographic research, the images available in the Pierre Lefèvre-Pontalis archives were digitized by Basile Évrard. For the "Siamese" part of the manuscript, Boonpissit Srihong, a doctoral student at Bangkok's Chulalongkorn University, carried out a highly efficient and relevant search of Thailand's national archives. We also benefited from the kindness and hospitality of Professor Yongyuth Chuwaen, a historian specializing in Thailand's southern regions, during a trip in the footsteps of Pierre Lefèvre-Pontalis to the provinces of Songkhla, Phatthalung and Trang in December 2020.

Financial support from the Unité Mixte de Recherche Patrimoines Locaux, Environnement et Globalisation (CNRS/IRD/MNHN) enabled us to fund the proofreading of the manuscript and the preparation of the lexicon and glossary, which was carried out with the help of Bertrand Bayet (IRASEC). The final stages of the book's publication, promotion and distribution received financial and logistical support from the French Embassy in Bangkok, thanks to Ambassador Jean-Claude Poinboeuf and his Cooperation and Cultural Action Department. The IRD's Mission for Scientific and Technological Culture, under the direction of Marie-Lise Sabrié, also provided financial support for the book's distribution. Finally, we owe a special thanks to Narisa Chakrabongse, director of River Books, for her interest in our project and for her trust and kindness during the editorial process.

Glossary

Aceh – Province in northern Sumatra, called Achen in the original text by Pierre Lefèvre-Pontalis.

Adhipaccaya – Name given after the 18th century to the region to the west of the Shwedagon pagoda (according to Lefèvre-Pontalis based on Forchhammer, 1883).

Ahlone – Town in the Sagaing region, on the left bank of the Chindwin River, Burma. Pierre Lefèvre-Pontalis spells it Alon in his notebooks.

Ai-Lao – Ailao, ancient confederation of south-western Yunnan, covering Dehong and part of northern Burma.

Aleppo – City in Syria.

Alexandrette – City in Turkey.

Amarapura – Former royal capital of Burma, adjoining the present-day city of Mandalay to the south, which Lefèvre-Pontalis francized as Amarapoura in his notebooks.

Amherst – Town founded by the British in 1826 not far from Moulmein (Mawlamyine), Burma.

ampheu – In Thai, อำเภอ is often transcribed as *amphoe*. Usually translated as district, the term refers to a subdivision of the province.

Arakan – A region in north-western Burma, bordering Bangladesh, now known as the Rakhine State within the Republic of the Union of Myanmar. Pierre Lefèvre-Pontalis spells it Arrakan in his notebooks.

Assam – Assam lies in the centre of India's north-eastern region. It is an Indian state in the same way as Nagaland, Arunachal Pradesh, Manipur, Mizoram and Tripura, which border it.

Attharam (river) [also called Uttaran, when Lefèvre-Pontalis followed Leal's spelling, 1826] – Ataran river (Kasat Noi in Thailand), a tributary of the Gyaing river, Moulmein (Mawlamyine), Burma.

Ava – Inwa, an ancient royal city in central Burma, close to present-day Mandalay, founded in the 15th century.

Ayetthema – Village 30 kilometres north of Thaton in Burma, near the site of the ancient city of Golanagara or Taikkala. Pierre Lefèvre-Pontalis spells it Ayetthima in his notebooks.

Ayutthaya – City in Thailand, capital of the province of the same name and former royal capital of Siam. Pierre Lefèvre-Pontalis spells it Ajuthia in his notebooks.

Bacala – European name for the city of Pokkhara, formerly known as Adhipaccaya, located to the west of Rangoon (Yangon) according to Lefèvre-Pontalis (based on Forchhammer, 1883).

Ban Chang – Bang Khonthi (?) (source: Sternstein, 1993: 68). One of Leal's stops (1826) on the Mae Klong river (Thailand).

Ban Chiom – One of Leal's stops (1826) at the confluence of the Khwae Noi (which he descended) and the Khwae Yai in Siam.

Bandon – Also sometimes spelt Ban Don, former name of Surat Thani.

Bang Saphan – District in Thailand, situated to the south of the province of Prachuap Khiri Khan. Pierre Lefèvre-Pontalis spells it Ban Tapan in his notebooks.

Bangkok – Capital of the Kingdom of Thailand (Siam until 1939).

Bangnarom – Prachuap Khiri Khan (source: Sternstein, 1993).

Bantam – Kingdom of Banten, Indonesia.

Bassein – Now Pathein, two hundred kilometres west of Yangon (Rangoon).

Basra – City in Iraq.

Baw Baw Gyi (stupa) – Bawbawyi, pyu stupa located in Pyay (Prome).

Bebegyi – see Baw Baw Gyi.

Bengal – Bangladesh

Bentik (island) – Bentinck, island in the Mergui (Myeik) archipelago, Burma.

Bhamo – Town in Kachin State, Burma.

Bibby line – Shipping company operating between Great Britain and Rangoon (Yangon) via Colombo to Ceylon (Sri Lanka).

Bombay Burmah – Bombay Burmah Trading Company (BBTC), a trading company created in the 1860s in Bombay to trade tea and then teak in the British Indian Empire.

Boribat – Boat belonging to the Siam Navigation Co, Ltd., operated by the Danish East Asiatic Company. She made regular trips between Bangkok and Singapore along the west coast of the Gulf of Siam.

bot (โบสถ์) – Short form of *ubosot* (อุโบสถ), a building dedicated to certain religious rites, particularly ordination ceremonies.

Boxer Rebellion – A revolt by a Chinese secret society following China's defeat by Japan in 1895 and in protest against the demands of the European powers in 1898. This violent nationalist movement attacked the foreign missions and led, in June 1900, to the assassination of the German minister and the siege of the foreign legations in Peking.

British India – British East India Company, founded in 1600 and dissolved in 1874.

Cachar – District of the State of Assam, India.

Chance (island) – Colonial name for one of the islands in the Mergui (Myeik) archipelago, off the mouth of the Kraburi/Pak Chan river.

Chantaboun – Town in Chanthaburi province, in the south-east of modern-day Thailand.

Chaiya – District in what is now Surat Thani province, Thailand.

Chayok – Sai Yok district, Kanchanaburi, Thailand. One of the stops along the way for Leal (1826), who travelled up the Ataran/Kasat Noi river from Moulmein (Burma) and then down the Khwae Noi (Thailand).

chedi – (เจดีย์) Thai term for a stupa.

cherouk – cheroot, the Burmese cigar.

Chersonese (also called Khrysé by Lefèvre-Pontalis) – Ptolemy's Golden Chersonese, associated with the toponym Suvaṇṇabhūmi in Thailand.

Chiang Hung – Jinghong (Chiang Hung, Sipsongpanna, Keng Hung), Yunnan, China, spelt Xieng-hung, Xieng Hung, Xieng-Hung and Xien Houng by Lefèvre-Pontalis. One of the nine ancient Tai Dai kingdoms of Yunnan (bordering northern Shan state, Burma).

Chiang Mai – City in northern Thailand (spelt Xieng Mai in the original version of the Lefèvre-Pontalis notebooks).

Chiang Rai – City in northern Thailand (spelt Xieng Hai in the original version of the Lefèvre-Pontalis notebooks).

Chiang Saen – Former Shan principality on the border between Burma and Laos (spelt Xieng Sen in the original version of the Lefèvre-Pontalis notebooks).

Chiang Tung – Kyaing Tong, Shan State, Burma (spelt Xieng Tung in the original version of the Lefèvre-Pontalis notebooks).

Chindwin (river) – Chindwin River, tributary of the Irrawaddy, Sagaing region, Burma.

Chittagong – Chattogram, first port of Bangladesh.

Cholon – Ho Chi Minh City district in southern Vietnam.

Chom Si – That Chom Si, a religious monument at the top of Phu Si hill, in the historic centre of the town of Luang Prabang in Laos.

Chumphon – Province in southern Thailand, spelt Choumphon in the Lefèvre-Pontalis notebooks.

Circuit house – Residence reserved for civil servants and government officers passing through British colonial towns.

Coromandel – Coromandel Coast, India

Couir (Koney, Couli, Kin) – On the road from Mergui (Myeik) to Ayutthaya.

Court (island) – Courts island, island in the Mergui (Myeik) archipelago, Burma.

Dala – Another name for the city of Pokkhara, formerly known as Adhipaccaya, west of Rangoon according to Lefèvre-Pontalis (based on Forchhammer, 1883).

Danclai – One of Leal's stops (1826) between the Chao Phraya basin and Mergui (Myeik).

Dhannavati – Pāli name for the capital of the first Arakanese kingdom and the Twante region south of Rangoon (Yangon) according to Burmese historical tradition (Forchhammer, 1883). Name given after the 15th century to the region south of the Shwedagon pagoda (according to Lefèvre-Pontalis, based on Forchhammer, 1883).

Dreadnought – Predominant type of battleship of the 20th century.

Dusit – The district of Bangkok that has housed royal palaces since the time of King Chulalongkorn (r.1868-1910).

Fu Kien – Fukien, province in south-east China.

Golamattikanagara – The name given to an ancient city near the village of Ayetthema, 30 kilometres north of Thaton, Burma.

Golconde – Golkonda, India, Telangana state.

Gothek – Gokteik, a town in Shan State, where a viaduct was built to link the towns of Pyin Oo Lwin (Maymyo) and Lashio by train. It was inaugurated in 1901.

Hainan – China's southernmost island province.

Haiphong – Hải Phòng, Vietnam.

Halong – Halong Bay, in the north of Vietnam.

Hangsawadi – Hanthawaddy, Pāli name for the present-day town of Bago (Pegu), Burma.

Hanoi – Capital of Tonkin during the French colonial period, then of modern-day Vietnam.

Hatien – Hà Tiên, port of southern Vietnam.

Hindus – Indians of the Hindu religion.

Hotha – Ho Hsa, Yunnan, China. One of the nine ancient Tai Dai kingdoms of Yunnan (bordering northern Shan state, Burma).

Indochina – Indochinese Peninsula or continental Southeast Asia, today comprising seven countries: Vietnam, Laos, Cambodia, Thailand, Myanmar (Burma), the northern part of Malaysia and Singapore.

Inywa – Town at the junction of the Irrawaddy and Shweli rivers in Burma, spelt Inoua in the Lefèvre-Pontalis notebooks.

Irrawaddy – The Ayeyarwady River, Burma's main north-south artery.

Irrawaddy Flotilla (also spelt Irraouaddy flotilla by Lefèvre-Pontalis) – Irrawaddy Flotilla Company (IFC), a British river shipping company established in 1865 to transport troops, then goods and passengers on the Irrawaddy River.

Jelinga – Village on the border between Burma and Siam, on the road from Mergui (Myeik) to Ayutthaya (and accessible via the Tenasserim river).

Junk Ceylon – Former name of the island of Phuket.

Kachin – Ethnic group mainly found in northern Burma.

Kaing Ma (also called Xieng Ma by Lefèvre-Pontalis) – One of the nine ancient Tai Dai kingdoms of Yunnan (bordering northern Shan state, Burma)

Kalah (Kuleh, Kuleh, Kola) – Other names for the ancient city of Golanagara (Takkala, Taikkala) located thirty kilometres north of Thaton.

Kalinga (kingdom) – Ancient kingdom of east-central India (now Odisha and northern Andhra Pradesh).

Kalyanisima – Kalyani Sima (ordination hall) built by King Dhammazedi (r. 1471-1492) in Pegu (Bago), which contains the so-called Kalyani inscriptions (in Mon and Pāli), major sources for the history of Theravādin Buddhism.

Kamphaeng – Current province of Kamphaeng Phet in Thailand, spelt Kampeng in the Lefèvre-Pontalis notebooks.

Kanburi – Current province of Kanchanaburi in Thailand, spelt Kanbouri in the Lefèvre-Pontalis notebooks.

Kapilavistu – Kapilavastu, former capital of the Śākya clan, from which the Buddha of our era, Siddhārta Gautama, descended (the remains of which lie near the border between India and Nepal).

Karen (sometimes *kariang* in Thai) – Generic term applied to four ethnic groups (Sgaw, Pwo, Kayah and Pa-O), speaking Tibeto-Burmese, living on either side of the Thai-Burmese border.

Kasoun (Mount) – A mountain in the Tennasserim range, on the edge of the Sing Khon pass, on the border between Burma and Thailand.

Katha – Sagaing Division, on the right bank of the Irrawaddy, Burma.

Katigara – Town in the state of Assam, India.

Kedah – State in Malaysia.

Kelantan – State in Malaysia.

Khamti – Khamti town, Sagaing division, Burma.

Khsatrya – The *kṣatriya* are the 'warrior-kings' and represent one of the four classes of the primordial hierarchy, born of the sacrifice of the great man according to Vedic cosmogony: the *brāhmaṇa* of his mouth, the *kṣatriya* of his arms, the *vaiśya* of his thighs, the *śūdra* of his feet.

Kindat – Sagaing region, Mawlaik district, Burma.

King (island) or Kings Island – Colonial name for Kadan Kyun, the largest of the islands in the Mergui (Myeik) archipelago.

Kinywa – Village in Mon state, Burma, about 30 kilometres north of Thaton.

Kioc pié [name given by Leal, 1826, reproduced by Lefèvre-Pontalis] – Phaya Thone Zu, the Three Pagodas

Pass on the Thai-Burmese border.

Kisserang (island) – island in the Mergui (Myeik) archipelago.

Klings – Name given to people of Indian origin in Malaysia and Indonesia.

Klong Bangwilai – One of Leal's stops (1826) on his way up the Ataran/Kasat Noi river (from Moulmein to Siam).

Klong Menang Luong – Phitthaya Long Kong /Khlong sahakon /Sapphasamit (?). A waterway linking the mouths of the Tha Chin and Chao Phraya rivers, used by Leal to reach Bangkok in 1826.

Klong Mykut – One of Leal's stops (1826) on his way up the Ataran/Kasat Noi river (from Moulmein to Siam).

Klong Mysikleet – One of Leal's stops (1826) on his way up the Ataran/Kasat Noi river (from Moulmein to Siam).

Klong Peli – One of Leal's stops (1826) on his way up the Ataran/Kasat Noi river (from Moulmein to Siam).

Koh Kut – Island in south-east Thailand, close to the Cambodian border, in the province of Trat.

Koh Lak (bay) – Bay located near the small town of Prachuap Khiri Khan, in the province of the same name in Thailand.

Kokain (hills) – Kokine, former name of Kabar Aye Pagoda Road, Rangoon (Yangon), Burma.

Kokarit – Kawkareik, Karen state, Burma.

Koney (Couli, Kin, Couir) – Thailand, on the road from Mergui (Myeik) to Ayutthaya.

Ko Shan Pri (also known as the nine Shan states, Koshambi, Kosambi, Kopyidoung) – The nine ancient Tai Dai kingdoms of Yunnan (on the border with the northern Shan state of Burma) which the Burmese and Shan people of Burma refer to in Burmese as Ko-shan-pyi ("the nine Shan countries").

Kra (isthmus of) – Narrowest part of the Indochinese peninsula (around forty kilometres) between the Gulf of Siam and the Andaman Sea.

Kratieh – City of Kratie, northern Cambodia.

Kulanagara – Another name for the ancient city of Golanagara (Takkala, Taikkala) located 30 kilometres north of Thaton, Burma.

Kulataik – Burmese name for the ancient city of Golanagara (Takkala, Taikkala) located 30 kilometres north of Thaton, Burma.

Kunlong – Shan state, Burma.

Kursaal – German word meaning "health spa".

Kusima – Pāli name for the town of Pathein (Bassein), Burma.

Kyauk Myaung – Town in the Sagaing region, on the right bank of the Irrawaddy, Burma.

Kyauk Taw (pagoda) – Kyauktawgyi Pagoda, Mandalay, Burma.

Lai Chau – Lai Châu, province in northeast Vietnam.

Lakhon – Lefèvre-Pontalis uses this term to refer to Nakhon Sri Thammarat (also known as Ligor).

Langkawi – Malaysian archipelago in the northern part of the Strait of Malacca.

langouti – A piece of cotton used as a loincloth.

Lang Suan – A town slightly south of Chumphon in Thailand, spelt Lang Souan in the Lefèvre-Pontalis notebooks.

Laos – Current People's Democratic Republic of Laos.

Laotian – Inhabitant of Laos.

Lashio – Town in Shan State, Burma.

laterite – Clusters of microcrystalline iron hydroxides. Used as a building material.

Latha – Mong Hsa, Yunnan, China. One of the nine ancient Tai Dai kingdoms of Yunnan (bordering Northern Shan State, Burma).

Lem Chong Pra – Cape (*laem* in Thai) along the coast near Chumphon.

Ligor – Former name of Nakhon Sri Thammarat.

Long Chuien (also called Long Chwan by Lefèvre-Pontalis) – Mong Mao (Luchuan), one of the nine ancient Tai Dai kingdoms of Yunnan (border with the Shan State of the North, Burma).

Lopburi – City in central Thailand.

Lu Kiang – Chinese city.

Luang Prabang – Former royal capital of Laos.

Macau – City on the south coast of China, Portuguese territory until 1999.

Madaya – Town in the Mandalay region, Pyin Oo Lwin district, Burma.

Mae Ping – Ping, river rising in Chiang Dao, north of Chiang Mai and flowing to Nakhon Sawan where its confluence with the Nan river forms the Chao Phraya.

Mae Sot – Town on the border between Thailand and Burma, in the province of Tak, spelt Mesot in the Lefèvre-Pontalis notebooks.

Mai yang – Rubber tree with latex.

Maing Lung – Monglon, Kyaukme division, Northern Shan state, Burma.

Maing Lyin (also called Maing Len Gyi, Mong Lien and Muong Lem by Lefèvre-Pontalis) – Mong Lien, one of the nine ancient Tai Dai kingdoms of Yunnan (bordering the northern Shan state of Burma).

Maing Maing – Momein (?), Tengchong, Yunnan.

Malabar – Name given by Westerners to the inhabitants of the Kerala and Karnataka coasts in India.

Malacca (or Bandar Melaka) – Capital of the coastal state of Malacca in south-west Malaysia. The Strait of Malacca separates the northern part of Malaysia from the island of Sumatra in Indonesia.

Malay – Inhabitants of Malaysia.

Malais Siamois, Siamese Malays – The author refers here to the Muslim populations living in the south of Siam and claiming a Malay origin.

English Malaya, Siamese Malaya – The Anglo-Siamese Treaty of 1909 established the border between Siam and the northern states of Malaya, which were under British influence at the time. Under the treaty, Siam relinquished its claim to the states of Kedah, Kelantan, Perlis and Teregganu, transferring sovereignty over them to the British. However, Siam retained sovereignty over a region corresponding to the present-day provinces of Narathiwat, Pattani, Satun, Songkhla and Yala. British recognition of Siamese sovereignty over the northern part of the "Malay Country" was justified by the desire to create an ally to face the French in Indochina. This treaty sealed the border between modern-day Malaya and Thailand.

Male – Sagaing region, on the right bank of the Irrawaddy, Burma. The term is gallicised as "Malé" in the Lefèvre-Pontalis notebooks.

Manipur – State in north-east India bordering Burma.

Martaban – Mottama (Martaban), Burma.

Masulipatam – Machilipatnam, port on the Coromandel coast, India.

Meerawaddi – see Myawadi.

Meklong (river) – Mae Klong River, Thailand. Originates in Kanchanaburi, at the confluence of the Mae Nam Khwae Noi and Khwae Yai rivers.

Mekong (river) – The Mekong River (*mae nam khong* in Lao) originates on the Tibetan plateau and flows into the sea between Cambodia and Vietnam.

Menam – Chao Phraya River (*mae nam chao phraya*), which irrigates central Thailand.

Menam Noi – Place on the Mae Nam Khwae Noi river (Kanchanaburi, Thailand) where the Siamese built a fort.

Meng Ting – City of Yunnan.

Mergui – Archipelago located in southern Burma, in the Andaman Sea. Also known as Myeik.

Meiktila – A town in the Mandalay region of central Burma, spelt Métheila in Lefèvre-Pontalis' notebooks.

Mingun (pagoda) – Pagoda in the town of Mingun, Mandalay region, Burma, spelt Mingohn in Lefèvre-Pontalis' notebooks. The pagoda was begun by King Bodawphaya (1782-1819), but never completed.

Minto Mansions – Colonial hotel in Rangoon (Yangon), contemporary with the Strand, but now destroyed.

Mogaung – Kachin state, Burma.

Mogok – Town in the Pyin Oo Lwin district, Mandalay region, Burma, famous for its precious and semi-precious stone mines.

Momiet – Mong Mit, Kyaukme division, Northern Shan state, Burma.

Mon – Mon ethnic group, found mainly in southern Burma. Pierre Lefèvre-Pontalis writes Môn and also refers to them as Talaing or Pégouan (the Môn of the Pegu region).

Mona – Mong Na, Yunnan, China. One of the nine ancient Tai Dai kingdoms of Yunnan (bordering Northern Shan State, Burma).

Mong Lien – One of the nine ancient Tai Dai kingdoms of Yunnan (northern Shan state border, Burma).

Mong Nai – Division of Loilen, Southern Shan State, Burma, spelt Monei in Lefèvre-Pontalis' notebooks.

monthon – The *monthon*, in Thai มณฑล, from the Sanskrit *māṇḍala* or "circles", was a subdivision of the Kingdom of Siam (now Thailand) in the early 20th century. The *monthons* were created as part of an administrative system, the *thesaphiban* (เทศาภิบาล, literally "territorial control") set up by Prince Damrong Rajanubhab, at the same time as the provinces or *changwat*, and the districts or *amphoe*.

A *monthon* was headed by a royal commissioner, also known as a *thesaphiban*, appointed by Bangkok. The system was officially adopted in 1897. However, it was not implemented throughout the kingdom until around 1910. The main reason for this delay was the lack of competent personnel, as well as resistance from local traditional chiefs.

Monyin – Mohnyin (Mong Yang), Kachin state, Burma.

Monywa – Sagaing region, left bank of the Chindwin river, Burma.

Moscos (islands) – Group of islands off Dawei (Tavoy), Thaninthayi (Tenasserim), Burma.

Moulmein – Mawlamyine, Burma.

Mowun (also called Muong Woun by Lefèvre-Pontalis) – Mong Wan, one of the nine ancient Tai Dai kingdoms of Yunnan (bordering the northern Shan state of Burma).

muong – (เมือง) The term (also spelt *muang* or *mueang*) refers to the level of political hierarchy immediately above that of the village. Traditionally, a *muong* was formed by several *ban* villages surrounding a larger village, *ban louang*, which was sometimes fortified and in this case called *vièng* or *xièng* [also spelt *chiang, xiang, chièng*] if a very important person resided there. However, *muong* can also refer to the canton, district, principality or country as a whole. It is a fundamental element of Tai identity, insofar as it can be found both within the great principalities of Yuan (Lan Na), Siam (Ayutthaya) or Lao (Lan Xang) and in regions where the degree of political hierarchy, for historical reasons, is lower or less stable, notably among the Shan of Burma and the Lue of southern Yunnan. The term is not linked to Buddhism, but to the cult of the tutelary spirits *phi*, whose hierarchy reproduces that of the *muong*.

Muong-Hou – Muong Ou, northern Laos.

Muong La – Mong La, Northern Shan State, Burma (Yunnan border).

Muong Mau – Mong Mao (Luchuan), one of the nine ancient Tai Dai kingdoms of Yunnan (border with Northern Shan State, Burma).

Muong Sing – Muang Sing, northern Laos, declared an autonomous principality under French protection in 1904.

Muong Tak – The town of Tak, in the centre of the province of the same name, Thailand.

Muttima – Mottama (Martaban), Burma.

Myawadi – Myawaddy, Karen state, Burma. Town bordering Thailand, near Mae Sot.

Myi-Kya-Kyauptein – Point on the road from Tavoy to Siam, via the Nayé Daung pass, where there is a pillar demarcating the border between the two countries (Source: Low, 1835).

Myingyan – Town in the Mandalay region, Burma.

Myitkyina – Capital of Kachin State, Burma.

Mykesath – One of Leal's stops on his way up the Ataran/Kasat Noi river from Moulmein to Siam in 1826.

naga – Mythical serpent-dragon.

Nagasaki – Japanese city.

Nakhon Sri Thammarat – City in southern Thailand, formerly known as Ligor.

Nam Kouei (river) – Mae Nam Khwae Noi River, Kanchanaburi, Thailand.

Nam Mun – River in north-east Thailand, a tributary of the Mekong, known as Sé Moun in the Lefèvre-Pontalis notebooks.

Nantchao – Nanzhao, ancient kingdom of Yunnan in the 8th and 9th centuries.

Nayé Daung (pass-) – Maw Daung/ Sing Khon pass (Thailand-Burma border).

Negritos – A pejorative term for the hunter-gatherer forest dwellers of southern Thailand and northern Malaysia. They are known as the Mani in Thailand and the Kensiu in Malaysia. They are considered to be the oldest inhabitants of the land in these regions, closely related to certain indigenous populations of the Andaman Islands.

Nha Trang – City in central Vietnam.

Nicobar – Part of the Andaman archipelago.

Noire (river) – River Da, main tributary of the Red River, Vietnam.

Ormuz – Hormuz, Iran.

Pagan – Bagan, capital of the Burmese kingdom from the 9th to 13th centuries.

Pak Chan – The border river between Thailand and Burma, named Kraburi on the Thai side and Pak Chan on the Burmese side.

Pak Payun – Village at the entrance to the Phatthalung lagoon in Thailand.

Pak Prek – Pak Phraek, Kanchanaburi, Thailand.

Paknam – Located at the mouth of the Chao Phraya in the Gulf of Siam.

Paknampho – Nakhon Sawan (Pak Nam Pho), Thailand. Where the Nan and Ping rivers converge to form the Chao Phraya.

Palembang – Sumatra, Indonesia.

panung – Generic term for the traditional garment (tube of fabric tied at the waist) known as *sarung* (Malay), *sin* (Lao) or *longyi* in Burmese.

Panya – Kingdom of Pinya, a fortified centre of 14th century central Burma, located south of present-day Mandalay.

Patani – City in southern Thailand, centre of the province of the same name.

Paunglaung (river) – Paunglaung River, which flows through the southern Shan states before emptying into the Sittang river.

Pegu – Bago, Burma, called Pegou by Pierre Lefèvre-Pontalis.

Peguans – Inhabitants of Bago (Pegu), Burma.

Penang – The city of Penang, on the island of the same name.

Perlis – State of Malaysia, neighbouring Kedah, bordering Thailand. Declared a British protectorate under the Treaty of Bangkok in 1909.

Phatthalung – Town of Phatthalung, centre of the province of the same name in southern Thailand, spelt Patalung in Lefèvre-Pontalis' notebooks.

phi – (ผี) Spirit, genie, ghost. The expression refers to a supernatural entity of which there are an infinite number of forms and names in Thai (but also Lao) popular culture. In Thai, *phi* refers more to a malevolent, wandering entity, as opposed to the *chao thi*, genies who are masters of the land, guardians of the soil, houses, trees, and so on.

Phixai – Phetchaburi, Thailand (source: Sternstein, 1993).

Phra Chedi Sam Ong – Siamese name for the Three Pagoda pass on the Thai-Burmese border.

Phra Mongue – One of Leal's stops (1826) on his way up the Ataran/Kasat Noi river (from Moulmein to Siam).

Phra Song Chu – Phaya Thone Zu, the Burmese name for the Three Pagoda pass on the Thai-Burmese border.

Phu-Quoc – Phú Quốc (Vietnamese) or Koh Tral / Koh Trol (Khmer) is the largest island in Vietnam, part of an archipelago of twenty-two islands, located in the extreme south-west of the country and belonging to the province of Kiên Giang.

Phuket – Phuket Island, Thailand.

phya – title of nobility, Pontalis' spelling corresponds to the northern language (*phya* พญา) but the term is pronounced *phraya* (พระยา) in central Thai.

picul – Traditional unit of measurement equivalent to about sixty kilograms.

pla tu – Small fish in the mackerel family.

Pokkhara – Another name for the city of Dala, formerly known as Adhipaccaya, west of Rangoon (according to Lefèvre-Pontalis based on Forchhammer, 1883).

Pondicherry – City on the south-east coast of India, a French colony until 1954.

Pram or Prang – Town in Thailand, on the road from Mergui to Ayutthaya.

Prome – Colonial name for the present-day town of Pyay, Burma.

Pulao Langkawi – Pulau Langkawi, Malaysia.

Pulao Pinang – Island of Penang, Malaysia (deformation of *pulao*: island in Malay).

Pulao Teratau – Tarutau Island, Thailand.

Pulao Telibong – Libong Island in Thailand.

Pyu – Name given to an ancient Tibeto-Burman language group who lived in the Irrawaddy basin. Their territory was centred on the present-day town of Pyay (Prome). They gradually merged with the present-day Burmese, to whom they passed on much of their culture.

Raheng – Town located between Tak and Mae Sot, in Thailand.

Ramanadesa – Ramañña, ancient name for Lower Burma, which is currently covered by the regions of Bago (Pegu), Yangon (Rangoon), Bassein (Pathein) and the Mon state. From the point of view of Burmese apocryphal geography (Candier, 2020: 347), Ramañña is included in Suvaṇṇabhūmi and happens to be the place where the Buddhist missionaries Sona and Uttara, sent by the Indian king Aśoka (3rd century BC) to propagate Theravādin Buddhism, landed (Kalyani inscription, Bago).

Rammavati – Corresponds to several ancient cities in India (including the birthplace of Kondana Buddha), Arakan and Burma (Taungdwin according to the *Chronicle of the Glass Palace*). Name given after the 15th century to the region to the east of the Shwedagon pagoda, Rangoon, Burma (according to Lefèvre-Pontalis, based on Forchhammer, 1883).

Rangoon – Yangon. Capital of Burma until 2005, replaced by Naypyidaw.

Ranong – City and province in Thailand.

Ratburi – Ratchaburi, Thailand.

Remyo – Probably Maymyo, now Pyin Oo Lwin, which was a high-altitude resort in the Shan States that allowed Europeans living in Burma to cool off during the hot season.

Sachanalai – Sri Satchanalai, forty-five kilometres north of Sukhotai, is home to temple ruins dating back to the 13th century.

Saddhammanagara – Pāli name for the ancient royal city of Thaton.

Sagaing – Town in the Sagaing division, on the right bank of the Irrawaddy.

Saigon – Ho Chi Minh City, Vietnam.

sala – Common Thai and Lao term for small pavilions used for rest or pleasure.

Salween (river) – Thanlwin river, Burma, called Salouen by Lefèvre-Pontalis.

Sanda (also called Tsanta, Thanta and Santafau by Lefèvre-Pontalis) – Mong Santa, one of the nine ancient Tai (or Dai) kingdoms of Yunnan (bordering the northern Shan state of Burma).

Sat Dharma – Sanskrit name from which, according to Lefèvre-Pontalis, the Pāli name of the town of Thaton, Saddhammanagara, is derived.

Satan or Saton (another spelling of Thaton) – Thaton, Burma.

Sawbwa, – rulers of the Shan principalities.

Sea Gypsies – Literally "sea nomads", a term used to describe a number of coastal populations along the Burmese, Thai and Malay coasts who speak languages of Malay origin and are more or less mobile depending on the season: Moken, Moklen, Urak Lawoi, Urang Laut etc.

Selung – Burmese name for the Moken, a nomadic seafaring people.

Setchuen – Sichuan, China.

Shan – Tai-speaking people living in north-east Burma. Also known as Tai-Yai in Thailand.

Sheinmaga – Village in the Sagaing division, on the Irrawaddy, Burma.

Shui Madu – Shwemawdaw Pagoda, Bago (Pegu), Burma.

Shway Gyeen – Shwegyin Pagoda, Bago (Pegu) region, Burma.

Shwe Dagon – Shwedagon Pagoda, Yangon (Rangoon), Burma.

Shwegu – Town in Kachin state, on the left bank of the Irrawaddy, Burma, spelt Shwé Gu in Lefèvre-Pontalis' notebooks.

Shwe Gyi Bie – Shwe In Bin monastery, south-west of Mandalay, built in 1895.

Shweli (river) – A tributary of the Irrawaddy, the Shweli (Burmese) – Nam Mao (in Shan) and Ruili (in Chinese) – forms part of the border between Burma and China.

Siam – Former name of Thailand, given to the Thai people by the Khmers. Founded in 1350 by King Ramathibodi (r. 1351-1369), Siam became Thailand in 1939 after General Phibun Songkhram (1897-1964) took power.

Sim Jan Bine – Chaung Wa Pyin, village at the mouth of the Dawei (Tavoy) river, Burma.

sin – see *panung*.

Sing Khon Tha Pe – Sing Khon /Maw Daung pass (Thailand-Burma border).

Singapore – City and State of Singapore.

Singora – former name of present-day Songkhla, a town in southern Thailand.

Sissovat (river) – Mae Nam Mae Klong (Khwae Yai), Thailand.

Sittang (river) – Burmese river that rises on the Shan plateau, south-east of Mandalay, and flows south to the Gulf of Martaban, between the Irrawaddy and Salween rivers.

sra (สระ) – Water reservoir, sacred pond.

Steel brothers – Steel Brothers & Co Ltd, founded in Rangoon in 1870 to trade in rice and teak.

Straits – The Straits Settlements are a group of territories administered from 1826 by the British East India Company – Malacca, Singapore and Penang – then grouped together as a single British colony in 1867.

Strand Hotel – Located in the heart of Rangoon (Yangon) in Burma, this is one of the most famous hotels in Southeast Asia, built in 1901 and owned by the Sarkies brothers (also of Raffles hotel, Singapore).

Sukhothai – Former Siamese royal city, spelt Sukhotai in Lefèvre-Pontalis' notebooks.

Suphan Buri – A town in central Thailand where the moats and walls of an ancient city can be found, spelt Soupan in the notebooks of Lefèvre-Pontalis.

Suvannabhumi – Suvaṇṇabhūmi. Pāli toponym found in several ancient sources, referring to territories in eastern India. According to the Sinhalese chronicle Mahāvaṃsa, the Indian king Aśoka (IIIe century BC) delegated two monks, Sona and Uttara, to Suvaṇṇabhūmi, to propagate Theravādin orthodox Buddhism, that of the Pāli canon. In Burma, Suvaṇṇabhūmi is located south of the Sittang (Thaton) river.

Tagala or Tegala – The name given to the ancient city of Golanagara, 30 kilometres north of Thaton, by the Portuguese explorer Hernandez Pinto in the 17th century.

Tagaung – Town of Takaung, Mandalay region, left bank of the Irrawaddy, Burma. The ancient city was a Pyu city-state founded in the first millennium.

Tai – Current name for citizens of Thailand. Speakers of the Tai language (which includes several closely related languages: Lao, Shan, Lue, etc.).

Tai Noi – Name given, probably by the Siamese, to the Tai-speaking populations of the north of the country, also known as Tai Yuan or Khon Mueang.

Tai Yai – Thai name for the Shan people.

Takkala or Taikkala – Other names for the ancient city of Golanagara, located 30 kilometres north of Thaton near the village of Ayetthema, Burma.

Talaings – One of the names of the Mon ethnic group, present mainly in southern Burma.

Tali – Dali, Yunnan.

Tang San – Probably the present-day Ban San Tang, north-west of the town of Trang, Thailand.

Tap Thieng – Quarter of the present-day town of Trang in southern Thailand.

Taping (river) – Taping River, rises in Yunnan and flows into the Irrawaddy north of Bhamo, Kachin state, Burma.

Taungthu – Burmese word for mountain people. According to Burmese historical tradition, this people originated from Thaton (source: Forchhammer, 1883). It is also one of the Burmese exonyms for the Pa-O.

Tavoy – Dawei, Burma.

Tchang – Resort turned royal botanical garden to the east of the town of Trang, Thailand.

Tehong – Toponym between Phatthalung and Trang in southern Thailand.

Tenasserim – The Tanintharyi region or Tenasserim region is a subdivision of southern Burma. It is located on the Malay Peninsula, between the Andaman Sea to the west and Thailand to the east. To the north, it borders the Mon state. Its capital is Dawei (Tavoy) and another major city is Myeik (Mergui).

Teratan (island of) – Island to the north of Pulau Langkawi.

Tha Chin (river) – Tha Chin River, branch of the Chao Phraya.

Thabeikkyin – Town and district of the same name on the left bank of the Irrawaddy, Mandalay region, Burma, spelt Thabeikhyin in Lefèvre-Pontalis' notebooks.

Thai – Current name for citizens of Thailand.

Thakuto – One of Leal's stops (1826) on the Mae Klong river (Siam).

Thalang – Name of the boat Pierre Lefèvre-Pontalis took from Penang to sail back to Burma. A distortion of the name Selung, the Burmese name for the Moken, a nomadic seafaring people.

Thale Noi – Northern part of the lagoon stretching from Songkhla to Phatthalung, Thailand.

Tham Kou Ha – Cave in the centre of Phatthalung, Thailand.

Tharekkettara – Thayekhittaya (Sri Ksetra), Burma. Ancient Pyu city located near the present-day town of Pyay (Prome).

Thaton – Town in Mon state, southern Burma.

Thazi – Town in Thazi township, Meiktila district, Mandalay region, central Burma.

Theinni (also called Hwen Win, Kien-Hung and Tchéli/Tcheli by Lefèvre-Pontalis) – Hsenwi, northern Shan state, Burma.

tical – Weight of silver alloy coins used in Burma and Siam. The coins take their

GLOSSARY 247

name from this unit of mass, which is not the same from one country to another.

Tigyaing – Town in Sagaing division, right bank of the Irrawaddy, Burma.

Toungoo – Town and former royal city in the region of Bago (Pegu), Burma, spelt Toungou or Taungu by Lefèvre-Pontalis.

Tourane-Savannakhet – Road linking Da Nang (called Tourane by the French colonisers) in Vietnam to Savannakhet in Laos.

Trang – City in southern Thailand, administrative centre of the province of the same name.

Tripitaka – The three *piṭaka*, literally the "baskets", are the texts forming the dogma of Theravādin Buddhism. They include the Pāli canon, its commentaries (*aṭṭakathā*), postcanonical texts and treatises on Pāli grammar.

Tsanta (also called Sanda, Thanta and Santafau by Lefèvre-Pontalis) – Mong Santa, one of the nine ancient Tai Dai kingdoms of Yunnan (bordering the northern Shan state of Burma).

Tsiguen – Hsikwan (Hsi-gwin), Yunnan, China. One of the nine ancient Tai Dai kingdoms of Yunnan (bordering northern Shan state, Burma).

Ubon – Ubon Ratchathani, a town in north-east Thailand, spelt Oubone in the Lefèvre-Pontalis notebooks.

Ukkala – Utkala (Orissa). In Burmese Buddhist tradition, this toponym refers to the region of the Irrawaddy delta where two merchants are said to have brought strands of the Buddha's hair and built the Shwedagon pagoda in Rangoon (Yangon). This is the name given after the 15th century to the region north of the Shwedagon pagoda (according to Lefèvre-Pontalis, based on Forchhammer, 1883).

Ukkalanagara – Another name for the town of Ukkala, north of the Shwedagon pagoda, Rangoon (Yangon), Burma.

Uttaran (river) [also called Attharam by Lefèvre-Pontalis] – Ataran river (Kasat Noi in Thailand), a tributary of the Gyaing river, Mawlamyine (Moulmein), Burma.

Victoria point (Lefèvre-Pontalis also writes Point Victoria) – Colonial name for the present-day town of Kawthaung, Burma.

vieng – Circular ditch delimiting the main towns of a *muang* (เมือง) and sometimes forming the root of their name (Vieng Tian for contemporary Vientiane, capital city of Lao P.D.R). The form Chiang or Xieng is also found in the north.

Wan Tien – Wan-tien, Yunnan.

Wellesley province (north of Penang) – Seberang Perai.

wolfram (mine) – Tungsten mine.

Xatan (another spelling of Thaton) – Thaton, Burma.

Xieng Ma (also called Laing Ma by Lefèvre-Pontalis) – One of the nine ancient Tai Dai kingdoms of Yunnan (bordering northern Shan state, Burma).

Yamethin – A town in the Mandalay region of Burma, francized to Yamethin in Lefèvre-Pontalis' notebooks.

Ye – Town in the Mon state of Burma, gallicised to Yé in Lefèvre-Pontalis' notebooks.

Yunnan – Province in south-west China, with Kunming as its capital.

Yunnanese – Inhabitants of Yunnan.

Yunnanfou or Yunnan Sen – Kunming, Yunnan.

Zelaya – Name of a boat borrowed by Lefèvre-Pontalis.

Zingyaik – Zin Kyaik, Mon State, Burma.

Sources used to compile the glossary

Candier, Aurore (2020) *La réforme politique en Birmanie pendant le premier moment colonial (1819-1878)*, Paris, EFEO.

Condominas, Georges (1980) *L'espace social à propos de l'Asie du Sud-Est*, Paris, Flammarion.

Forchhammer, Emmanuel (1883), *Notes on the early history and geography of British Burma: the Shwe Dagon pagoda*, Rangoon, Governement Press, available at https://archive.org/stream/b2935125x/b2935125x_djvu.txt

Low, James (1835, 1836) "History of Tennasserim," *Journal of the Royal Asiatic Society of Great-Britain and Ireland*, 1835, pp. 248-275; 1836, pp. 287-336.

Sternstein, Larry (1993) "The London Company's Envoys Plot Siam," *The Journal of the Siam Society*, 81(2), pp. 11-95.

Biographies of personalities

ABBEY, W. (major) – Chief of the Thaton district, Burma, during Pierre Lefèvre-Pontalis' trip.

ALLEGRI, Carlos – Italian engineer who became chief engineer to King Chulalongkorn (Rama V, r. 1868-1910). He supervised the construction of many roads and bridges in Siam.

ALOMPRA – King Alaungphaya or Alaungmintaya (r. 1752-1760), Konbaung dynasty, royal city of Shwebo, Burma.

ANURATHA (king) – Anawratha, king of Pagan (r. 1044-1077), Burma.

BEAUREGARD – Chevalier de Beauregard (1665-1692), French governor in Bangkok, then in Mergui (Myeik) during the reign of King Narai (r. 1656-1688).

BHANURANGSI – Prince Bhanurangsi Savangwongse (1859-1928), one of the sons of King Mongkut (Rama IV, r. 1851-1868) and Queen Debsirindra, younger brother of King Chulalongkorn (Rama V, r. 1868-1910).

BOURDONNAIS, Bertrand François Mahé de la – French admiral and engineer (1699-1753).

de BRUAN – French commander at Mergui (Myeik) in 1688 (reign of Narai, 1656-1688) who built a port there.

BURENG NAUNG (king) – Bayinnaung reigned in Burma from 1550 to 1581.

BURNABY, Richard – Governor of Mergui (Myeik), killed the Siamese revolt against the British in 1687.

BURNEY, Henry (1792-1845) – Major Henry Burney, British resident at the Court of Ava between 1830 and 1838, his stay recorded in a diary which was subsequently published.

CĀLUKYA (dynasty) – Royal dynasty that ruled southern India between the 6th and 12th centuries.

CHAKRABONGSE, Bhunavath, (Prince) (1883-1920) – son of King Chulalongkorn (Rama V, r. 1868-1910) and Queen Saovabha. Secretary General of the Royal Army and founder of the Royal Air Force.

CHAO UTHONG – King Uthong (Ramathibodhi I), founder of Ayutthaya (r. 1351-1369).

CHARBONNEAU, René (1643-1727) – lay missionary and doctor, made governor of Phuket for between 1682 and 1685 by King Narai (r. 1656-1688).

CHAROON (Prince) – Charoonsak Kridakorn (1877-1947), grandson of King Mongkut (Rama IV, r. 1851-1868), son of Prince Naret; Siam's ambassador to Paris 1912-1927.

CHIRAC, Pierre de, (1863-1929) – Priest of the Society of Foreign Missions posted to Moulmein (Mawlamyine), Burma, from 1886 until his death in 1929.

CHULALONGKORN – King Rama V (1853-1910) reigned in Siam from 1868 to 1910.

COOK – Thomas Cook (1808-1892), a British businessman and one of the first travel agents, starting out in 1841 and thirty years later founding a company bearing his name.

CURZON, George Nathaniel (1859-1925) – Viceroy of the British Indian Empire from 1899 to 1905.

DAMRONG, Rajanubhab, (Prince) (1862-1943) – Brother of King

Chulalongkorn (Rama V, r. 1868-1910), founder of the modern Siamese education system and provincial administration.

DELONCLE, François (1856-1922) – French MP.

DESFARGES, (Marshal) – Commander (French) of the fortress of Bangkok in 1688 at the time of the death of King Narai (r. 1656-1688).

DHAMMACETI (king) – Dhammazedi (r. 1471-1492), king of Hanthawaddy (Pegu, Bago), Burma.

DUROISELLE, Charles (1871-1951) – Correspondent of the École française d'Extrême-Orient, director of the archaeological department of Burma (successor to Taw Sein Ko), professor of Pāli at Rangoon University and co-founder of the Burma Research Society.

ELIAS, Ney (1844-1877) – British explorer, appointed assistant to the British resident in Mandalay in 1874. He was part of the Burma-China double expedition of 1875, aborted after the murder of Margary in Yunnan.

FAROUA – See Wareru.

FEDERICI, Caesar dei (c. 1530-c. 1600) – Italian merchant and traveller.

FITZMAURICE, Henry – British consular assistant in Siam, vice consul in Phuket and Chiang Mai.

FORCHHAMMER, Emmanuel (1851-1890) – Swiss Indologist and Pāli scholar who held the chair of Pāli at Rangoon College in the late 1870s and was appointed head of the archaeological department of British Burma at the beginning of the following decade.

FOURNEREAU, Lucien (1846-1906) – French archaeologist, architect, explorer and photographer who led excavations in Indochina and Siam.

GERVAISE, Nicolas (1662-1729) – Priest of the Foreign Missions of Paris and author of a natural and political history of Siam (1689).

HANNAY – Captain Hannay visited the amber mines of the Hukong valley, Kachin country, Burma on the Assam border, in 1836 (Pemberton, 1837).

HARDOUIN, Sent by the French colonial authorities from Laos to set up a consular post in Nan province in 1895. He then stayed in Siam where he became consul in Bangkok before retiring to Penang.

JAMES II – King of England and Ireland (r. 1685-1688).

KING, Hamilton – American ambassador (consul general then minister plenipotentiary) in Bangkok from 1898 to 1912.

de LAJONQUIÈRE, Étienne Lunet de Lajonquière (1861-1833) – Military officer, explorer, archaeologist and writer, posted to French Indochina and appointed member of the École française d'Extrême-Orient in 1899.

LA LOUBÈRE – Simon de La Loubère (1642-1729), French poet and diplomat sent by King Louis XIV (r. 1643-1715) to Siam in 1687-1688.

LASSEN, Christian (1800-1876) – Norwegian indianist.

LEAL, Francis Joseph – Interpreter for Henri Burney, the British East India Company's special envoy to Siam in 1826. On Burney's orders, Leal made several crossings between the Andaman coast, the Gulf of Siam and Bangkok, and took the route from Martaban to Bangkok in 1826. His notes are recorded in *The Burney Papers, 1910*, Bangkok: Vajirañāna National Library. Reprinted 1971. London: Gregg International Publishers Limited.

LOW, James (Lieutenant, then Captain) – (1795-1852), Scottish officer in

BIOGRAPHIES OF PERSONALITIES 251

the service of the British East India Company, in charge of Wellesley province in the Straits Settlements; author of several reports and maps of the province.

MACLEOD (Captain) – Last British resident appointed to Ava (Inwa), then Rangoon (Yangon), 1839-1840.

MAHIBAL – Phya Mahibal Borirak (1867-1927), was first assistant to the Siamese ambassador in Paris in 1888. Then was tutor Prince Chakrabongse Saint Petersburg in 1898, before becoming Siamese ambassador to Russia. Governor of *monthon* Chumphon from 1905. As his administrative residence was in Bandon, he was called Governor of Bandon. He retired in 1911 and devoted himself to his business ventures until his death.

MANOHARI / MANUHA (king) – Manuha, last king of Thaton, southern Burma, defeated and taken captive to Pagan during the reign of Anawratha (r. 1044-1077).

MAUGRAS, François Gustave Gaston (1884-1965) – French diplomat.

MENG KYINIA (king) – King Mingyi Nyo (1485-1530), founder of the Taungoo dynasty.

MIDON (King) – King Mindon (r. 1852-1878), Konbaung dynasty, royal cities of Amarapura and Mandalay, Burma.

NANDA BURENG (king) – King Nanda Bayin (r. 1581-1599), son and successor of Bayinnaung, Burma.

NARATHA JEDI MEN – Nawratha Zadi Min (?), prince of Tavoy who embellished Ye in 1438 (source: Low, 1835: 255)

NARET (King of Siam) – Naresuan (1555-1605), King of Ayutthaya, from 1590 to 1605.

NARET (prince) – Prince Nares Varariddhi, Siam's first ambassador to Washington.

NARAI, King – Narai, (1632-1688), often referred to as Phra Narai (Thai: สมเด็จพระนารายณ์มหาราช), was one of the most important rulers of Ayutthaya (Siam, reigning from 1656) until his death under the name of Ramathibodi III.

NOTTON, Camille (1881-1961) – French diplomat and historian, consul in Chiang Mai from the First to the Second World War. He was responsible for numerous translations and studies of northern Tai manuscripts.

PEEL, Arthur – British Ambassador to Siam from 1909 to 1915.

PETITHUGUENIN, Paul (1876-1955) – Correspondent of the École Française d'Extrême-Orient (EFEO), Consul of France in Bangkok and Advisor to the Siamese government (in charge of the liquor industry). He lived in Siam from 1902 to 1919 and took part in the Bernard mission which, in 1905, demarcated the border between French Indochina and Siam.

PHAULKON, Constantin, born Costantin Gerachi (1647-1688) – a Greek adventurer who became the first adviser to the Ayutthaya King Narai (r. 1656-1688) before being assassinated after the king's death.

SATHORN SATHAN PHITHAK, Phra – Nephew of Phya Ratsada, who was assassinated with him in Penang in 1913.

PINTO, Fernão Mendes (1511-1583) – Portuguese writer, soldier, diplomat, adventurer and explorer who spent time in Siam between 1530 and 1540.

PTOLEMY (c. 100- c. 168) – Greek astronomer, astrologer, mathematician and geographer who lived in

Alexandria (Egypt).

RAMKHAMHAENG, King – Ramkhamhaeng, king of Sukhothai (r. 1279-1298).

RATSADA – The last son of the governor of Ranong (Khaw Soo Cheng), Phraya Ratsadanupradit Mahitsaraphakdi (born Khaw Sim Bee, 1857-1913, in an influential Chinese family). He was appointed governor of Kraburi in 1882 and then, after the visit of King Chulalongkorn (Rama V, r. 1868-1910), governor of Trang in 1890. Trang became the symbol of King Chulalongkorn's modernist policy. In 1896, Phuket became the *monthon* (super-province) of all the west coast provinces and Khaw Sim Bee was appointed its governor in 1900, when he was given the title of Phaya Ratsada. He was assassinated in early February 1913 in the port of Trang.

SCOTT, James George (1851-1935) – British journalist, writer and colonial administrator.

SIRI DHAMMASOKA (king) – Indian king Aśoka (c. 304 – 232 BC).

SONA – According to the Buddhist historical tradition, one of the two missionaries sent to Ramañña/Suvaṇṇabhūmi by the Indian king Aśoka (IIIe century BC) to propagate Theravādin Buddhism there.

STIRLING – High Commissioner of Lashio, former member of the Muong Sing demarcation commission (1894) in which Lefèvre-Pontalis participated (for details see Gosha, 2003: 54-55).

TABENG SHWEHTI (king) – King Tabinshwehti (r. 1530-1550), Toungoo dynasty, Burma.

TACHARD, Guy (1648-1712) – Jesuit priest who accompanied the French missions to Siam in 1685 and 1687.

TAVERNIER – Jean-Baptiste Tavernier (1605-1689), merchant, adventurer and author of several travel accounts in the Orient.

TONKINSON, Harry – Secretary General to the Government of British Burma, appointed in 1904 (source: India List, 1905).

UTTARA – According to Buddhist historical tradition, one of the two missionaries sent to Ramañña/Suvaṇṇabhūmi by the Indian king Aśoka (3rd century BC) to propagate Theravādin Buddhism there.

DES VOEUX, Herbert – *Deputy Commissioner*, Burma (source: India List, 1905: 480).

VILMORIN, Philippe de (1872-1917) – French botanist, travelling companion of Pierre Lefèvre-Pontalis on the Burmese section of the diary.

WARERU – Wareru, king of Martaban (r. 1287-1307), southern Burma, also called Fa roua by Pierre Lefèvre-Pontalis.

WHITE, Samuel – Governor of Mergui (Myeik) during the reign of Phra Narai (r. 1656-1688).

WITTANAKIT – Phya Wittanakit Picharana, governor of Phatthalung from 1909 to 1913.

YUGALA – Prince Yugala Dighambara (1882-1932), also known as the Prince of Lopburi. Son of King Chulalongkorn and HRH Princess Saisavali Bhiromya.

YULE, Henry (1820-1889) – Scottish orientalist who accompanied the British envoy Arthur Phayre (1812-1885) on his mission to Burma in 1855. Author of *A Narrative of the Mission Sent by the Governor General of India to the Court of Ava in 1855, with Notices of the Country, Government and People* (1858), London, Smith Elder.

Sources used to compile the biographies

Gosha, Christopher, and Soren Ivarson (eds. 2003), *Contesting Vision of the Lao Past: Laos Historiography at the Crossroads*, Copenhagen, NIAS Press.

The India List and India Office List for 1905 (1905), London, Harrison and sons.

Low, James (1835, 1836) "History of Tennasserim", *Journal of the Royal Asiatic Society of Great-Britain and Ireland*, 1835, pp. 248-275; 1836, pp. 287-336.

Index

Abbey, Major W. 120, 122, 124-6, 145, 147
Aceh 99
Adhipaccaya 121
Ahlone 143,
Ai-Lao 155
Alaungpra 168, 172, 174
Allegri, Carlos 26, 46, 67
Alompra 132, 192
Amarapura 155, 158, 163-4, 168-70, 172
American Missions 73, 77, 82
Amherst 112-3
Ampheu (อำเภอ) 68, 75, 209, 221, 231
Ananda pagoda 176-78, 180, 184, 224
Angkor 17, 57, 179, 184
Angkor Wat 163, 186, 226
Anglo-American 105
Anglo-French 97
Anglo-Saxon, The 28, 83
Andaman Sea 25
Annam 30, 38, 64, 173
Aanuratha, King 20, 120-1, 173, 180-1, 183, 185, 191, 228
Arakan 108, 163-5, 168, 181, 183
Arcachon 46
Arimaddana 180
Arramana 191
Aryans 119
Assam 125, 143, 147, 154, 181
Attharam, River 111
Ava 133, 144, 155, 158, 160, 165, 168-72, 174, 182-3
Ayetthima, 121
Ayutthaya 15, 19, 23, 26-7, 95, 100, 135, 171, 225, 227, 228-9, 233

Bacala 121

Bactau 78
Ban Chang 112
Ban Chiang Khong 213
Ban Chiom 112
Ban Dok Mai 222
Ban Huay Sak 213
Ban Pha Nu 230
Ban Tapan 100
Bandon 7, 22, 24-5, 38, 40, 41-5, 50, 53, 72, 74-5, 78, 92
Bandon River 41-2
Bangkok 10, 12, 15-6, 19, 22-3, 25-9, 31, 32, 36, 39, 41, 46, 52-4, 58, 61, 63-5, 73, 76, 78, 82, 85-6, 90, 92, 94, 96-7, 99, 104, 106-7, 109, 111-2, 114, 118, 130, 138, 144, 153, 157, 174-5, 187, 190, 205, 209, 219-21, 227, 229, 231-5
Bangnarom 100
Bantam 96
Bassein 121
Battambang 17, 27
Baw Baw Gyi, stupa 163, 173
Beauregard 97
Bébégyi 173
Bentik, Island 98
Bengal, Bay of 23, 41, 43-4, 66, 77, 90, 92, 94-6, 99, 101, 106, 109, 117, 119, 143-4, 212
Bhamo 125-6, 129, 137-8, 143-4, 146-50, 151, 152-3, 167-8, 174-5, 186
Bhamo (boat) 167-8, 174-5, 186
Bhanurangsi, Prince 49
Bibby line 124, 129
Black River 140, 148
Bodawpaya, King 164, 183
Bombay Burmah 115, 147, 156, 193, 196, 215, 221

Boribat (boat) 36, 37-8, 41-2, 45-6
Bonnafous 37
Borobudur 17
Bourdonnais, Bertrand François Mahe de la 92
Bowring Treaty, The 27, 29
Boxers Revolt 174
British 18-9, 24-5, 27-30, 50, 56, 81-2, 92, 94, 105, 108, 111, 115, 126, 136-7, 144, 147, 166, 169, 194, 197, 207
British India 84, 105-6, 190
Buddha 56, 70, 78, 117, 122, 128, 159-60, 162, 164, 168, 178-9, 181, 184-5, 191, 224-5
Buddhism 20, 44, 74, 120-1, 181
Bureng Naung, King 95, 133, 145, 155, 171, 191, 199
Burnaby, Richard 96
Burney, Henry 146

Cachar 143
Calukya dynasty 119
Cambodia 17, 27, 44, 101, 106, 179, 186
Chaiya 24
Chakrabongse, Prince 49, 64, 209, 214, 216
Chance Island 98
Chandoo 194-5
Chang 29-30, 61, 62-3, 64-6, 67, 68-9
Chantabun 51
Chao Phraya river 15-6, 233
Chao Uthong 227
Charbonneau, René 27, 96
Charoon, Prince 49, 76-7, 80
Château d'Aulnaie 10, 13
Chayok 108-9, 112
Chersonèse 122
Chiang Hai 83, 228
Chiang Hung 145-6

Chiang Mai 11-2, 43, 83, 133, 171, 205, 219, 221, 228-9
Chiang Rai 227-8
Chiang Saen 12, 147
Chiang Tung 146-7
China 25, 51-3, 73, 135, 143-8, 151, 181, 198
Chindwin River 143-4, 155, 161, 169, 175-6, 188
Chinese 16, 18-21, 23, 25-7, 29-31, 38, 40-3, 45, 47-8, 62, 65, 68-9, 71-6, 78-82, 84-7, 90, 104-6, 108, 112-3, 118, 143-55, 157, 171, 180, 182, 186, 193, 195, 199, 201, 208, 210, 215, 220-1, 232-3
Chinese Shan 146, 150
Chira, Prince 48, 49
Chirac, Pierre de 115, 193-4
Circuit house 134, 137, 158, 162, 178, 184
Chittagong 144, 157
Cholon 79
Chulalongkorn, King 16, 22, 46
Chumphon 7, 22, 25, 38, 40, 53, 74, 78, 92
Chumphon Bay 24, 40
Cochinchina 45, 85, 87
Colombo 79, 124
Comité de l'Asie Française 9
Conti, Nicolo di 170
Cook 15, 126, 130, 190
Coromandel 96
Couir (Koney) 99-100
Court Island 98
Curzon, Viceroy George Nathaniel 134

Dala 121
Dali 147, 152
Damrong Rajanubhab, Prince 16, 40, 46, 52, 58, 60, 65, 69-70, 76, 81, 83, 91, 227-8
Danclai 112

Danish 26, 196
Danish East Asiatic Company 37, 45
Darwin, Charles 18
Dawson, Commissioner. 114-6, 118, 122-3, 126, 138, 150, 188-90, 192, 194, 197-8, 220
Dhammaceti, King 121-2, 132
de Bruan 97, 106
De Reuth 66
Deloncle, François 65, 92
Desfarges, Marechal 96, 106
Des Voeux, Herbert 189-90
Dewana hills 200-2, 205
Dreadnought 124
Doi Tai Chan 216
Dunlop, Dr. 73-4, 77-8
Duroiselle, Charles 134, 159, 163-4, 166, 173, 176, 186
Dusit 57, 65
Dutch 23-4, 26, 95-6, 106
Dvaravati 19

East Asia 23, 95
East Asiatic Company 43
East Indies 97
Eastern and Oriental Hotel, The 84-5
École Française d'Extrême-Orient 17
École Spéciale des langues orientales 9
Elias, Ney 146
England 28, 96, 110, 115, 189, 193, 196
English 16, 19, 24-5, 27-8, 41, 43, 46, 49, 51, 57, 61-2, 64, 66, 76, 81, 83, 85-6, 90-2, 94-8, 102-6, 108-9, 111, 113-4, 116-7, 125-6, 134, 136-7, 140, 143-7, 149, 152, 156-7, 163, 167, 174-5, 182, 189-90, 193-5, 197-8, 201, 204, 217, 220, 232
English East India Company 95-6, 99
English Quarter 129
Europe 18, 21, 70, 76, 92, 220
Europeans 17, 26, 28-9, 41, 45, 48-9, 51, 57, 60, 62, 65-6, 75, 80, 84-6, 89-91, 95-6, 112, 121, 135, 170, 195, 229

Federici, Cesar dei 109
Fitzmaurice, Henry 49, 56-7, 60, 73, 76-8
Forchhammer, Emmanuel 19-20, 122, 165
Fournereau, Lucien 226
France 10-2, 25, 28, 96, 106, 188, 202, 208, 220
Franco-British 24
French 16-7, 19, 24-9, 31, 65, 74, 83, 86, 91-92, 96-7, 99-100, 102-3, 106, 115, 117, 124, 128-9, 132, 147, 159, 165-6, 168, 192, 194, 197, 220
French Indochina 17, 45, 86
Freya (boat) 45
Fu Kien 85

Germans 17, 41, 50 54, 66
Gervaise, Nicolas 229
Goa 89, 95
Gobineau, Arthur de 18
Golamattikanagara 122
Golanagara 121-2
Golconde 96, 99
Gothek 137, 156
Goudineau, Yves 11
Gulf of Siam 15, 25, 43, 92, 94, 100-1, 106, 110, 174

Hà Tiên canal 57
Hainan 85, 143, 210
Haiphong 144
Haiphong-Yunnan Sen 144
Halong Bay 78
Hamilton King 82-4
Hangsawadi 20, 119-21, 132, 171, 173, 182, 191-2, 207
Hannay 146

INDEX 257

Hanoi 145, 182
Hardouin, Raoul 64, 69, 212
Hindu 17, 20, 44, 78, 82, 85, 87, 89-90, 100-1, 104, 119-21, 123-4, 128, 130, 134, 139, 141, 143, 149, 156-7, 161, 163, 165, 173, 175, 184-5, 190-1, 193, 195, 197-8, 204, 210, 221, 223-4, 227-8
Hindu-Buddhist 19
Hinduisation 20
Hong Kong 76, 79, 90, 97
Hotha 146

India 17, 44, 89, 95-7, 99-100, 119, 121, 124-5, 130, 136, 141-2, 144, 147, 149, 163, 166, 174-5, 179, 185, 198
Indian 17-20, 26-7, 29, 96, 144, 179, 198, 205
Indian coast 23-4, 95
Indian Empire 146
Indian Ocean 23, 29, 92
Indo-Aryan 17, 20
Indo-Burmese 142
Indo-Pacific 25
Indochina 9, 17, 44, 50-1, 57, 60, 64, 68, 76, 80, 83, 86, 103, 114, 122, 144, 147, 149-50, 155, 163, 171-2, 184, 215
Inywa 154
Irrawaddy 114, 119-20, 122, 125, 138, 139, 140, 141-4, 146, 148, 149, 152-7, 160, 163, 168-72, 174, 176-77, 180, 182-3, 187-8, 198, 223
Irrawaddy Flotilla 194
Isthmus of Kra 15, 41, 65, 87, 93
Italian 26, 46, 62-3, 66, 165

James II, King 97
Japan 28, 51, 73
Japanese 26, 50, 105
Java 49, 76

Jelinga 99
Junk Ceylon 49, 79, 96-97, 101

Kachin 149, 151-3
Kaing Ma 146
Kalah (Kuleh, Kuleh, Kola) 121
Kalamani 206
Kalinga 100, 119
Kalyanisima 132
Kamphaeng Phet 222, 223, 225, 226-31
Kanburi 107, 110-2, 229
Kao Chay Son 52, 56
Kao Tang Kuan, Hill 50
Kapilavistu 141
Karen 102, 114, 120, 123, 132, 200, 204, 206, 208, 214, 215, 221
Kasun, Mount 100
Katha 143, 147, 152, 162
Katigara 143
Kaupalene 206
Kedah 47, 82, 94
Kelantan 94
Kennedy 78
Khamti 146
Khao Kao 68-9, 70, 71-2, 76, 78
Khata 143, 152-3
Khryse 122
Khsatrya 142, 179
King, Hamilton 82-84
Kings Island 106
Kinywa 121
Kisserang Island 102
Klings 104
Klong Bangwilai 111
Klong Menang Luong 112
Klong Mykut 111
Klong Mysikleet 111
Klong Peli 111
Kodak 15, 151, 204-5, 207, 224
Kokain 121

Kokarit 115, 150, 189, 193
Ko Shan pri 146, 154
Koh Kut 51
Koh Lak 37-8
Ko Si Ko Ha Islands 52, 53
Khaw Soo Cheang 30
Khamuk 207
Khawa 211
Khmer 10, 27, 165
Kraburi 24
Kra Isthmus 15, 41, 65, 87, 93
Kratieh road 64
Kublai Khan 182
Kulanagara 121
Kulataik 121
Kunlong 125, 144
Kursaal 64
Kusima 121
Kyanhyat 140
Kyauk Myaung 156
Kyauk Taw, pagoda 159, 161-2
Kyoaewa 182

La Loubère, Simon de 96, 229-30
Labong 205
Lai Châu 140
Lak Muong 226
Lamar 24
Lampang 12
Lan Chang 171
Langkawi 81, 89
Lang Suan 38, 41
Laos 9-11, 16, 64, 88, 165
Laotien 9
Lashio 125, 129, 144, 147
Lassen, Christian 122
Latha 146
Lawa, Kingdoms 205-6
Leal, Francis Joseph 100, 108, 111-2
Lefèvre-Pontalis, Amédé 9
Lefèvre-Pontalis, Henriette 9, 15, 78, 124, 129-30, 132, 138, 143, 150-1, 177, 188-90, 193, 195, 199-203, 208, 210-1, 213-4, 216, 220, 223, 231-2, 234
Lefèvre-Pontalis, Jean-Bertrand 11
Lefèvre-Pontalis, Patrick 10-2, 235
Lefèvre-Pontalis, Pierre 8, 9-11, 15, 18, 31, 37, 235
Lem Chong Pra 38
Lesseps, Ferdinand de 24
Ligor (Nakhon Sri Thammarat) 17, 21, 23-4, 43-4, 52, 56, 68, 100-2
limonite 123
Lopburi 46, 135, 225, 233
Louis XIV, King 24, 106
Low, James 97, 108, 111, 182
Lu Kiang 146,
Luang Peo 51
Luang Pitchak 220
Luang Prabang 50, 83
Lumchang 112

Macao 75
MacLeod, Captain 146
Madaya 158
Mae Ping 16, 218, 219, 220, 222, 223, 226-8, 230-2
Mae Sot 15, 196, 205-7, 208-9, 210, 211, 215-6
Mahibal, Phya 22, 38, 40-3, 53
mai yang 216
Mainlaunggyee 206
Maing Lung 146
Maing Lyin 146
Maing Maing 146
Malabar 59, 85, 104, 157
Malacca 23-5, 75, 95, 109
Malays 23, 25, 28, 38, 45, 68, 74, 81, 84-5, 90, 94, 101, 104, 196, 228
Malaysian 26
Male 140, 155-6, 182
Malta 99

INDEX 259

Manaud, Dr 46
Mandalay 15, 126, 129-30, 132, 134, 136-41, 143-4, 147, 150, 155-8, 159, 160, 161, 162, 165-9, 172, 176-7, 188-9, 197-8
Mandalay-Lashio 144
Manipur 142-3, 169, 176, 181
Manohari (Manuha), King 122, 181, 185
Marseille 99-100
Martaban 20, 23, 95, 101-2, 108, 110-1, 113, 116-9, 121-2, 124-5, 133, 173, 181, 191-2, 206, 212, 227-8
Masulipatam 99
Mathieu, Mr. 68
Maugras, François 37, 62, 138, 190, 205, 220, 230, 234
Maymyo 189
Meerawaddi 205-7
Meiktila 188
Meklong 108, 110-2
Mekong 9, 125, 139, 141, 145, 147, 151
Melamao 213, 215
Menam 99-102, 108, 111-2, 196, 214, 228-33
Menam Noi 108, 111-2
Menam Pho 228
Meng Kyinia, King 133
Meng Ting 144, 146
Mergui (now Myeik) 15, 23-4, 27, 89, 92, 95-100, 102-6, 108-110, 117, 123
Metho 217-8
Metok 215-7
Mindat 143
Mindon, King 136, 161
Mingla Sedi 184
Mingun pagoda 139
Minto Mansions 129, 132, 188
Misty Hollow 198, 200-1
Mogaung 125, 138, 146, 170

Mogok 139, 156, 163
Momiet 146
Mon 12, 18-20, 23-4, 27, 120, 132, 171
Mon-Khmer 230
Mona 146
Mong Lien 146
Mong Nai 146
Mongkut, King 29-30
Mongols 156, 182
Monyin 146, 170-1
Monywa 143
Moscos 109
Motte Lambert, Mgr de la 99
Moulmein (now Mawlamyine) 15, 20, 97, 99, 103, 109-11, 113-9, 123, 125-6, 130, 138, 143, 150, 160, 188-93, 194, 195-6, 198, 201, 207-8, 212, 215, 220-1
Moulmein-Raheng 196
Mowun 146
Muang (เมือง) 22, 229
Muong Chaiya 77
Muong La 145-6
Muong Mau 145-6, 154
Muong Sing 147, 165
Muong Tak 222
Muong Woun 146
Muslim Malays 29
Muttima 141
Mya Thein Dau 206
Myawadi (now Myawaddy) 15, 115, 138, 150, 198, 199, 202, 203, 205-8, 209, 213, 218
Myi-Kya-Kyauptein 108
Myingyan 126, 134, 144, 158, 186-8
Myitkyina 143
Mykesath 111
Myndoon 134
Myngoon 140, 169, 197

Naga 135, 161
Naga (people) 168, 176, 181
Nagasaki 50
Nak Boa 211
Nakhon Sawan 220, 222, 232
Nam Kuei Noi 108
Nam Meuy 207-8, 211, 213
Nam Tha Valley 10
Nam Mun 83
Nanda Bureng, King 145
Nanzhao 146
Napoleonic Wars 21
Narai, Phra 24, 96-7, 106, 229
Narapatisithu, King 184
Naratha Jedi Men 110
Naret, Prince 77, 80
Naret, King 207
Na Wang 59-61, 68
Nayé Daung 108, 111
Negritos (Mani) 18, 64, 77
Newbrunner, Mr. 84-5
Nha Trang 173
Nicobar 98
Nile 141, 176
Nord German Lloyd 190
Notton, Camille 37

Ormuz 99

Paetongtarn Shinawatra, Prime Minister 26
Pagan 15, 20, 101, 120, 125-6, 129-30, 133, 137, 142, 155, 158, 161, 163, 165, 167, 169-71, 173-86, 188, 191, 210, 224-5, 228
Pahang State of 94
Pak Chan 41, 74, 78, 90-2, 94, 98, 104, 118, 174
Paklène 211
Paknam 37
Paknampho 138, 190, 219, 221, 230-3

Pak Nam Tako 38
Pak Payun 52, 53
Pak Prek 112
Peking Gazette 146
Palembang 101
Paleolithicist 19
Palot 209, 213-6
Panya 155, 169, 170, 172, 182
Patani 47, 94
Patte (cook) 132, 158, 199-200, 202-3, 224
Paunglaung 132
Pavie Mission 9, 12, 15
Peel, Arthur 114
Pegu (Bago) 20, 101, 119, 122-3, 132-3, 170-1, 181, 191-2
Peguans 20, 102, 108, 112, 120, 171, 174, 182, 191, 230
Penang 15, 23-4, 30-1, 47, 49, 57, 59, 63-5, 68-9, 73-6, 78-82, 84-7, 90, 92, 94-7, 99, 103, 106, 109
Perlis 81-2, 90
Persia, The Shah of 99
Persian 26-7, 29, 173
Petithuguenin, Paul 37, 186, 231
Phang Nga 24
Phang Nga Bay 24
Phatthalung 16, 23, 28-9, 49, 51-2, 53, 54, 57-9, 61-3, 68
Phaulkon, Constantin 96, 106
Phayre, Arthur 19
Phetburi (Phipri) 23, 100
Phitsanulok 229
Phixaie 51
Phra Chedi Sam Ong 111
Phra Ruang 212
Phra Song Chu 111
Phra Sak Ta Ruong Lit 209, 219
Phra Tcha Koun 209
Phra Nhiun 224-5
Phra Non 224-5
Phu-Quoc 85

INDEX 261

Phuket (Junk Ceylon) 20, 23-4, 27-8, 31, 43, 49, 56, 61, 64-5, 71, 75-7, 79, 83, 90-1, 96-7, 101
Pinto, Mendes 98, 121
Pissanumyo 172
Pokkhara 121
Polo, Marco 181
Pondicherry 106
Pontalis, Jean-Bertrand 11
Portuguese 24, 89, 95, 98, 109, 118
Pranburi (Kuiburi) 23
Pram (Prang) 100
Pratique des Hautes Études (EPHE), École 11
Prinsep 195-8
Prome 119-20, 129-30, 132-3, 142, 154-6, 163, 172-4, 179-80
Ptolemy 121, 173
Pulao Langkawi 81, 89
Pulo Penang 85, 90, 94, 117
Pulo Telibong 81
Pulo Teratau 81
Pyu 156, 172-3, 179-80

Raheng (now Tak) 15-6, 23, 26, 37, 114-5, 138, 196, 205, 209-12, 218-23, 226, 230
Ramanadesa 121
Ramkhamhaeng, King 101, 181
Rammavati 121
Rangoon (now Yangon) 15, 19, 105, 108, 113-6, 118, 121-2, 124, 126, 128-30, 132, 136-7, 143, 147, 158, 164-6, 173, 175, 178, 188-91, 234
Ranong 21, 25, 30-1, 78, 92
Rapi, Prince 48, 49
Ratburi 110-2
Ratnapura 170
Ratsada (Khaw Sim Bee), Phya 23, 30-1, 43, 49, 56, 58, 61-64, 66-7, 71, 73-4, 76, 78-9, 84, 86, 90-2
Remyo 126

Russel, Mr. 114-6, 193-4
Russia 78

Saddhammanagara 119
Sagaing 159-60, 169-70, 172, 180, 197-8
Saigon 45, 47, 76, 79, 109
Saint François Xavier, College 86
Salween 101, 112-3, 117-21, 123, 125, 144, 146, 153-4, 190, 193, 201, 212, 228
Sam Sing 112
Sanda 145-6
Sandjak 78
Santafau 146
Sarong 68, 104, 123
Sat Dharma 119
Satan 119
Sathorn Sathan Phithak, Phra 73
Saton 119
Sawbwa 144
Scott, James George 122, 163, 180
Sea Gypsies 81
Shan 114, 120, 122-3, 125, 129, 133-4, 138, 140, 142, 144-6, 148-55, 157, 161, 165, 169-72, 174, 181-2, 188, 197, 206, 215, 217-8, 221, 229
Sheinmaga 157
Shui Madu 132
Shway Gyeen 132
Shwe Dagon 121-2, 126, 127, 129-30, 132, 136, 189-90
Shwé Gyi Bié 162
Shwe Madu 192
Shweli 144, 148, 154, 186
Siamese Malaya 86, 94
Siamese Malays 47, 52, 90
Siem Reap 17, 27, 29
Sim Jan Bine 107
Sing Khon Tha Pe 100
Singapore 24-5, 28, 37, 41-2, 48, 59,

75, 84-6, 90, 92, 93, 96-7, 104, 190
Singora 45-7, 49, 50, 51-2, 54, 56, 58, 66, 68, 74-5, 82-3, 94-5, 106, 109
Siri Dhammasoka, King 122
Sissovat 112
Sittang 120-1, 132-3
Smithies, Michael 27
Sona 121-2
Songkhla 15, 21-2, 24-5, 28, 36, 235
Srettha Thavisin, Prime Minister 26
Sri Satchanalai 101, 226
Srikshetra 172
St Maur 194
Steel Brothers 147
Stirling, Mr. 122, 125
Straits 104-5, 122, 124
Strand Hotel 124
Sukhothai 19, 37, 95, 101, 130, 138, 212, 220, 226, 228-9, 231
Sukli 198, 201, 204, 217
Sumatra 75, 96
Suphan Buri 228-9
Surate 99
Suvannabhumi 20, 119, 121-2
Swiss 19

Ta Chane 218
Tabeng Shwehti, King 133, 155, 174
Tachard, Guy 106
Tagala 121
Tagaung 141-2, 154-5, 170, 172-3
Taikkala 121
Takkala 121-2
Tai 16, 28, 142, 145-6, 153-5, 191, 206, 212, 214, 216, 226-30
Tai Noi 227-8, 230
Tai Yai 230
Tai-yuan 12
Tan Nyen 165

Tang San 68
Tap Thieng 61, 68, 73-5, 79
Taping 148, 153
Taungthu 118, 120, 123
Tavernier, Jean-Baptiste 95
Tavoy 89, 99, 101, 103-4, 107-112, 173, 196, 206
Tayokpyi, King 182
Tcheli 145
Tchioum 37
Teak 23, 42, 111 114, 135. 141. 147. 152-54, 156, 162, 192-93, 195-96, 205, 207, 214-15, 222
Tegala 121
Tehong 58, 61, 65, 73, 77
Tenasserim 23, 41, 92, 95, 97, 99-103, 107, 109-111, 113, 118, 173-4, 182, 196, 207, 212, 229
Teratan 90
Tha Chin, River 111-2
Thabeikhyin 139-40, 156
Thado Men Bya 170
Thakuto 112
Thalang (boat) 79, 80, 82, 84, 89, 98
Thale Noi 54
Tham Ha 56
Thamala 191
Thanta 146
Tharekkettara 119-21, 179
Thaton 20, 114, 116-24, 142, 145, 173, 179, 181, 185, 191, 227-8
Thazi 134, 144, 188
Theinni 144-6
Theravadin 20
Thibaw, King 134-5, 166, 197-8
Thiripitsaya 180
Thonburi 19
Tibet 153
Tigyaing 142, 154
Tiom Si 50
Tonkinson, Harry 126, 129-30

Toungoo 132-3, 155, 171, 174
Tourane-Savannakhet 63
Trang 15-6, 18, 23, 26, 28-30, 44-5, 52, 55-6, 59, 61, 63, 65-8, 73-6, 78-80, 83-4, 94, 235
Trang, River 77, 92, 94
Trinidad 86
Tripitaka 120, 161
Tsanta 146
Tsiguen 146
Turk 27

Ubon 57, 74
Ukkala 121
Ukkalanagara 121
United States 18, 83
Uttara 121-2
Uttaradit 233
Uttaran 111

Vajiravudh, King 16, 22
Versailles 96, 166
Victoria point 104, 106, 118, 174
Vieng 226
Vienna 10
Vilmorin, Mélanie de 193, 195, 203, 208, 211, 216-8, 220, 231
Vilmorin, Philippe de 15, 79, 124, 129, 132, 137-8, 150, 156, 158, 189-90, 192, 195, 199-201, 214, 216, 218, 222, 231-2
Vishnu 172

Wan Tien 146
Wareru 118, 133, 181, 191, 206, 212, 228
Washington 9, 166
Wat Doi 202
Wat Phra Keo 224
Wat Xang Pheuk 226
Wellesley 94
Whites, 29, 96

Wimala 191
Winchester 45
Wittanakit, Phya 58-60

Xang Phala 226
Xatan 119

Yamethin 133, 188
Ye 89, 110, 112
Yugala, Prince 46, 49, 231
Yule, Henry 122, 146, 168, 170
Yunnan 115, 125, 140, 145-7, 150, 152, 155
Yunnanfou 147
Yunnan Sen 144

Zedel 67
Zelaya (boat) 89, 91, 103, 113-4
Zingyaik 124
Zo Moun Nit 182
Zonit 182